MURASAKI SHIKIBU'S *THE TALE OF GENJI*

OXFORD STUDIES IN PHILOSOPHY AND LITERATURE

Richard Eldridge, Philosophy, Swarthmore College

EDITORIAL BOARD

PUBLISHED IN THE SERIES:

MURASAKI SHIKIBU'S
THE TALE OF GENJI

Philosophical Perspectives

Edited by James McMullen

OXFORD
UNIVERSITY PRESS

OXFORD

UNIVERSITY PRESS

Oxford University Press is a department of the University of Oxford. It furthers
the University's objective of excellence in research, scholarship, and education
by publishing worldwide. Oxford is a registered trade mark of Oxford University
Press in the UK and certain other countries.

Published in the United States of America by Oxford University Press
198 Madison Avenue, New York, NY 10016, United States of America.

Library of Congress Cataloging-in-Publication Data
Names: McMullen, James, 1939– editor.
Title: Murasaki Shikibu's The tale of genji : philosophical perspectives /
edited by James McMullen.
Description: New York : Oxford University Press, 2019. |
Includes bibliographical references and index.
Identifiers: LCCN 2018038471 (print) | LCCN 2018048448 (ebook) |
ISBN 9780190655013 (online content) | ISBN 9780190654993 (updf) |
ISBN 9780190655006 (epub) | ISBN 9780190654986 (pbk. : alk. paper) |
ISBN 9780190654979 (cloth : alk. paper)
Subjects: LCSH: Murasaki Shikibu, 978?– Genji monogatari. | Philosophy in literature.
Classification: LCC PL788.4.G43 (ebook) | LCC PL788.4.G43 M68 2019 (print) |
DDC 895.63/14—dc23

CONTENTS

SERIES EDITOR'S FOREWORD

At least since Plato had Socrates criticize the poets and attempt to displace Homer as the authoritative articulator and transmitter of human experience and values, philosophy and literature have developed as partly competing, partly complementary enterprises. Both literary writers and philosophers have frequently studied and commented on each other's texts and ideas, sometimes with approval, sometimes with disapproval, in their efforts to become clearer about human life and about valuable commitments—moral, artistic, political, epistemic, metaphysical, and religious, as may be. Plato's texts themselves register the complexity and importance of these interactions in being dialogues in which both deductive argumentation and dramatic narration do central work in furthering a complex body of views.

While these relations have been widely recognized, they have also frequently been ignored or misunderstood, as academic disciplines have gone their separate ways within their modern institutional settings. Philosophy has often turned to science or mathematics as providing models of knowledge; in doing so it has often explicitly set itself against cultural entanglements and literary devices, rejecting, at least officially, the importance of plot, figuration, and imagery in favor of supposedly plain speech about the truth. Literary study has moved variously through formalism, structuralism, post-structuralism, and cultural studies, among other movements, as modes of approach to a literary text. In doing so it has understood literary texts as sample instances of images, structures, personal styles, or failures of consciousness, or it has seen the literary text as a largely fungible product, fundamentally shaped by wider pressures and patterns of consumption and expectation that affect and figure in non-literary textual production as well. It has thus set itself against the idea that major literary texts productively and originally address philosophical problems of value and commitment precisely through their form, diction, imagery, and development, even while these works also resist claiming conclusively to solve the problems that occupy them.

These distinct academic traditions have yielded important perspectives and insights. But in the end none of them has been kind to the idea of major literary works as achievements in thinking about values and human life, often in distinctive, open, self-revising, self-critical ways. At the same time readers outside institutional settings, and often enough philosophers and literary scholars too, have turned to major literary texts precisely in order to engage with their productive, materially and medially specific patterns and processes of thinking. These turns to literature have, however, not so far been systematically encouraged within disciplines, and they have generally occurred independently of each other.

The aim of this series is to make manifest the multiple, complex engagements with philosophical ideas and problems that lie at the hearts of major literary texts. In doing so, its volumes aim not only to help philosophers and literary scholars of various kinds to find rich affinities and provocations to further thought and work, they also aim to bridge various gaps between academic disciplines and between those disciplines and the experiences of extra-institutional readers.

Each volume focuses on a single, undisputedly major literary text. Both philosophers with training and experience in literary study and literary scholars with training and experience in philosophy are invited to engage with themes, details, images, and incidents in the focal text, through which philosophical problems are held in view, worried at, and reformulated. Decidedly not a project simply to formulate A's philosophy of X as a finished product, merely illustrated in the text, and decidedly not a project to explain the literary work entirely by reference to external social configurations and forces, the effort is instead to track the work of open thinking in literary forms, as they lie both neighbor to and aslant from philosophy. As Walter Benjamin once wrote, "new centers of reflection are continually forming," as problems of commitment and value of all kinds take on new shapes for human agents in relation to changing historical circumstances, where reflective address remains possible. By considering how such centers of reflection are formed and expressed in and through literary works, as they engage with philosophical problems of agency, knowledge, commitment, and value, these volumes undertake to present both literature and philosophy as, at times, productive forms of reflective, medial work in relation both to each other and to social circumstances and to show how this work is specifically undertaken and developed in distinctive and original ways in exemplary works of literary art.

Richard Eldridge
Swarthmore College

ACKNOWLEDGMENTS

For help, patience, encouragement, and useful suggestions, the Editor is grateful to Richard Eldridge, Series Editor of the Oxford University Press Philosophy and Literature series; Lucy Randall, Commissioning Editor, and Hannah Doyle, Editorial Assistant, at Oxford University Press, New York; Lincy Priya and her Production Team; Mary Becker and Victoria Danahy, Copyeditors; and to the seven contributors to this volume for their patience and goodwill. For their advice and encouragement, I am also grateful to Gaye Rowley, School of Law, Waseda University; Thomas Harper, retired from University of Leiden; Nicholas Bunnin, Director, Chinese Philosophy Project, University of Oxford; my brother David McMullen, Professor Emeritus of Chinese, Faculty of Oriental Studies and St John's College, Cambridge; and my wife, Bonnie, scholar of English literature.

CONTRIBUTORS

Wiebke Denecke is Professor of East Asian Literatures & Comparative Literature at Boston University. Her research interests include premodern literature and thought of the Sinographic Sphere (China, Japan, Korea); comparative studies of East Asia and the premodern world; world literature; and the politics of cultural heritage and memory. She is the author of *The Dynamics of Masters Literature: Early Chinese Thought from Confucius to Han Feizi* (2010), *Classical World Literatures: Sino-Japanese and Greco-Roman Comparisons* (2014), and co-editor of *The Norton Anthology of World Literature* (2012, 2018), *The Oxford Handbook of Classical Chinese Literature* (2017) and a three-volume literary history of Japan and East Asia (*Nihon "bun"gakushi. A New History of Japanese "Letterature"*) (2015-19).

Edward Kamens is Sumitomo Professor of Japanese Studies in the Department of East Asian Languages and Literatures at Yale University, where he has been on the faculty since 1986. His areas of research include classical Japanese poetry and prose, Buddhist literature, and the interactions of literary and visual cultures. He has recently completed a book-length study of *waka* (the classical Japanese poem) in and as material culture. In the spring of 2015 he was a Robert and Lisa Sainsbury Fellow at the Sainsbury Institute for the Study of Japanese Arts and Cultures in Norwich, UK, and gave lectures in London, Cambridge, Norwich, and Leiden.

Melissa McCormick is Professor of Japanese Art and Culture, Harvard College Professor, Harvard University, BA in Art History and Japanese Language and Literature from the University of Michigan (1990), PhD in Art History, Princeton University (2000). Melissa McCormick's research focuses on art and social history and the interrelationship of painting and literature. Her publications include *Tosa Mitsunobu and the Small Scroll in Medieval Japan* (University of Washington Press, 2009), as well as several articles on Japanese narrative painting and communities of female readers, writers, and amateur artists. She is the author of *"The Tale of Genji": A Visual Companion* (Princeton University Press, 2018), and co-curator of the 2019 international exhibition *"The Tale of Genji": A Japanese Classic Illuminated* at the Metropolitan Museum of Art, New York.

James McMullen's research specializes in the history of Confucianism in Japan. He has a doctorate from the University of Cambridge and taught first at the University of Toronto, then, from 1972 until retirement, at Oxford, where he is now Fellow Emeritus at Pembroke and St Antony's Colleges. Among his publications are *Religion in Japan: Arrows to Heaven and Earth* (ed., with Peter Kornicki, Cambridge University Press, 1996) and *Idealism, Protest and "The Tale of Genji"* (Oxford University Press, 1999). A monograph, *The Worship of Confucius in Japan,* is forthcoming. He was elected Fellow of the British Academy in 2001.

Rajyashree Pandey is Reader in Asian Studies at the Politics Department of Goldsmiths, University of London. She received her education in India, the United Kingdom, the United States, and Australia and has taught in many academic institutions across the world. She is the author of *Perfumed Sleeves and Tangled Hair: Body, Woman, and Desire in Medieval Japanese Narratives* (University of Hawai'i Press, 2016) and *Writing and Renunciation in Medieval Japan: The Works of the Poet-Priest Kamo no Chōmei* (University of Michigan, Japanese Monograph Series, 1998). She has also published articles in a wide range of journals, from *Monumenta Nipponica* to *Postcolonial Studies* on medieval Japanese literature and Buddhism, as well as on sexuality and popular culture in Japan.

Tomoko Sakomura is Associate Professor of Art History at Swarthmore College. Her work explores the relationships between text and image in Japanese art and design. Her recent publication, *Poetry as Image: The Visual Culture of Waka in Sixteenth-Century Japan* (Brill, 2016), examines pictorial representations of Japanese court poetry and the ways they functioned as elegant instruments of elite self-representation and promoted the courtly present. Sakomura holds a PhD in art history and archaeology from Columbia University.

Ivo Smits is Professor of Arts and Cultures at Leiden University, the Netherlands. He teaches on literature and film in Japan. He studied at the Universities of Leiden, Cambridge, and Tokyo, as well as Waseda University, and was Visiting Associate Professor at Yale University. He specializes in traditional Japanese literature, especially classical court poetry in both Japanese and Chinese. His research focuses on issues of multilingualism, sociopolitical contexts, and questions of imagination in relation to texts and poetic practices of premodern literature in Japan.

Royall Tyler was born in London but spent his early years in the United States and graduated from L'École des Roches in Normandy (1954). He received a BA degree in Japanese from Harvard (1957) and a PhD in Japanese literature from Columbia (1977). After teaching at the University of Oslo and elsewhere, he moved to the Australian National University in Canberra (1990) and retired in 2000. He now lives on a farm in New South Wales. He has translated *The Tale of Genji* (Viking Penguin, 2001) and *The Tale of the Heike* (Viking Penguin, 2012).

EDITOR'S NOTE

References to the original Japanese or English translations of *The Tale of Genji* are given in the text of this volume in the following style.

JAPANESE TEXT

g 00/00 [vol no./page no.]: Quotations and references to the Japanese text of *Genji monogatari*. Abe Akio, Akiyama Ken, and Imai Gen'e, eds. *Genji monogatari*. By Murasaki Shikibu. 6 vols. In *Shinpen Nihon koten bungaku zenshū*, vols. 20–25. Tokyo: Shōgakukan, 1994–98.

ENGLISH TRANSLATIONS

t000: Tyler, Royall, tr. *The Tale of Genji*. By Murasaki Shikibu. 2 vols.; through pagination. New York: Viking Penguin, 2001.
w000: Washburn, Dennis, tr. *The Tale of Genji*. By Murasaki Shikibu. New York: W. W. Norton, 2015.

CHAPTER TITLES OF *THE TALE OF GENJI*

Chapter	Japanese title	Tyler	Washburn
1	Kiritsubo	The Paulonia Pavilion	The Lady of the Paulonia-Courtyard Chambers
2	Hahakigi	The Broom Tree	Broom Cypress
3	Utsusemi	The Cicada Shell	A Molted Cicada Shell
4	Yūgao	The Twilight Beauty	The Lady of the Evening Faces
5	Wakamurasaki	Young Murasaki	Little Purple Gromwell
6	Suetsumuhana	The Safflower	The Safflower
7	Momiji no ga	Beneath the Autumn leaves	An Imperial Celebration of Autumn Foliage

Chapter	Japanese title	Tyler	Washburn
8	Hana no en	Under the Cherry Blossoms	A Banquet Celebrating Cherry Blossoms
9	Aoi	Heart-to-Heart	Leaves of Wild Ginger
10	Sakaki	The Green Branch	A Branch of Sacred Evergreen
11	Hanachirusato	Falling Flowers	The Lady at the Villa of Scattering Orange Blossoms
12	Suma	Suma	Exile to Suma
13	Akashi	Akashi	The Lady at Akashi
14	Miotsukushi	The Pilgrimage to Sumiyoshi	Channel Markers
15	Yomogiu	A Waste of Weeds	A Ruined Villa of Tangled Gardens
16	Sekiya	At the Pass	The Barrier Gate
17	Eawase	The Picture Contest	A Contest of Illustrations
18	Matsukaze	Wind in the Pines	Wind in the Pines
19	Usugumo	Wisps of Cloud	A Thin Veil of Clouds
20	Asagao	The Bluebell	Bellflowers
21	Otome	The Maidens	Maidens of the Dance
22	Tamakazura	The Tendril Wreath	A Lovely Garland

Chapter	Japanese title	Tyler	Washburn
23	Hatsune	The Warbler's First Song	First Song of Spring
24	Kochō	Butterflies	Butterflies
25	Hotaru	The Fireflies	Fireflies
26	Tokonatsu	The Pink	Wild Pinks
27	Kagaribi	The Cressets	Cresset Fires
28	Nowaki	The Typhoon	An Autumn Tempest
29	Miyuki	The Imperial Progress	An Imperial Excursion
30	Fujibakama	Thoroughwort Flowers	Mistflowers
31	Makibashira	The Handsome Pillar	A Beloved Pillar of Cypress
32	Umegae	The Plum Tree Branch	A Branch of Plum
33	Fuji no Uraba	New Wisteria Leaves	Shoots of Wisteria Leaves
34	Wakana I	Spring Shoots I	Early Spring Greens: Part 1
35	Wakana II	Spring Shoots II	Early Spring Greens: Part 2
36	Kashiwagi	The Oak Tree	The Oak Tree
37	Yokobue	The Flute	The Transverse Flute
38	Suzumushi	The Bell Cricket	Bell Crickets
39	Yūgiri	Evening Mist	Evening Mist
40	Minori	The Law	Rites of the Sacred Law

Chapter	Japanese title	Tyler	Washburn
41	Maboroshi	The Seer	Spirit Summoner [Kumogakure] [Vanished into the Clouds]
42	Niou Miya	The Perfumed Prince	The Fragrant Prince
43	Kōbai	Red Plum Blossoms	Red Plum
44	Takekawa	Bamboo River	Bamboo River
45	Hashihime	The Maiden of the Bridge	Divine Princess at Uji Bridge
46	Shii ga moto	Beneath the Oak	At the Foot of the Oak Tree
47	Agemaki	Trefoil Knots	A Bowknot Tied in Maiden's Loops
48	Sawarabi	Bracken Shoots	Early Fiddlehead Greens
49	Yadorigi	The Ivy	Trees Encoiled in Vines of Ivy
50	Azumaya	The Eastern Cottage	A Hut in the Eastern Provinces
51	Ukifune	A Drifting Boat	A Boat Cast Adrift
52	Kagerō	The Mayfly	Ephemerids
53	Tenarai	Writing Practice	Practicing Calligraphy
54	Yume no ukihashi	The Floating Bridge	A Floating Bridge in a Dream

MURASAKI SHIKIBU'S *THE TALE OF GENJI*

Introduction

The Tale of Genji is described by Kawabata Yasunari (1899–1972), Japan's first winner of the Nobel Prize for Literature, as "the highest pinnacle of Japanese literature" and "a miracle."[1] Seldom has a work of literature so deeply and permanently colored its nation's cultural and aesthetic heritage. Since its creation in the early eleventh century, the *Genji* has cast a spell on its readers. Some two centuries after its completion, the Juntoku Emperor (r. 1210–21) referred to it as "the supreme treasure of Japan."[2] Estimated to be twice as long as *War and Peace*, it has the capacity to subvert the reader's sense of reality.[3] A seventeenth-century samurai described what he called "*Genji* people": "Their whole lives they study nothing else but remain concerned exclusively with the *Genji*. When they do study something different, they treat it as ancillary to the *Genji*. . . . So what is fiction has become real."[4]

---

1. Kawabata, *Japan the Beautiful and Myself*, pp. 47–48.
2. Quoted in the medieval commentary *Kakaishō*; see Harper, *Reading "The Tale of Genji,"* p. 530, note 13.
3. Morris, *The World of the Shining Prince*, p. 275.
4. Kumazawa, *Yakaiki*, p. 182.

The eight essays of this book offer a fresh exploration of the *Genji* from a philosophical point of view. The author, known to posterity as Murasaki Shikibu, was a lady-in-waiting to the Imperial Consort Shōshi (988–1074), in the reign of the Emperor Ichijō (r. 986–1011). As a woman, she was denied formal education and did not know philosophy as a discrete discipline. Yet her writing depicts a community of sophisticated men and women, and she had a grasp of the contemporary East Asian literary and intellectual tradition and of East Asian history. She was deeply influenced by many of the metaphysical assumptions of Buddhism, but also seems to have accepted a world of spirits and spirit possession. Her compellingly realistic narrative is informed by implicit but coherent assumptions about, and insights into, matters of both universal and historical interest, such as the exercise of power; space and time; morality in human relationships; freedom and causality; the nature of the cultural skills so important in her society; nature itself; gender roles; the nature of reality; and the role of literature. As Wiebke Denecke argues in her essay, these assumptions, often different from those of the modern West, and are amenable to philosophical exploration. With the rare exception of Genji's "defense of fiction" analyzed in Melissa McCormick's essay, they are "narrativized" in the *Genji*, that is, articulated implicitly through the narrative rather than raised as discrete or abstract philosophical problems. They are presented as lived experience, subject to success or failure and to the reaction of characters within the narrative and from time to time also to the narrator's comment.

Murasaki Shikibu was born around 973 into the middle rank of aristocracy qualified to serve the imperial family in person.[5] Her father, Fujiwara no Tametoki (dates uncertain), served as a provincial governor, but won a reputation for learning and as a poet. In

---

5. For further details, see Bowring, *The Diary of Lady Murasaki*, pp. xxxii–xxxix.

996, Murasaki accompanied him to his appointment as governor of the northwestern province of Echizen, where he participated in poetry exchanges with Chinese immigrants. It has been speculated that Murasaki Shikibu herself might have had some contact with representatives of a land not "bookish [and] foreign... but "living."[6] It is certain that she developed a facility with written Chinese and knowledge of Chinese literature and history rare among women of her period.

From around 1006 she was back in the capital and in service to Shōshi. Some details of her life at court and a sense of her watchful and sometimes seemingly depressive temperament can be gathered from her fragmentarily preserved diary. She became known for her storytelling. Parts of *The Tale of Genji* were read to the Emperor.[7] Her vast and panoramic work was written with care; she refers to a revised copy, which she evidently felt to be an improvement over an earlier version.[8] Within the Japanese tradition, the *Genji* has been seen as a repository of cultural and aesthetic wisdom, depicting a society of great elegance and sophistication. For most readers, it is a creation of dazzling and sustained narrative skill and compelling characterization. Yet the work has also posed difficulties both in Japan and in the West and continues to do so for modern readers. As is touched upon in several essays here, some have considered it a repetitious and salacious story of seduction and even rape, a response still encountered even among sophisticated readers.

One preliminary question concerns genre. The Japanese term *monogatari* is normally understood to refer to a narrative of indeterminate length, whether historical or fictional. "Tale," established as the title of the work in English, seems too redolent of fireside coziness to

---

6. Sasakawa, "*Honchō Reisō* no sekiten shi to '*Genji monogatari*,'" p. 54.
7. Bowring, *The Diary of Lady Murasaki*, p. 57.
8. Ibid., p. 33.

categorize this panoramic, often unsettling or even subversive work. "Novel," *faut de mieux*, seems preferable. It was as a "novel" comparable to the *À la recerche du temps perdu of* Marcel Proust (1871–1922) that the work was greeted by Arthur Waley (1889–1966), the first translator of the whole work into English, and his contemporary, the critic Raymond Mortimer (1895–1980). Another methodological difficulty arises from the status of the novel as the most extensive witness to its own time and society. This raises the danger of circularity: to what extent are the tensions and questions raised in the novel characteristic of the world that produced it and to what extent do they reflect Murasaki's own insight and skill in challenging or even protesting the usages of her own society? The text is also linguistically difficult, and few, beyond specialists, can claim to have read it all closely in the original. Fortunately, several good modern translations into English and other languages, most recently in Dutch, are available.[9]

HISTORICAL BACKGROUND

A more serious challenge is posed by the historical and geographical remoteness of the society reflected in the novel. Since the seventh century, the archipelago had been affected by the expansion of Chinese influence across the East Asian region that accompanied the reunification of China following the disunion of the Six Dynasties (229–589). The period marked an interlude in Japanese history during which, starting from a decentralized tribal society based on

---

9. Waley, tr., *The Tale of Genji*, vol. 2, pp. 30–31. Mortimer, "A New Planet," p. 371. An earlier English translation of the first seventeen chapters by Suematsu Kenchō (1855–1920; later Baron) while studying at St. John's College, Cambridge, was published in London by Trübner & Co., in 1882. For the Dutch translation, see Vos, tr., *Her verhaal van Genji*.

kinship, a centralized bureaucratic state and court under a hereditary emperor developed on the Chinese pattern.

The major physical manifestation of this state-building in Murasaki Shikibu's time was the metropolitan capital city of Heiankyō, the scene of Genji's exploits and residence of the elite society depicted in the novel. Most of the action of the narrative takes place here and in its immediate environs. Central was the palace, residence of the reigning emperor and the location of his court and the national administration, replete with ministries and offices and a system of official Confucian-style state education. This was the site of a highly sophisticated civilization advanced in the fields of urban planning, architecture, dress, literature, writing, art, and music. This community was dominated by an elite of aristocratic lineages and their entourages, numbering some thousands. Within it, status was determined by genealogical and physical proximity to the emperor and the palace.

Outside the capital, the provincial Japanese world was negatively viewed in proportion to its distance from the capital as generally uncivilized and dangerous. Closest at varying distances are special sites that are associated with alternative histories and values. These are exploited by the novelist to interrogate the emperor-centered order of prestige. Such sites are the Northern Hills, where in a monastery Genji encounters the girl-child who is to be the love of his life; Suma and Akashi, the scene of his exile but also associated with alternatives to secular metropolitan values. Kyūshū, the southwest island, is depicted as the home of rough, uncivilized men. In the final sequence of the novel, in the following generation, the scene shifts to Uji, a private world deeply associated with Buddhism, a day's journey from the capital but distanced from the public rituals and cultural splendor of the emperor's court.

Beyond the archipelago lay the foreign land of China and further still India, the source of the Buddhism that colored the world of the novel. By the end of the tenth century, official relations with China had been suspended for a century, and opportunities for direct encounters with representatives of foreign cultures had become rare. The early eleventh century was a complex time in Japanese history. In the broadest terms, this was the period in which, across many fields, sociopolitical, cultural, religious, and linguistic resolutions were negotiated between indigenous insular and continental or peninsular influences. Ostensibly Japan possessed a Chinese-style public polity. And indeed, as Denecke shows, Chinese culture and values still exerted magnetism among the elite. However, behind the Chinese-style facade, Japanese society retained its earlier kin-based organization. Though bearing the titles of Chinese-style bureaucratic offices, court society coalesced into an oligarchic structure of elite kindreds. At its apex a limited coterie of aristocratic families enjoyed marital relations with the imperial lineage. Access to office tended to be based on hereditary status rather than a merit-based system determined by examinations, as was becoming established in China. So was created a relatively small, inward-looking community, highly conscious of hereditary status, rank, and privilege, many members of which were mutually well acquainted. The courtly society of Heian Japan was characterized by a sharp distinction between those within the court and others, overwhelming importance attached to rank and parentage, and elaborate ritual and etiquette. In these respects, even though it did not share their feudal origins, it had much in common with the medieval and Renaissance courts of Europe. This sophisticated and leisured elite occupied itself with such cultural practices as verse composition, calligraphy, and garden construction, of which the philosophical aspects are explored in this volume in the respective essays by Edward Kamens, Tomoko Sakomura, and Ivo Smits. The upper echelons of the court community that feature in the *Genji* derived their considerable wealth from complex landholding and fiscal arrangements. Wealth was channeled to them by taxation, which by the eleventh century had devolved into a part private patronage, part residual Chinese-style public fiscal system. Genji himself commanded great wealth.

RELIGION AND THOUGHT

Like the institutional structure, the intellectual and social climate in which Murasaki Shikibu wrote the *Genji* owed much to foreign influences. An overwhelming influence was Buddhism, filtered through its Chinese interpretation. In many ways, eleventh-century Japan was a client culture of China and drew on the pluralist intellectual world of the continent. In China, popular belief in spirits merged into a range of world-denying and world-affirming systems of thought and political philosophies. There existed well-defined schools, such as Daoism, Legalism, Confucianism, and Mohism. Much of this world of belief and thought had been transmitted to Japan by the time of Murasaki Shikibu, but did not form separate philosophical schools. One systematic category of learning with some kinship to philosophy, however, was Onmyōdō (Yinyang studies), really a kind of astrology, geomancy, and divination of Chinese origin, whose influence is apparent in the novel mainly in the form of taboos against moving in certain directions at certain times and, as Ivo Smit's essay shows, in the construction of gardens.

Formally, the Heian state was founded on a Chinese Confucian order, its institutional and legal structures modeled after those of the Tang Dynasty (618–907). Education, based on the Chinese language needed for the operation of the Chinese-style institutions of government, was provided in the Chinese manner by the state, at a state institution of learning, the Academy (*Daigakuryō*). The curriculum was based on Confucianism, and access to office was, formally, allocated on the basis of examination on a Confucian curriculum.

Confucius was worshipped in a twice-annual ceremony at a shrine in the Academy. By the eleventh century, however, a social distance had opened between the Academy and the elite social world of the court itself. The meritocratic functioning of the Academy had been subverted by hereditary privilege. The Academy community was regarded with disdain by the higher aristocracy; it commanded respect only in nostalgic retrospect; to the courtly elite in Genji's world, it was a "rabble" (t384). Outside the formal structures of the bureaucratic state, Confucian influence was also thin, though some Confucian practices were adopted as law in the eighth century, for instance aspects of family law and, in modified form, of mourning. Law itself, let alone courts or judicial procedures, however, is rarely mentioned in the novel.

Though China was a pervasive presence, specifically Confucian influence appears to have obtruded little. Confucianism is referred to teasingly by a grandee as "the teachings of what's his name" or "so and so" (*nanigashi*; g3/438; cf. t563). Japanese elite society, however, found some support in Confucianism for its disprivileging of women. For instance, the Confucian "three subordinations" (t518) of women to men (successively father, husband, and son) are endorsed by an otherwise sometimes more liberal Genji (t473). Yet, though high status and nubile woman were secluded, gender roles were complex and to some extent flexible, as Rajyashree Pandey argues in her essay.

THE RITUAL STATE

In one respect, however, there was a major congruence between eleventh-century elite society and Confucianism: Heian court society conformed with Confucian principles in respect of the fundamental importance of ritual. Rituals absorbed much of the energy of the court society of the time. Ancestral, apotropaic, petitionary, purificatory, or

Buddhistic, they drew on various traditions, many of continental origin. Yet it was an indication of growing cultural self-confidence that many ritual practices legitimated indigenous tradition and mythology. A century before Murasaki Shikibu began writing her novel, a committee of scholars began to compile the *Engishiki* (Procedures of the Engi era), the last of a series of ritual compendia. This text brings together some five hundred rituals and a larger number of protocols prescribing a vast spectrum of activities ranging from enthronements through state-sponsored Buddhist rites to rituals concerned with other matters. The rich pomp, ceremony, and etiquette of the Heian court were its own end. In the words of the historical sociologist Norbert Elias (1897–1990) describing the comparable court societies of Europe, they constituted the "exhibition of court society to itself."[10] It has been claimed that "Japan existed predominantly in a ritual mode."[11] The Japanese state has been described as a "liturgical community" in which "ritual [was] soteriological in and of itself."[12] James McMullen's essay argues that ritual performance was a key element also in the formation of personhood in the world of the *Genji*.

BUDDHISM

Coexisting with these features and contributing to the rich ritual life of the Heian court was the powerful religious influence of Buddhism. The teaching offered the deepest analysis of human experience in East Asia. Introduced to Japan from the sixth century, it had taken root institutionally with organization into sects, physically with dignified temples, socially through rituals and

10. Elias, *The Court Society,* p. 101.
11. Grapard, "The Economics of Ritual Power," p. 71.
12. Miller, "Ritsuryō Japan," p. 119.

through medical activities, and intellectually through elaborate metaphysical, often mystical, doctrines. Buddhism has a profound and pervasive, but also complex and ambivalent, impact on *The Tale of Genji*. The teaching offered a basically negative view of the world and of human sensory experience. It provided a metaphysical framework, epistemology, and method for achieving liberation from the world and its attachments; it also offered individuals a path to salvation through renunciation. Its grand metaphysical speculations and logical discipline were, in theory, available through Chinese translations of Sanskrit Buddhist writings. Its doctrine that the world is ephemeral and illusory combines with its view that the Heian period coincided with an era of cosmic decline to promote an atmosphere of melancholy that intensifies over the course of the narrative. This pessimism contrasts oddly with the celebration of cultural grandeur of Part I. The Buddhist doctrine of transgenerational karma, a form of predestination, however, is used ambivalently. It is invoked to explain Genji's extraordinary gifts and the glories of his age. At the same time, it exonerates the characters of the novel from inappropriate conduct, misjudgments, unhappy outcomes, and suffering.

For most people, the Buddhist tradition, its ultimate postulates inexpressible in language, was known largely through devolved Mahayana interpretations or "conventional truths" and through petitionary and other forms of ritual, chiefly apotropaic or in quest of favorable rebirth. This tradition is reflected throughout the novel; it was also associated with a pantheon of anthropomorphic and other beings. Increasingly, Buddhist practice took the form of invoking the name of Amida, a divinity associated with granting rebirth in paradise. There is a strain of misogyny in Buddhism. The influence of the tradition on the construction of gender in the novel is among the themes explored in Pandey's wide-ranging essay on gender roles. Its influence both on the *Genji* itself and on how it was read in the centuries after its creation is analyzed in the essay by Melissa McCormick.

SUPERNATURAL AGENCIES AND SPIRIT POSSESSION

These Buddhistic traditions coexisted and often merged with belief in an animistic, occult world of spirits, both human and associated with natural phenomena. Much of this was of continental or Korean peninsula origin. One such belief saw Heaven or "the sky" as an all-seeing monitor of human activity that intruded into the human realm with judgments and warnings against improper conduct. The supernatural world was also populated by animistic nature spirits, ancestral spirits, and other supernatural agents. This seething, sometimes anarchic-seeming occult world intruded destructively into the human realm, causing adversities in the form of spirit possession emanating from the living or dead. In a society in which women lived much of their lives passively in seclusion and restricted mobility, the activity of spirits formed an unseen but dynamic force field in which wronged or jealous persons or disprized lovers could inflict vengeance on the object of their resentment. In the *Genji*, dramatic spirit possessions are an important mode for articulating relationships, particularly affecting women. Ritual exorcism administered by Buddhist monks, in which spirits were transferred to shamanic mediums, offered a means to propitiate such interventions. In contrast to karmic influence, spirit possession sometimes explicitly identified its cause through these mediums, who could articulate grievances. Whether Murasaki Shikibu believed literally in this phenomenon has been questioned, but retributive spirit possession is a major feature of her work and essential to its plot. This theme is explored in McMullen's essay.

THE *GENJI* NARRATIVE

Such were the forms and pressures of the courtly world of Murasaki Shikibu. The community that she depicts, however, was not immediately contemporary. She shared the common East Asian reflex that looked to the past as an authority for a better society. Her mise-en-scène was informed by nostalgia among her contemporaries for the reign of the Daigo Emperor (r. 897–930) of about a century before her time, a historical distance that enabled her to idealize her fictional world and its central figure in some respects.[13]

The Tale of Genji consists of fifty-four chapters of uneven length and covers four generations of a family associated with the imperial lineage. It is usually divided into three parts, the first two of which focus on the career of the eponymous hero, Genji, a son of the reigning emperor by a much loved, but hierarchically junior, consort. In Part I (Chapters 1–33 "Kiritsubo" to "Fuji no uraba"), the child Genji is made a commoner for political reasons, but an illustrious future is foretold of him by a Korean soothsayer. His career is traced through his love affairs, including his most transgressive relationship with his father's consort, his abduction of the girl Murasaki, who will become his most loved, but secondary wife, exile, his triumphal return, and subsequent ascendancy in court. In Part II (Chapters 34–41 "Wakana I" to "Maboroshi"), Genji's world comes under strain. He maintains his dominance, but his personal life begins to unravel. He marries his half-brother's daughter and deeply offends Murasaki. His own cuckolding of his father is revisited on Genji himself. An angry spirit surviving like mycelium from Genji's youthful injury to its long-dead owner afflicts Murasaki, and she eventually dies.

---

13. Sasagawa, "*Honchō Reisō* no Sekiten shi to '*Genji monogatari*,'" p. 56. For the historical basis, see the fourteenth-century commentary *Kakaishō* quoted in Harper, *Reading "The Tale of Genji*," p. 344.

In Part III (Chapters 42–54 "Niou Miya" to "Yume no ukihashi"), after a gap of eight years following Genji's death, the public world of Genji and his great rituals recedes, the narrative contracts, and the scene shifts from the capital to the Buddhist-centered community of Uji and to two secluded but nubile princesses, later joined by a newly discovered third half-sister. This part pursues many of the themes of Parts I and II, but the tone is different, and it has been regarded by some as a discrete work and even by a different author. The main themes are summarized in the first essay, Royall Tyler's overview of the novel.

THE PRESENT BOOK

Murasaki Shikibu's long narrative confronts human behavior in all its complexity, contradictions, and ambiguities. Its dazzling literary skill deploys interior monologue, subtle and oblique dialogue, close description and evocative scene setting, exploitation of Chinese and indigenous topoi, and compelling characterization. Like all literary masterpieces, her work has been read in many ways, among them: as a picaresque novel of gallantry; a protest on behalf of women; a quest for Buddhist salvation; a Confucian record of high aesthetic culture and ritual; a plea for achievement rather than ascription as the basis of prestige; an evocation of intense human affect; a historical novel; a sustained love story between two fallible human beings. It has been seen as comparable to Proust's magnum opus; as a multivocal postmodern production, an intertextual masterpiece, and a narrative laced with Freudian significance. The eight essays of this volume both describe the *Genji* and interrogate the text to identify some of its philosophical challenges. They reflect contemporary intellectual movements such as postmodern views on authorship, intertextualism, deconstruction, and cultural history. The focus is mainly on

Parts I and II. Many also refer to Part III. This section of the *Genji* has, however, already been the subject of a collection of essays; limits of space preclude more thorough treatment here.[14]

The sequence of the essays is designed both to introduce the novel descriptively and to analyze its philosophical assumptions. The first two are concerned with the coordinates of time and place. The first essay (Tyler) outlines the story, its scope, and the dynamic that impels it; the second (Denecke) sets the stage for the main spatial and temporal aspects of the narrative. The third essay (McMullen) glances at the construction of the self and moral personhood. Three further essays examine the distinctive cultural practices of poetry (Kamens), calligraphy (Sakomura), and garden-making (Smits) that reveal many of the assumptions concerning art and human life. Finally, two essays revisit two salient but paradoxical features of the *Genji* that have emerged in the preceding essays and are distinctive in world literature: its female authorship in a society in which women were virtually imprisoned in the court harem (Pandey) and its emanation from a society deeply imbued with the fundamentally world-denying philosophy of Buddhism (McCormick).

"The Structure of Genji's Career: Myth, Politics, and Pride" (Tyler)

The *Genji* is frequently represented as a narrative of courtly philandering. This reading is common in the reception history in Japan and reflected also in the critical response in the West. Already, W. G. Aston's *A History of Japanese literature* (1899) found it "mainly an account of [Genji's] numerous love affairs."[15] Virginia Woolf (1882–1941), in her turn, saw in *Genji* a world in which "the interests of men

---

14. Pekarik, *Ukifune: Love in "The Tale of Genji."*
15. Aston, *A History of Japanese Literature*, p. 93.

did not centre upon politics."[16] Most recently, Ian Buruma, reviewing Dennis Washburn's new translation for the *New Yorker* under the title of "The Sensualist," focuses on Genji as "a typical Don Juan" and "the great seducer, as vain as a diva." Royall Tyler's essay must be read as a corrective to these reductive views, but it also serves the introductory function of familiarizing the reader with the *Genji* narrative. Tyler draws on a gifted translator's intimate knowledge of the text to expose motivations in its central character far more complex than mere philandering. Genji has two main projects, sometimes in mutual tension: political ambition and gallantry. His amorous adventures themselves do not disqualify him from political advancement, though it is important that his public liaisons should be with women qualified by birth to enhance his proximity to the Emperor. But love affairs can be dangerous. Little immediate damage need result if they remain secret, but over time the resentment of disprized or jealous lovers, projected in spirit form, can inflict sickness and even death.

However, Genji's interests extend beyond libidinal gratification. His purpose, supported by cosmic powers that protect him through to his middle age, is to correct the wrong of his father's preferment of his elder half-brother to succeed to the throne. Parts I and II are built around the rivalry with this brother, later the Suzaku Emperor. Tyler documents indigenous mythical authority behind this fraternal political struggle. In the medium term, Genji wins, not least by marriage politics; by Chapter 33 "Fuji no Uraba" he has attained quasi-imperial status. Yet he is unsatisfied. His most loved partner, Murasaki, is not of a rank appropriate to consolidate his political ascendancy. As the polygamy of the court allowed, Genji looks elsewhere and chooses as his main wife the Third Princess, the higher-status favorite daughter of the Retired Emperor Suzaku. Politically, this might potentially work, but personally it proves to be a blunder. Genji's neglect of her

16. In Harper, *Reading "The Tale of Genji,"* p. 567.

precipitates a decline in his fortunes, damages those close to him, and leads to his own despair. Tyler points to Genji's vanity and overreaching ambition as the cause.

Genji is remembered in the world of the novel as a paragon and his ascendancy as a golden age of rituals, high culture, and political achievement. Tyler quotes his half-brother's description of a man of "so commanding a presence that one hardly dares to approach him" (t578–79). Yet the insubstantial nature of his authority raises questions. The narrative does not provide much material for philosophical analysis here. The narrator is unconcerned with Genji's exercise of political authority in the wider world. There is no trace of any preoccupation with the moral function of sovereignty, a major concern of Chinese political thought. His power does not conform to any theory of legitimacy, justice, or concern for popular welfare, let alone the expectations or rights of the governed. Nor is it expressed through law, though a Chinese-style legal system was formally in place in the Japan of the period. No coercive mode of enforcement is invoked. There is no mention of delegation or the bureaucratic councils that historically made decisions at the time. If Genji's dominance over his world is to be associated with any East Asian model, it must be with the soft, almost Daoistic notion of charismatic sovereignty found in some Confucian texts. This theory does not require the ruler to engage hands-on with control over his realm. His personal virtue suffices to secure order in the realm. This suggests an idealized representation of the primarily sacerdotal role that historians attribute to emperors in the Heian period. But perhaps the truth is that the author of the novel simply did not engage with the question of political control beyond the limited world of the court she knew.

Genji's professed spiritual aspirations are Buddhist; he studies Buddhist texts and even goes on retreat. Serious asceticism, however, is not his style, or not at least until the final years of his life. True, he has empathy, even for his paramours, though, as Tyler notes, he is possessively unwilling to let them pursue their own liberation through the tonsure. He is, however, tactful when necessary, as Tyler shows with a subtle analysis of the elaborate and indirect negotiations leading to Genji's late marriage to the Third Princess.

After Genji's death, the narrative centers on the Buddhist community in Uji. Tyler surveys the final chapters of Part III, touching on the main controversies surrounding this part of the novel.

"The Epistemology of Space in The Tale of Genji" (Denecke)

The spatial world of the *Genji* has two main centers. Wiebke Denecke shows that the Japanese center was formed concentrically around the emperor and his palace; thence it extends to aristocratic residences, to the capital and its environs, and beyond that to the provinces. The second center is formed by China, and to a lesser extent Korea and even to India, the source of Buddhism. By the end of the tenth century, China and the Korean peninsula have become unreachable in person, yet close enough through cultural memory, physical artifacts, and literary tradition to impinge pervasively on the consciousness of the novelist and her characters. Denecke points out that the role of China in the novel tended to be underestimated during the decades when nationalism intensified, from the late nineteenth century until the end of the Pacific War. Her essay redresses that distortion. It is concerned chiefly with how Heian period Japanese experienced space and in particular explores the philosophical and literary function of China in the novel.

China is represented in the *Genji* in several different modes serving various literary purposes. Materially, treasured foreign artifacts, silk, paper, ceramics, confer dignity or symbolic significance on the occasions when they are presented or used, as do Chinese and Korean music and dance. In nonmaterial culture, the Chinese world was the source of wisdom, admonitory experience, and much in the world of art. In the intellectual and literary realms, China supplies many of the topoi and archetypes of the novel. Denecke describes how references to Chinese historical experience recorded in famous works of literature add depth to the narrative. Closer to hand, Genji's brilliant mastery of Chinese poetry and prose competition enhance his stature. Yet changing fashion also operates: rigid attachment to the China of the past could signify a deplorable outdatedness, as with the pilloried lowly scholars of the Academy, or the comical red-nosed Suetsumuhana.

The copious, various, and mutating influences stemming from the Japan–China spatial dualities lead Denecke to take issue with the practice of analyzing the China–Japan duality as binary, for this practice leads to difficulty with exceptions and the danger of essentialization. Rather, spatial duality and difference should be seen "operationally" as aesthetic "juxtapositions" through which their complexity better emerges. In this way, what a binary scheme represents as intractable "exceptions" "disappear into the pleasure of ever new combinations, recombinations, permutations with variations" into which "any Japanese or Chinese 'essence' disappears." One example is the famous *shinasadame* (identifying categories [of women]) scene of Chapter 2 "Hahakigi," which invites juxtaposition with a scene in Chapter 21 "Otome" describing mockery of the Confucian scholars of the Academy. Such juxtaposition, Denecke argues, yields appreciation of "Murasaki Shikibu's narrative crafting" that "play in more complex ways [than the binary approach] with spatial duality."

In an important coda to her essay, Denecke addresses a concern fundamental to this volume: the relationship of her inquiry (and those of other contributors) to what is regarded as "philosophy" in the Anglo-American tradition. She is particularly concerned with the "epistemology" of her title and admits that "thetical, conceptual, and systematic inquiry" is not to be found in East Asia, at least until the

Neo-Confucianism of the Song Dynasty (960–1279). Any fruitless search for this makes the Japanese cultural tradition look "deficient." Rather, Denecke links "juxtaposition" with what she refers to as "philosophizability," an obvious potential justification of the project of this book. With reference to the concept of space, she finds that this concept resonates with the "rich and complex concept of 'place' " of the well-known post-Restoration Japanese philosopher Nishida Kitarō (1870–1945), which draws on the concept of "nondualism" of Daoism and Buddhist metaphysics. In turn, this opens up the "possibility" of a "nondualistic but also not subjectivist philosophy in a world that has grown challengingly multicultural and pluralistic." For the *Genji*, she concludes, this new "epistemology of space" would allow for "an ever more complex aestheticizing play with spatial dualities in Heian social reality and its artistic representation." Thus Murasaki Shikibu's use of "juxtaposition" in the novel and its understanding as a heuristic device facilitate philosophical analysis of how China figures not only as "a foreign realm or exotic ornament," but, more significantly, is also situated at "the heart of *Genji*'s brilliant narrative art and psychological depth."

"Ritual, Moral Personhood, and Spirit Possession in The Tale of Genji" (McMullen)

Over the long reception history of the *Genji*, many in Japan and beyond have found Genji's persistently libidinal behavior offensive or difficult to reconcile with his reputation in his world. In the West, the British diplomat and student of Japanese culture W.G. Aston (1841–1911) early indicted its "laxity of morals" as "indefensible."[17] James McMullen's essay adapts the philosophical analysis of early Confucian thought by the American philosopher Herbert Fingarette

---

17. Aston, *A History of Japanese Literature*, p. 97.

(b. 1921) and others to explore the moral personhood implicit in the world of the *Genji*. McMullen argues that this moral world is centered on ritual, is pluralistic and evolving, but ultimately coherent. Genji himself, he argues, goes on a moral journey.

First, particularly in Part I but persisting through the entire narrative, the society of the Heian court is based on an "aesthetic order." Conduct is evaluated not against universal or transcendent laws, or as the expression of a particular view of human nature, as found in later Chinese philosophy. Rather, as is typical of courtly communities, men and women are judged by external criteria—by others' perception of their discrete acts and their appearance. Basic to this view is the role of ritual in the *Genji*. Mastery of ritual is the principal mode of person formation, and its effective performance establishes the person in society. Ritual addresses both society and the interface with the occult worlds. It includes the conventions governing civilized social intercourse, courtship, and the usages that articulate hierarchical distinctions in this highly status-conscious society. But it also extends to religious, petitionary, and apotropaic rites, many of which are Buddhist.

Ritual can assume a moral dimension, so that egregious sexual misconduct such as Genji's toward his father and half-brother may be thought of as both immoral and an offense against ritual propriety. Most important, however, an "aesthetic order" is oriented to the external world, and the sense of an inner core of moral personhood subsisting through time is weak. Genji's personhood suffers little tainting from his offenses. The main sanction against offense is shame; it incurs resentment, mockery, or censure and associated loss of self-estimation. Shame is privileged over internally oriented guilt. Concomitantly, secrecy is highly valued and is an important theme in the narrative. McMullen argues that this feature of the *Genji* affects the moral vocabulary when the text is translated into Western languages. The use of such English terms as "guilt" and "sin" may distort the nuance of the original Japanese. In the sense that conduct and reputation are molded through external social sanctions and shame, this process of person formation also resonates with Ruth Benedict's influential analysis of more recent Japanese society in *The Chrysanthemum and the Sword* and with modern behaviorist models of socialization.

But the "aesthetic order" and its concomitant shame, though a permanent feature of the world of the *Genji*, are not the only influences informing its moral field. Buddhism exerts a powerful but ambivalent influence over the minds and aspirations of its characters. In one direction, Buddhist deterministic karma can be invoked to exonerate offenses. In another, however, Buddhist pessimism and its ascetic and renunciatory imperatives address behavior at the individual rather than the social level, creating the possibility of individual responsibility and thus guilt rather than shame. As Genji grows older, Buddhism exerts a stronger influence, inclining him to compunction and even an internal sense of penitence, self-accusation, or guilt over his youthful indiscretions. This syndrome exists uneasily with the outward-looking fear of social opprobrium and the secrecy associated with the "aesthetic order," a tension that Genji is unable to resolve. In Part III, the main character, Kaoru, who seems to inherit an intensification of Genji's middle-aged Buddhist inclinations, is crippled by a sense of guilt.

Other influences contribute in important ways to the moral field around Genji's behavior. He himself enjoys supernatural protection from rather nebulously characterized powers that seemingly forestall retribution for his offenses. However, as he approaches middle age, this protection weakens and he and those closest to him are exposed to the vulnerabilities of less privileged mortals. McMullen argues that spirit possession intervenes in Genji's life to administer retribution, damage his fortune, and confer moral coherence on the novel.

The second half of McMullen's essay pursues the playing out of these themes through analysis of three episodes from Parts I and II of the novel. These episodes show that, while the "aesthetic order" persists, Buddhist sensibilities intensify and spirit possession remains an important means of articulating the moral world of the novel. It is argued that, despite his laudable concern for his paramours, Genji's self-indulgent exploitation of women comes home in the spirit possession and death of his most loved partner and his own despair.

"Flares in the Garden, Darkness in the Heart: Exteriority, Interiority, and the Role of Poems in The Tale of Genji" (Kamens)

From the underlying considerations of time, space, and human nature, the focus of the next three essays turns to three important cultural practices that preoccupy the characters, determine their standing, and illustrate their assumptions concerning value. Of these practices, verse composition is probably most prominent in the *Genji*, and the main subject of Edward Kamens's essay.

Like Denecke, Edward Kamens is concerned with dualities. He calls them "dyads" and claims that they are pervasive in the world of the novel. Like Denecke, he is wary of their function; insufficiently understood, they may "short-circuit our perception of nuance, subtlety, shades of difference, and the shifting, slippery character and significance of all things that are not fixed." Kamens's principal dyad here is interiority and exteriority. He explores this from the perspective of the subjectivity of readers, whose relationship with it is dynamic and changeable; he writes of "oscillation" between exteriority and interiority and readers' continuing development in reading the text. Another theme of his essay is the intertextual and paratextual nature of *Genji* as modern readers encounter it. He approaches these topics through a preliminary excursion into a pictorial analogue to *Genji* provided by the multi-panel pictorial "Kyoto screens" produced in Japan from the sixteenth century. These well-known screens, which incidentally also depict the erstwhile scene of Genji's exploits, convey an all-embracing vision "composed of disparate, noncontiguous but carefully chosen elements," including both interiors and exteriors. Another pair of screens from the Yale museum, he finds, illustrate selected scenes from the *Genji* itself in a similar way; the viewer is "simultaneously held outside the world that they create, yet drawn . . . into that world and beyond . . . into the imaginary that the *Tale, as a whole,* creates and opens up to us."

In a different direction, Kamens next takes up another instance of interiority and exteriority that usefully addresses an aspect of the *Genji* that many readers find confusing: the different ways by which the characters are named in the original and in modern Japanese- and Western-language translations. Basic to modern naming is a view of the *Genji* as a continuing, permeable, and multivocal project. Some names of characters are interior to the text from its original formation. Others, however, are exterior or paratextual, like that applied retrospectively by readers, commentators, and translators to Genji's doppelganger, Tō no Chūjō; they are the product of later readers' search for clarity. Nonetheless, they have become an established feature of the *Genji* as now read.

Kamens's principal declared chief topic is the use of verse in the novel. This is another dyad; he is concerned both internally with the nearly eight hundred poems original to the text, composed as exchanges between characters, and externally with quotations or echoes of the vast body of verse both Chinese and Japanese that is an inheritance of Heian courtly culture. These are "a huge presence in the text, demanding an alteration of readerly attention as they slow or halt or divert its forward movement . . . that bring narrative sub-arcs to emotional peaks . . . or . . . conclude certain phases of action, interaction, or contemplation." He describes this use of verse as to "reach out . . . to the vast intertextual matrices of the entirety of the rest of the text and to the whole of Japanese poesy, Chinese poesy, Buddhist lore and more." In a striking phrase he describes a multivocal *Genji* as a "housing for verse." Drawing on a deep knowledge of the *waka* corpus, he cites the figure of "darkness of the heart" to refer to parental attachment, particularly to daughters, from a poem by Murasaki Shikibu's great grandfather. Kamens traces its mutations, passing through the Kiritsubo Emperor's troubled parenthood of Genji himself to the "misogynist hypocrisy and egotism" of Prince Hachi in the final Uji chapters.

The essay ends with an example of interiority and exteriority that encapsulates Kamens's breadth of reference and view of reading *Genji* as an open-ended evolving project. The final chapter of the novel bears the evocative title "Yume no ukihashi," an expression that does not occur in the text and is of uncertain origin. Kamens quotes its use in a poem by the noted poet and *Genji* scholar Fujiwara no Teika (1162–1241); he describes this as "outside of and exterior to the *Tale*, yet deeply engaged with and *of* it." Used for the title of its last chapter, the poem "absorbs [the novel], reproduces it, and, . . . propels [it], and itself, once more out into the world."

"Calligraphy, Aesthetics, and Character in The Tale of Genji" (Sakomura)

Rivaling poetry in importance as an expressive cultural practice in the world of the *Genji*, but set apart by its materiality, is the art of calligraphy. For Raymond Mortimer, indeed, the "accomplishment" of calligraphy in the novel is important "above all."[18] Exemplary calligraphy by earlier emperors and others is treasured, deemed suitable as dowry gifts. Its prominence in the narrative justifies the treatment

18. Mortimer, "A New Planet," p. 371.

of calligraphy as a separate topic. It is the subject of the essay by the cultural historian Tomoko Sakomura.

Tomoko Sakomura identifies a dual function: calligraphy functions as a vehicle of semantic content, but it is also much more, an expressive art and visible evidence of the writer's moral status, aesthetic discrimination, and social standing. Like speech, calligraphy is the medium in which much poetry is communicated. Its particular importance as self-expression for women is intensified by the convention that elite nubile women lived in seclusion; for the physical person to be seen by a man was tantamount to being sexually possessed. In the physical absence of its author, calligraphy, as Sakomura indicates, stood as "proxy." Thus for women, it was a vital but oblique form of presentation of the self. For Genji himself, in his constant quest for satisfactory amatory partners, a woman's calligraphy has an erotic interest; it is an important indication of her character, standing, and desirability.

Sakomura provides helpful background information on the Japanese calligraphic tradition in the lifetime of Murasaki. This complicated system had evolved from Chinese characters over the fifth to ninth centuries. It featured several styles, differentiated by their degree of cursiveness and to some extent by gendered usage and function: formal, square writing of Chinese characters was used by men for official purposes; a graphically simpler cursive script derived from the square style was used to represent syllables rather than for its original Chinese logographic purpose; this was employed by women and by men for personal communication and writing Japanese verse. An important aspect of calligraphy was the choice of paper; Chinese, Japanese, and Korean papers in various colors were available, and each carried subtle associations.

The property of calligraphy as a vehicle for self-expression not necessarily directly connected to its semantic content led to an intense connoisseurship. An extended passage in Chapter 32 "Ume ga e" is devoted to this activity, in which Genji, the supreme arbiter of taste and himself a distinguished calligrapher and practitioner of the related art of painting, comments on past and contemporary examples. Sakomura offers an extended analysis of this key passage. For her, the practice of calligraphy is an example of the "aestheticiziation of everyday life" in the world of the novel. She is undoubtedly correct. Yet she also points out that despite this intense interest and attention, the criteria applied by Genji and others to individual cases do not yield a consistent or objective scheme of value. Genji's judgments are personal, inconsistent, and particularistic. What is surprising, perhaps, is that the rank of the writer is deemed an essential aspect of the value of any given example, apparently transcending artistic merit. It is tempting to see here a cross-binding between Sakomura's artistic use of the term and its extension beyond artistic value to the "aesthetic order" in the sense identified in McMullen's essay; not only artistic merit, but conduct more widely is judged not by transcendent or universal norms, but particularistically, as a discrete aspect of the behavior of individuals.

"Genji's Gardens: Negotiating Nature at the Heian Court" (Smits)

The Japanese garden of the Heian period was important for the cultural and affective life of the aristocracy. The residences of aristocratic families opened directly onto their gardens; space flowed between house and garden. For many, the garden represented their most intimate contact with the natural world. But as the cultural historian Ivor Smits shows, the relationship, though often personalized, was of a highly codified, self-conscious, and literary kind.

Smits's essay starts from his observation that unmediated Nature was not an object of contemplation in the *Genji*. True, there is a nebulous conception of natural forces, including storms, and of an all-seeing Heaven that intervenes in the human realm, but this is only sporadically featured in the narrative and is viewed solely with reference to its impact on human affairs, particularly Genji's. Geomancy, Chinese in origin and associated with directional taboos, is also predicated on natural forces but is used in the novel not least to justify wayward behavior. There is no sense of Nature as a realm ontologically separate from the human order, let alone as a productive source sustaining human society. No doubt this reflects the prevailing horizons of sensibility in the courtly and urbanized elite society of the period. Smits quotes a revealing Chinese-language poem by Renzen, a descendent of the onetime Minister of the Left Fujiwara no Saneyori (900–70), writing perhaps a century after Murasaki's time. The poet refers to *zōka* 造化, a Chinese locution commonly translated as "creation," which, the poem runs, brings into being such beautiful natural phenomena as "light through catalpa and mulberry tree" and "a line of geese bonding with clouds." In Chinese canonical sources, *zōka* refers broadly to the creative processes by which Heaven and Earth produce the phenomenal world, and the concept had political significance; it was the function of the ideal moral person to "assist" creation through his moral perfection and insight and thus to benefit the human order. Renzen's poem, however, ends with the couplet

The beauty of this place is all because of Creation
Any human effort to add something is pointless here.

Just so, natural phenomena in the Heian courtly world are the object of detached aesthetic appreciation rather than the responsibility of human "assistance" or management. Smits shows how natural phenomena in the *Genji* are viewed through the lens of prosodic convention. This operated dialectically in two ways: the mood of a character, for instance Yūgiri, on his way through wild country to court Ochiba no Miya and troubled over infidelity to his main wife, can be intensified by symbols in the background such as the belling of a stag; alternatively, phenomena already present in the scene could arouse feelings in characters. In either case, however, the natural phenomena are broadly prescribed by prosodic practice established in influential Chinese and Japanese anthologies and handbooks. This view of nature informs the attitude to gardens in *The Tale of Genji*. Murasaki Shikibu's characters lavish care and expense on their gardens and spend time contemplating them for their aesthetic quality and literary associations. For her the garden was in effect a reordered improvement on nature at its most aesthetically and affectively resonant. Gardens are human constructs that arrange nature to form a sort of sounding board to give vibrancy and depth to the narrative. This perception of gardens is borne out by authorial praise comparing gardens to paintings.

How this intimate relationship between garden and sophisticated society works out in practice is illustrated in Smits's masterly analysis of Genji's great Rokujō garden. This elaborate project is more a symbolic recapitulation of Genji's personal ascendancy than a project of horticulture. The plan follows several separate schemes: its four sections house the womenfolk with whom Genji has had romantic relationships or to whom he has shown compassion. Spatially, the sections were dedicated to the four seasons. The planting was redolent of special symbolism; individual species of trees and flowers consciously marked the poetically ordered progression of the seasons, but also had symbolic meaning for the individual female residents of each section. But that was not all; the buildings, Smits shows, were also arranged auspiciously according to notions from Chinese geomancy. Finally, the garden evoked a famous historical precedent in which the arrangement of rocks, streams, and a lake gave a glimpse of a sublunary paradise, evoking associations with long life and good fortune. Appropriately, Genji's lake is on occasion host to extravagant revels that transport participants by boat to a paradise, neither purely Daoist nor Buddhist. Water, potentially a dangerous element in Japan, is tamed to form a scene of aesthetic delight. In this sense, there is a fugitive atmosphere to this great garden, not inappropriate to the rarefied, courtly consciousness of its residents. Thus the garden, in the words of Smits's conclusion, serves "as a fundamental means to unlock the world that *The Tale of Genji* represents.

"Rethinking Gender in The Tale of Genji" (Pandey)

The structure of this volume requires that two motifs recurrently featured in the foregoing analyses be explored further. They are the female authorship of the *Genji* within a society that severely restricted the role of women and the intrusion of the beliefs and practices of Buddhism. These encompassing aspects of the *Genji* define its uniqueness in world literary history; they challenge expectation and present paradoxes. The final two essays step back from the more highly focused preceding discussions to explore these themes. First, given the restrictions as a woman to which she was subjected, how could Murasaki Shikibu have created a literary masterpiece of such broad scope and transcendent merit? An established culture of storytelling in the Heian court and Murasaki Shikibu's own superordinate talent are partial explanations. Rajyashree Pandey, who has written insightfully and extensively on gender in classical Japanese literature, approaches this apparent paradox philosophically through an original deconstruction of gender in ancient Japan with special reference to *Genji*.

Pandey, like Denecke and Kamens, argues against binary categorizations; she, too, wishes to "defamiliarize" "the way we read the *Genji*." She starts from a useful survey of the relationship between biological sex and gender in West and East. Overall, her argument is that in the East Asian tradition but in the *Genji* in particular, the relationship between biological sex and culturally constructed gender is unstable; markers of gendered behavior are less fixed than in the Western tradition. Through careful analysis, Pandey exposes the loose, blurred, and situationally determined nature of gender distinctions in the novel. As she puts it, "How gender comes to be coded depends on the context in which it is performed."

One area concerns the relationship between status, gender, and sexuality. Pandey compares two different male reactions to *désahabillé* women: Genji's critical view of the low-ranking Nokiba no Ogi and Kaoru's positive response of the exalted First Princess. It is not so much gender as status that determines the difference between the two responses and creates the "asymmetries that are constitutive of all relationships in the text." Other circumstances offer parallel cases in which gender markers are blurred. One is that of dress, where cross-dressing occurs and "lovers often exchange and wear each other's robes." In *waka* verse, poetic voices are distinguished by gender, but, she argues, this is a stylized "persona" rather than the projection of a real person; gendered distinctions do not reflect actual situations; the relation between prosodic persona and the sex of the poet is loose. For instance, a female persona connotes waiting and pining, and "a poet, regardless of his or her biological sex, . . . can slip seamlessly into the persona of the waiting female or the male who visits."

Cross-gender use of language provides another example. In a discussion that cross-binds with Denecke's use of "juxtaposition" in analyzing the same *shinasadame* scene from "Hahakigi," Pandey describes the vivid account of a young man whose ladylove, the daughter of a Chinese scholar, speaks in a highly sinicized language, criticized in the gathering as unattractive in a woman. Pandey comments, "By bringing to life women such as herself . . . learned in

Chinese," Murasaki exposes "the fictive nature of the assumed iso-morphism of gender and language."

Pandey's most arresting questioning of received interpre-tations of gender concerns the Buddhist tonsure. In the novel, entering Buddhist orders is more common among women than men. It has been a subject of controversy, interpreted by scholars "in terms of a binary framework of domination and subordina-tion." Some have seen it as a gendered response to subjection, a positive expression of female agency gaining a "space of free-dom." Others have taken an opposing view; the tonsure is "a form of death in life," symptomatic of women's helplessness. Pandey argues cogently that the worldview and understanding of suf-fering in Heian Japan do not warrant such a gendered view of tonsure. Suffering was metaphysically ordained, built into the Buddhist teaching that infuses the novel; the tonsure should not be seen simply in monochromatic terms of individual submis-sion or resistance, or on a gendered axis. These views "eviscer-ate the text of the Buddhist worldview." She points, rather, to "multiple significations" behind men as well as women taking this step. Buddhism, moreover, has a positive side as instanced by the celebratory nature of the rituals that Murasaki organizes for Genji's fortieth birthday and the exemplary Buddhist nature of Murasaki's own death in the novel.

Women in *Genji* emerge from her analysis as often empowered personalities capable of engagement with society and of cultural practices that overlap with and sometimes challenge those of men. Gender, she contends, is a matter of performance rather than of existential or biological constraints. Her analysis supports the view of performance as constitutive of personhood and of the "aesthetic order" as the social context of *The Tale of Genji*. It is also relevant to feminist discourse today.

"Murasaki's 'Mind Ground': A Buddhist Theory of the Novel" (McCormick)

A priori, the creation of a large-scale panoramic and compelling fictional world such as the *Genji* presumes a coherent view of the world and of humanity. The concept of personhood in that context has already been addressed, but what of more radical metaphysical assumptions concerning the nature of experience and of reality? As will be apparent from references in the preceding essays, Buddhism provided a pervasive interpretation of the world among Japanese of the eleventh century. But herein lay a problem for the author of a fiction concerning the relations between men and women. How did Murasaki Shikibu justify her great work in the context of the basically world-denying and ascetic system of beliefs that dominated her world? This question troubled the author herself; in Chapter 25 "Hotaru" she uses Genji as a spokesman to mount a famous justification for fiction, in which she attempts to establish the value of realistic fiction to those committed to Buddhism and its quest for liberation. Melissa McCormick's essay, appropriately for the last in this volume, starts from this fundamental problem and proceeds to the larger questions both of the influence of Buddhism on the novel and of the Buddhist reading of the novel by Japanese posterity.

Murasaki Shikibu, as her diary attests, was deeply familiar with Buddhism. Her hero himself is drawn to the teaching. Already, by Chapter 10 "Sakakigi," Genji, still in his early twenties, is on retreat at a temple, the Urin'in, studying Tendai Buddhist texts. More germane, Genji's defense of fiction to his ward Tamakazura draws on the teachings of the Tendai sect of Buddhism to claim that good and evil, as depicted in the Mahayana sutras, are not metaphysically distinct. Evil acts, in McCormick's exegesis, "cannot exist apart from Bodhi-wisdom; both are constitutive of each other." Evil, properly understood, acts as an "expedient means" in the pursuit of enlightenment.

This nonduality of good and evil can be extended to other fictional narratives such as, implicitly, the *Genji* itself.

The nondualist approach to the literary treatment of evil, the essay continues, informs a major tradition of *Genji* exegesis in premodern Japan. It becomes linked to a view of Murasaki Shikibu as possessing a state of mind termed *shikan* (cessation [of attachment] and insight [into nondualistic reality]). This image was reflected in a tradition of portrait icons of Murasaki Shikibu illustrated and analyzed in McCormick's essay: Murasaki is depicted under a cartouche inscribed with a tetralemma associated with the Indian Buddhist philosopher Nāgārjuna (c. 150 – c. 250 CE) that explained non-duality as a mental state that negated all predications about reality: all things "exist; do not exist; both exist and do not exist; neither exist nor do not exist." Also inscribed on the icon are two poems by Murasaki Shikibu that are "repurposed" to show the "negation of the conventional self" and the "mutability of existence." In the Buddhist view, these enlightened states of mind enabled the author to create a work chronicling these truths "through an entire arc of human life."

From these essentially Buddhological principles associated with traditions concerning Murasaki Shikibu's authorship, McCormick turns back in a final section to the Buddhist reading of the *Genji* text. Legend had it that Murasaki Shikibu conceived and started writing the work while staying near the capital in the Tendai temple of Ishiyama on the fifteenth day of the eighth month, a day associated with the fullest moon of the year and with Buddhist enlightenment. She was in a meditative state as she began her work with a description of Genji, in exile at Suma, gazing at the moon and fully conscious of the Buddhist significance of this day. The moon inspires Buddhist-style empathy in him, first for his nearest and dearest in the distant capital, but extending to his servants and others of low estate.

McCormick's arguments are cogent in respect of the place of Buddhism in the *Genji* itself and Genji's own moral journey. They also reflect the reception history of the novel by a medieval Japanese posterity deeply influenced by Buddhism. However, McCormick does not beatify Genji but accepts that he continues to "struggle with his own self-professed sexual proclivities." The depth and multilayered complexity of Murasaki Shikibu's literary skill, it may also be pointed out, are illustrated by the allusive resonance of this same episode of exile with indigenous mythical tradition, with the historical Ariwara no Yukihira and his brother Narihira, Sugawara no Michizane. Further, as both McCormick and Denecke indicate, they resonate also with influential Chinese literary exemplars of exile such as Qu Yuan, Bai Juyi, and others.

CONCLUSION

The essays in this volume extend the ways in which *The Tale of Genji* can be read. No effort has been made to impose a uniform methodology or point of view; the interpretations offered here may not always be mutually consistent. Variations differ across a spectrum from points of detail to wider issues. The typhoon of Chapter 28 "Nowaki," for instance, which toward the end of Part I damages Genji's great Rokujō garden, is interpreted both as an opportunity for his son Yūgiri to see his stepmother improperly and as a hint of Genji's own approaching misfortunes. More substantially, views of women taking the Buddhist tonsure and indeed of Buddhism itself have different nuances; these views are seen either as an acceptance of helplessness and as an escape or as an assertion of autonomy and claim to liberation. Similarly, the role and status of women are differently interpreted; misogyny is strong, but women may also be empowered. Such various interpretations are, of course, not necessarily mutually exclusive. All have cogency, and attentive readers should find a continuing dialogue among scholars of the novel here. Above all, in their variety, more than a millennium after its creation, these essays pay tribute to the depth and continued relevance of Murasaki Shikibu's extraordinary work.

WORKS CITED

Aston, W. G. *A History of Japanese Literature: With an Introduction to the New Edition by Terence Barlow, PhD*. Rutland, VT: Charles E. Tuttle, 1972.

Bowring, Richard, tr. *The Diary of Lady Murasaki*. London: Penguin Books, rpt., 2005.

Elias, Norbert. *The Civilizing Process*. Tr. Edmund Jephcott. Oxford: Blackwell, 1994.

Elias, Norbert. *The Court Society*. Tr. Edmund Jephcott. Oxford: Basil Blackwood, 1983.

Grapard, Alan. "The Economics of Ritual Power." In Jon Breen and Mark Teeuwen, eds., *Shinto in History: Ways of the Kami*. Richmond, Surrey: Curzon Press, 2000.

Harper, Thomas, and Haruo Shirane, eds. *Reading "The Tale of Genji": Sources from the First Millennium*. New York: Columbia University Press, 2015.

Kawabata Yasunari. *Japan the Beautiful and Myself*. Tr. Edward G. Seidensticker. Tokyo: Kōdansha, 1968.

Kumazawa Banzan. *Yakaiki*. In Masamune Atsuo et al., comps., *Teizō Banzan zenshū*, vol. 5. Tokyo: Meicho Shuppan, 1978.

Miller, Alan L. "Ritsuryō Japan: The State as Liturgical Community." *History of Religion* 11, no. 1 (August 1971).

Mortimer, Raymond. "A New Planet." In *The Nation & the Atheneum*, June 20, 1925.

Pekarik, Andrew, ed. *Ukifune: Love in "The Tale of Genji."* New York: Columbia University Press, 1982.

Sasakawa Isao. "*Honchō Reisō* no Sekiten shi to '*Genji monogatari*.'" *Higashi Ajia Hikaku Bunka Kenkyū* 13 (2014).

Vos, Jos tr., *Her verhaal van Genji*. Amsterdam: Athenaeum-Polak & Van Gennep. 2013.

Waley, Arthur, tr. *The Sacred Tree: Being the Second Part of "The Tale of Genji."* London: George Allen & Unwin, 1926.

Chapter 1

The Structure of Genji's Career

Myth, Politics, and Pride

ROYALL TYLER

The Tale of Genji is a magnificent, intricate, and perplexing wonder. Centuries of readers have fallen under its spell, yet the more one engages with it, the more intriguing it becomes. Seeking to grasp it as a whole resembles striving to capture in one picture a landscape that changes with every hour, season, and play of light, as well as with the viewer's own mood and interests. This outline has been reached only by setting aside most of the work's best known and most admired characters, scenes, and themes. Perhaps it could be called an attempt to discern, through fascinating tissue, the tale's bones.[1]

THE IRRESISTIBLE HERO

Hero or villain, Genji is for most readers the lover of endless charm and wandering fancy whose style and taste define a courtly age. Just

---

1. The issues raised below, among others, are discussed more fully in Tyler, *A Reading of "The Tale of Genji."*

offstage, however, he can also be a maker and breaker of men. His half-brother, Retired Emperor Suzaku, remarks of him during their mature years:

> "When grave and dignified he has so superbly commanding a presence that one hardly dares to approach him, and when relaxed and in a playful mood he is sweeter and more engagingly amusing than anyone in the world." (t579–80)

The enchanting lover can also inspire fear and awe. This Genji reveals himself in Chapter 35 "Wakana II." Kashiwagi has been making love to Genji's wife. Genji has nonetheless been expressing publicly the most generous affection for him, but the reader knows that he is outraged beyond forgiveness. At a gathering he singles Kashiwagi out for attention with a venomous show of friendly banter and peers into his eyes. Kashiwagi goes home ill and dies some months later. "As soon as I met his gaze that evening," he says near the end, "my soul fled in anguish, and it has never come back" (t677). As a late-twelfth-century woman reader put it, Genji had "killed him with a glance."[2] One does not trifle with such a man.

LOVE AND POLITICS

One goal of this essay is to disentangle in Genji the courtier-politician from the lover. The other, which follows from the first, is to suggest that Genji's life moves along a political (for want of a better word) trajectory—a continuous though seldom seen armature—that gives

---

2. She made the remark in her comments on the tale, calling Genji "despicable" (*muge ni keshikaranu ōnkokoro*). Higuchi and Kuboki, eds., *Mumyōzōshi*, p. 199.

the tale an underlying form distinct from simple acknowledgment of passing time. This form develops and extends a myth recorded in the earliest Japanese chronicles: that of two rival brothers, to whom Genji and Suzaku correspond.

In the *Genji* author's world the relations between men and women, dressed in the rhetoric of courtship, often merged with political considerations. Whether as individuals or as members of great families, courtiers were acutely aware of rank, and political marriages were normal. Genji's informal marriage to Murasaki is unusual because, unlike the earlier, advantageous marriage to Aoi arranged by his father, it offers no political gain.

Above all, however, it is the narrator who blurs before her audience the most self-interested aspects of Genji's career. She is a gentlewoman who serves the great in Genji's fictional world, just as her creator, the author, served in her own similar, historical one. She therefore owes Genji the respect due his rank. Even two centuries later a lady remarked in her appreciation of the tale that it was not for her to criticize Genji, despite the many things about him that one might wish otherwise.[3] As a woman the narrator is free to treat romance but not, as she reminds her audience more than once, political issues or affairs of state.[4] Matters of the heart were construed as politically disinterested, hence untainted by the more or less tawdry appetites involved in maneuvering for hierarchical or financial advantage. The tale's prose makes fine hierarchical distinctions, but not so the language of poetry, in which love is prominent. The more imposingly elevated a character, the more discreet the

---

3. Ibid., p. 198.

4. For example, the narrator remarks after the conversations between Genji and Reizei in Chapter 19 "Usugumo," "Genji marshaled all the arguments he could, but I should not have repeated any of them" (t357). Matters of history and government are not for a woman to discuss.

narrator must therefore be, in principle, about action or motivation; but love remains relatively safe and reliably appealing ground. This imperative influences her treatment of Genji on the one hand and of Suzaku on the other.

In the case of Genji, the early chapters certainly tell more or less scandalous stories of which the narrator claims to disapprove. However, these do not matter because Genji is relatively junior at the time and because, belonging as they do to the domain of love, they do not impugn his essential dignity. Besides, he is a commoner. As time goes by he comes to command greater caution.

In contrast, Suzaku moves from heir apparent to emperor and then to retired emperor. He is purely imperial, and his prestige (whether or not accompanied by effective power) is impossible to overstate. Genji achieves a dramatic rise, but Suzaku is beyond rank from the start. Both are no doubt subject, as men, to the usual human foibles, but since anger, jealousy, and so on are unworthy of an emperor, the narrator gives Suzaku no such feelings. At times he seems hardly more than a kindly, honorable wraith. Writers on the tale therefore make relatively little of him, although his relationship with Genji is the longest in the book.

Centuries of reception, too, have tended to obscure Genji's political side and overwhelmingly favor the lover, and modern scholars have done the same. After his youthful escapades Genji rises to high office and honor, yet most authorities would have those adventures prolonged not by the maneuvering for rank and prestige that one would expect of a successful figure at any court, but instead by nostalgic pursuit (Asagao) or acceptance (the Third Princess) of only coincidentally prestigious, wealthy, politically advantageous women—women who merely remind Genji of some earlier passion.

THE CHARACTER OF GENJI'S TRIUMPH

The practical issues of concern to the mature Genji are imperial succession, acquisition of decisive influence at court, and hierarchically advantageous marriage. Accumulation of wealth remains beneath discussion in the tale, but it, too, deserves mention. From the start Genji seems to have at his disposal whatever resources he needs, but he is undoubtedly richer at the end than at the beginning. His famous Rokujō estate probably comes to him from the Rokujō Haven in exchange for his undertaking to look after Akikonomu, her daughter. The Akashi Novice's enormous wealth, too, passes to him. When the Third Princess catches his interest, he certainly knows what she is worth.

His path follows that of a man who comes against great odds to dominate his world and then, through an error of judgment, overreaches himself and loses what he holds most dear. It begins in the tale's first chapter. The Emperor, his father, has two sons: Suzaku, the elder, and Genji, the younger. Social constraints force him to favor the lackluster Suzaku publicly and appoint him heir apparent. Privately, he does all he can to favor the brilliant Genji, but he must be content in the end with giving him a surname and so making him a commoner. Feeling cheated of the imperial honor to which his gifts properly destined him, Genji maneuvers over time to overcome those who relegated him to this position, and eventually he succeeds. Pride then undoes him. When last seen (Chapter 41 "Maboroshi"), he is the shell of a once-great man.

Together with Genji's natural gifts and charisma, two key episodes, one open and one hidden, ensure his unheard-of rise. Overtly, exile accompanied by supernatural intervention propels him to victory over his political opponents and makes him the grandfather of an empress. Secretly, his affair with his father's empress also makes him the father of an emperor who, in time, confers upon him the title of honorary retired emperor. He comes to dominate his world. However, he does not rule it.

Scholars have debated the nature of what they call Genji's *ōken* (kingship, regal authority), a term unusual otherwise in Japanese discourse. It signals the difficulty of the issue.[5] Genji is not the emperor, who in any case decided little on his own. He exerts no moral suasion and wields no armed might; nor does the tale associate him with the Chinese ideal, rhetorically accepted in Japan, of the sovereign whose virtue inspires such willing obedience that he need do nothing at all.[6] Instead, Genji owes his supreme standing to supernatural favor, the workings of which can be grasped in terms of known motifs, but the deeper reasons for which remain unfathomable except as a device to create a transcendent hero—one impossible in the author's real world. Despite Genji's risks and lapses, luck has been with him. His aura is a gift of the gods. "The gods dwell on an upright head," a saying common in medieval Japan, is reversible: the head is proven upright by the gods' presence upon it. Exceptional gifts and great fortune confirm unalloyed worth.

THE MYTH OF HIKOHOHODEMI

The Tale of Genji falls naturally into three parts. The first consists of Chapters 1–33 ("Kiritsubo" through "Fuji no uraba"), the second of Chapters 34–41 ("Wakana I" through "Maboroshi"), and the third of

---

5. The term *ō* 王, often translated "king" in the context of early Chinese history, now generally refers to the "king" of a monarchy, particularly a European one, other than Japan. In Heian Japanese it means an imperial descendant with perhaps a degree of residual prestige but otherwise no authority at all.

6. In the rhetoric associated with his office, a reigning emperor was understood to be "complete in goodness" (*jūzen*) and to preside, even in a time of war, over a spontaneously peaceful realm.

Chapters 42–54 ("Niou Miya" through "Yume no ukihashi"). Genji reaches his political pinnacle at the end of Part I when, as honorary retired emperor, he entertains the Retired Emperor Suzaku and the reigning Emperor (Reizei, his secret son) on his Rokujō estate. Early signs of trouble appear on the first page of Part II and build toward disaster. Genji dies during the eight-year gap between Parts II and III.

The author drew the underlying pattern of Part I from a myth that she transposed into her own world and then, in Part II, extended. This myth follows the rivalry between two divine brothers known as Hikohohodemi and Honosusori.[7]

Hikohohodemi (Genji in the tale) hunts successfully in the mountains, while his elder brother Honosusori (Suzaku) fishes with equal success in the sea. Then the two trade places, and Hikohohodemi borrows his brother's fishhook. When a fish makes off with it, Hikohohodemi offers Honosusori others, but his brother will have none but the original. Hikohohodemi returns to the shore to look for it, feeling ill-used. There Shiotsuchi no Oji (Old Man Spirit of the Tides) arranges passage for him to the palace of the sea god (the Akashi Novice). Hikohohodemi marries the god's elder daughter, Toyotama-hime (the Akashi Lady), whom he leaves pregnant to return to the land, bearing as the sea god's parting gift a pair of magic jewels. With these, in the upper realm, he subdues his elder brother. Toyotama-hime then emerges on the shore to give birth, forbidding Hikohohodemi to look at her while she does so. However, he spies on her anyway and sees that in truth she is a

---

7. The earliest written recognition of the myth's relevance appears in the fourteenth-century *Genji* commentaries *Kakaishō* (ed. Tamagami, p. 320) and *Kachō yosei* (ed. Ii, p. 99) in glosses on a sentence from Chapter 12 "Suma": "[Genji] woke up and understood that the Dragon King of the Sea, a great lover of beauty, must have his eye on him" (t253). The correspondence has been developed in modern times by such scholars as Ishikawa ("Hikaru Genji ryūtaku no kōsō no gensen") and, in English, Shirane, (*The Bridge of Dreams*, pp. 77–79). *Kachō yosei* explicitly likens Genji to Hikohohodemi, the Akashi Lady to Toyotama-hime, and her father to the dragon king.

creature of the deep. Shamed and angry, she returns forever to the sea after bearing a son (Genji's daughter), then sends her younger sister, Tamayori-hime (Murasaki), to care for the boy. The boy marries Tamayori-hime and fathers Jinmu, the founder of the imperial line. Genji's daughter corresponds to Hikohohodemi's son because no son of Genji, a commoner, could have acceded to the throne. Overtly, Genji could come no closer to the throne than to father an emperor's wife and so become the grandfather of that emperor's successor.

GENJI AND SUZAKU

Genji's birth and childhood prepare the way for his later career by situating the myth's abstract brothers in a political struggle between two court factions, one led by the Left Minister (by the end of the Chapter 1 "Kiritsubo" Genji's father-in-law) and the other by Kokiden, Suzaku's mother. By having Genji's father make his favored son a commoner who can eventually serve the realm in such civil offices as minister or regent, the author spares her hero the strictures that confine a ranking prince and gives his future experience maximum scope. His surname and birth even allow him over time to live, openly or secretly, on both sides of the line that separates common from imperial.

Genji and his allies have the reader's full attention from the start. The spotlight is always on him, while Suzaku, his older brother, remains in shadow. No wonder Suzaku's mother complains bitterly at the end of Chapter 10 "Sakaki" that "no one has ever granted him any respect" (t219). Genji has every gift but lacks political backing, while the undistinguished Suzaku enjoys powerful support. This pervasive contrast makes political tension and conflict inevitable in one form or another. Genji might seem better off in the end with his greater, commoner liberty, but the narrative frequently evokes the overwhelmingly desirable prestige of the imperial.

The opening chapter therefore establishes a political struggle surrounding succession to the throne and factional dominance over the court, and it leaves no doubt about the incumbent Emperor's feelings on the subject. The author was personally familiar with an analogous situation. Political pressure forced Emperor Ichijō (r. 986–1011), under whose reign the tale was written, to bypass a son he favored and to appoint instead, as heir apparent to his successor, a grandson of Fujiwara no Michinaga (966–1027). Genji's father's decisive intervention from the afterworld, in Genji's favor and against the Suzaku faction in Chapter 13 "Akashi," conveys a pattern present schematically in the myth and not unknown in life.

Anger and so on may be unmentionable in connection with an emperor, but several developments might move any man in Suzaku's place to resent not only the esteem won by his younger brother, but also Genji's repeated, personal victories. The first of these, in the opening chapter, involves Genji's marriage to Aoi, the Left Minister's beloved daughter. The Left Minister and Suzaku's maternal grandfather, the Right Minister, are political rivals, and the former therefore hopes to strengthen his hand by securing the Emperor's favorite son. Normally he would give his daughter to the heir apparent, as both his daughter and Suzaku's mother assume. However, he rightly judges that the Emperor will agree for the sake of his favorite son's future.

In this way Suzaku, who has already let it be known that he wants Aoi, loses her, and Genji gets her instead. Infuriated by this slight, Suzaku's mother goes on to complain bitterly of what Genji has done to Oborozukiyo.

Kokiden once planned to give Oborozukiyo, a much younger half-sister, to her son, then still heir apparent. Before she could do so, however, Genji made love to the young woman himself (Chapter 8 "Hana no En"), striking up with her a passionate, lasting affair. Genji knew at the time that she was one of the Right Minister's daughters, although not which one, and he certainly understood the risk he was taking. Apparently he took it deliberately, because later in the same chapter he accepts her father's invitation to a party and arrives ostentatiously late, dressed, unlike anyone else present, in the manner of an imperial prince. By then he suspects that his conquest may be the sister destined for Suzaku, and at the end of the evening he confirms this with outrageous nonchalance, having meanwhile, by his entrance, flaunted his contempt for his host and all his host's faction. Then Genji carries on with the young woman so rashly, in her own house, that her father finds them in bed them together in Chapter 10 "Sakaki." Enraged once more, and already convinced that Genji is plotting to overthrow Suzaku, Kokiden vows to bring him down. Oborozukiyo goes to Suzaku in the end, but her affair with Genji makes her unappointable as *nyōgo* (consort), the only title that Suzaku's mother felt to be worthy of her.

EXILE AND THE GREAT STORM

In the myth, the elder brother's anger forces Hikohohodemi down to the sea. In the *Genji* transposition, Kokiden's anger drives Genji to the shore at Suma. There a great storm engulfs him, and mantic dreams urge him to move farther along the coast, to Akashi, where the Akashi Novice welcomes him. One scholar described the account of this storm as "uniquely dynamic and marked by particularly intense supernatural interventions." He continued:

Only the [Hikohohodemi] myth was charged with sufficient energy to break through all references to historical figures comparable in their experience to Genji ... and to create the vital conditions for the hero's rise to unequaled glory."[8]

The political, broadly defined, here merges with the supernatural.

Near dawn, after the first night of the storm, Genji drops off to sleep. A mysterious being then comes to him and reminds him that he has been summoned to the palace. He understands upon awakening that the dragon king of the sea, "a great lover of beauty," is calling him (t253).[9] This dragon king, the sea god of the myth, inhabits an undersea palace. When agitated or covetous, he causes storms. Only a precious offering will calm him—sometimes a fine bronze mirror, sometimes a priceless jewel, sometimes a beautiful woman. The sea king created the storm in order to acquire a treasure beyond price: Genji himself.

However, Genji cannot descend like Hikohohodemi to the sea king's palace, which for a human belongs to an inaccessible realm. He therefore stays where he is until his father's spirit disposes him to heed the call of the deep by putting it in terms of plausible action. As the storm subsides, the late Emperor appears to Genji in a dream. "What are you doing in this terrible place?" he says. "Hasten to sail away from this coast, as the God of Sumiyoshi would have you do" (t259). He goes on to explain that, finding Genji's plight unbearable, "I dove into the sea, emerged on the strand, and despite my fatigue am now hurrying to the palace to have a word with [Emperor Suzaku] on the matter."

This "word" will address Suzaku's failure to recall Genji to the capital. Actually, Suzaku himself would rather recall Genji, but his mother forbids it. The brothers' father therefore confronts him in

8. Takada, "Suma, à la croisée du lyrisme et du destin," p. 67.
9. The mysterious being recalls Shiotsuchi no Oji, who facilitated Hikohohodemi's journey to the sea god's palace. The expression *ito itō mono-mede suru mono* (a great lover of beauty) could also be translated "one who lusts after high value." Genji's beauty, akin as it is to that of imagined kings, queens, princes, and princesses not only in Japan but the world over, signals his overwhelming rank and supreme value.

a vision and, with his gaze, temporarily blinds him. The alarmed Kokiden eventually relents and permits Genji's return.

In the meantime the brothers' father, the sea (dragon) king, and the Sumiyoshi deity, working together, bring Genji to Akashi after all. Genji accepts the hospitality of the Novice, the sea king's counterpart and agent on this accessible earth and, like Hikohohodemi, establishes a bond with his daughter. Her child will rise to be empress, although she herself, a sea woman like Toyotama-hime, will remain in the background. Because she lacks the court standing to be an empress's mother, Genji will instead have the childless Murasaki bring up his daughter.

Hikohohodemi first returns from the sea god's palace and subdues his older brother; only then does Toyotama-hime emerge on the shore and bear the progenitor of the Japanese imperial line. Similarly, the Akashi Lady is pregnant when Genji returns to the capital, and she comes up to the capital with her daughter only after the birth. By that time Genji's return has swept Suzaku from the throne and all his faction from office (Chapter 14 "Miotsukushi"). However, instead of accepting the exalted post of regent for the new Emperor Reizei, Genji cedes it, together with that of chancellor, to his father-in-law, who was cashiered with all his supporters when Suzaku's faction triumphed and Genji went into exile.

Genji's apparent modesty is typical. He avoids ostentation and shuns any vulgar display of obvious power. In Chapter 31 "Makibashira" Hotaru forbids his angry wife to abuse Genji, since "he receives not a breath of public criticism. . . . He always manages very skillfully, without betraying himself, to help or harm people according to how they behaved when he was in disgrace" (t534). Genji seems to aim less at the role of power behind the throne than that of exemplary influence above it. His is no ordinary destiny. He owes his triumph to his late father's spirit and to the gods.

Chapter 24 "Hotaru" chapter begins, "Genji's weighty dignity now relieved him of all care and left him so entirely at peace that those who depended on him were satisfied and lived secure, fortunate lives" (t455). By this time he is chancellor, an exalted sinecure still within the accepted framework of commoner appointments, but his destiny requires more. That more comes to him thanks to his desperate love for his father's empress. Genji's affair with Fujitsubo, in the early chapters of the tale, has long shocked some readers in Japan and, recently, in other countries of the world. A more purely and more scandalously erotic secret could hardly be imagined, yet in the end it lifts Genji higher than any appointment consequent upon his return from Suma.

By Genji, Fujitsubo has a son whose resemblance to him terrifies her. Genji's father notices it but says nothing. Does he know? Perhaps not; but perhaps he does. If he does, he approves, and approval commands silence. This child, born of an empress whom Genji's father loves and a son whom he admires, will succeed the mediocre Suzaku. The child's future will therefore benefit the realm, redress an injustice, and satisfy Genji's father's own worthiest hopes. Although impossible to prove, this reading explains his assertive intervention during Genji's exile.

Medieval readers accepted a legend about how Murasaki Shikibu conceived the tale. She was contemplating the moon's reflection in the waters of Lake Biwa when a vision rose before her, and in a rush of inspiration she wrote down Chapters 12 and 13 "Suma" and "Akashi." Later on she added the other chapters, one by one. Scholars dismiss this legend, but perhaps it makes sense to imagine the author, in an exalted state of mind, writing at least the key sections of those chapters first. Nothing else in the tale resembles the storm or the supernatural agencies connected with it, and nothing else draws so vividly on the myth. If some passages have long resisted satisfactory explanation, that might be because the density and urgency of the author's initial conception, coupled perhaps with her relative lack of experience then as a writer, left them in a less developed narrative state.

For example, the account of Genji's exile says next to nothing about what was going on meanwhile in the capital. Considering the ruthlessness of Suzaku's mother and the upheavals associated with one faction's victory over another, it is difficult to believe that Genji's secret son, appointed heir apparent by Genji's father, came through those years unscathed; and yet he did. Surely his very existence was anathema to Suzaku's mother, who would have moved heaven and earth to replace him with an heir apparent amenable to her will.

Thirty-two chapters after "Akashi," the author of Chapter 45 "Hashihime" exploited this doubt in order to begin a completely new story about a character unheard of earlier.

> [The Eighth Prince] was ... Genji's younger brother. In the days when ... Reizei was Heir Apparent, ... Suzaku's mother had plotted to have the imperial dignity pass to *him* instead, but the turmoil she caused by championing him while in power unfortunately led to the other side severing all relations with him, and since after that the world belonged entirely to [Genji]'s descendants, he had been unable to appear in society at all. (t831–32)

The Kokiden faction's failure to change the heir apparent is unintelligible, although of course not strictly impossible. What known ally of the future Reizei could have saved him?

This anomaly suggests a planned link between Genji's political rise, thanks to the process derived from the myth, and the transpolitical one made possible by the secret of Reizei's conception. Immediately after his return from Akashi (Chapter 14 "Miotsukushi"), the narrative presents Genji and his son as an identical pair: "His Highness, now eleven, was tall and dignified for his age, and his face appeared to be traced from Genji's own. Both shone so dazzlingly that everyone sang their praises" (t282). As before, Fujitsubo is terrified that others may grasp what the resemblance means, but no one does.

Reizei learns the secret of his birth after his mother's death (Chapter 19 "Usugumo"). Horrified and "overcome by pity and dismay that [Genji] should serve the realm as a mere commoner" (t356), he combs Japanese history in vain for a precedent to his predicament. Certain examples suggest to him that it might barely be possible to appoint Genji chancellor, then cede him the throne on the grounds of his superior ability; but Genji sternly rejects the idea and accepts only the office of chancellor. Once more the narrative stresses that the two look precisely alike (t357).

Six years and thirteen chapters after Reizei learns the truth, Chapter 33 "Fujinouraba" closes Part I. Its last pages complete the story of Genji's rise.

> That autumn he was granted a rank equivalent to Retired Emperor. His emoluments rose . . . and he acquired such awesome dignity that to his chagrin he could hardly call at the palace any more. (t570–71)

This historically unheard-of appointment, made by Reizei, resolves the problem of how to lift Genji beyond chancellor without somehow making him emperor. In practice, not even Reizei could have done that. Genji has skirted the throne to become a retired emperor who never reigned.

In the myth, Hikohohodemi and his brother lack any social context, apart from the question of which one dominates. However, Genji was born into such social complexity that no simple upward path could have lifted him high enough to parallel the myth to its end: that is to say, to triumph over Suzaku in prestige as well as power.

Part I traces for Genji two paths from subordination to sovereignty. One, overt, follows the rules of the court. Genji's return forces Suzaku from the throne, but he remains a commoner, and a commoner cannot rise beyond the nonimperial office of chancellor. Only the second, secret path, which violates the sacred imperial succession, opens for him the door to imperial standing.

Appointment as honorary retired emperor gives the final touch to Genji's rise. He brilliantly entertains Suzaku and Reizei together at his Rokujō residence. When he prepares to sit slightly below his guests, Reizei will not have it. "By His Majesty's decree," the narrator says, this arrangement was rectified" (t573). Genji's seat is raised to the level of his guests'. In a society so sensitive to the finest gradations of rank, inches can make all the difference in the world. Reizei means only to honor his father, but for Suzaku the consequence is that the incomparably more influential Genji now sits at the same level as himself. He soon sounds, in a poem, "perhaps a little piqued" (t574).

GENJI'S MODESTY

Genji's discretion, modesty, and even professed disdain for worldly affairs deserve further mention before the discussion passes to Part II. The narrator mentions these traits often, but they need not always be taken too seriously. An attitude like Genji's may easily serve to blunt the disappointment of being underappreciated, deflect accusations of self-serving ambition, or simply put others off guard. Moreover, honor unsought has a special gleam. Beyond what might be Genji's psychology if he were a living man, there are also the requirements of narratorial caution. Genji may speak of wishing to enter religion, but he never does, no matter how attractively he may picture to himself the rewards of the renunciate life. He clings too tightly to his world.

His treatment of Murasaki, when she herself wishes to become a nun, makes this clear. Suffice it to emphasize here Genji's unvoiced but still, for the reader, explicit regret that Reizei (who by this time has abdicated) lacks an heir. Already the grandfather of a future emperor in the female line, Genji is disappointed not to be the same in the male.

> Genji...nursed his disappointment that Retired Emperor Reizei had no successor of his own. The Heir Apparent was his direct descendant, too, it was true, but while no trouble had ever arisen to disturb [Reizei's] reign, so that Genji's transgression had not come to light and now would never be known, as fate would have it, that line was not to continue. Genji regretted this very much, and since he could hardly discuss the matter with anyone else it continued to weigh on his mind. (t631)

He has long wished to right the wrong done him as a boy and to found his own imperial line.

PART II

Chapter 34 "Wakana I" begins Part II so remarkably that style alone identifies it as a new beginning. The reader has never seen such writing before. In other respects, however, the transition from the last page of "Fujinouraba" is seamless. Having ended her development of the Hikohohodemi myth, the author now sets out to extend the story on her own. Genji's triumph will undo both brothers.

Danger faces the man at last unchallenged in his world, should pride subvert his judgment. He may feel above error, or at least its consequences, and indulge in pursuing risky conquests. Meanwhile his defeated opponent may feel driven by circumstance to seek his help and all too swiftly rue having done so. This is what happens in Part II. The fulcrum on which the relationship between Genji and his brother tips toward disaster is Suzaku's favorite daughter, whom the narrator has never mentioned before.

In the last pages of "Fujinouraba," Suzaku sounds "perhaps a little piqued." "Wakana I" begins, "His Eminence Suzaku began feeling unwell soon after His Majesty's visit to Rokujō" (t578). Although felicitous for Genji and Reizei, the visit did Suzaku no good. He has finally decided to leave the world, to prepare for death, but he cannot bear to do so until he finds a suitable husband for his beloved Third Princess.

At twelve or thirteen, Suzaku's favorite daughter (his others do not matter) is childish and small for her age. She is *onzo-gachi*, "lost in her clothes." Personally, she offers nothing. Nonetheless her father loves her so extravagantly that in preparation for renouncing the world he gives her everything of value that he owns. Her rank and wealth therefore make her a prize coveted by every ambitious gentlemen of the court. For Suzaku, only Genji will do.

Like Murasaki, the Third Princess is a niece of Fujitsubo. Genji's marriage to her estranges him first from Murasaki and then from Suzaku, and in the end ruins both brothers' lives. Together, Genji's helpless devotion to Murasaki and Suzaku's to his daughter precipitate the disaster. Genji's devotion to Murasaki needs no comment. It is Suzaku's to his daughter, somewhat puzzling at first, that moves the narrative on toward the end of the brothers' story.

Why does Genji marry the Third Princess? The common answer invokes erotic nostalgia, that is to say, erotic interest in the daughter (Akikonomu, Tamakazura) or even a niece (the Third Princess) of a woman he once loved. Therefore it is widely agreed that he accepts the Third Princess as a memento of Fujitsubo.[10] One authority also suggested that Genji hopes for a new Murasaki and called the marriage an attempt on his part to relive the past.[11] Some also have conceded an element of pity for Suzaku.

In the case of Akikonomu and Tamakazura, the full content of such a nostalgic attraction remains unclear. Why should Genji find both irresistible? No doubt they are handsome enough and call up memories, but he also might wish partly, in the case of Akikonomu, to possess yet another woman destined (like Oborozukiyo, but higher in rank) for Suzaku or, in that of Tamakazura, to leave his mark less on Yūgao's daughter than on Tō no Chūjō's. If such thoughts ever occurred to the author, her narrator could not have mentioned them.

More relevant to the matter of the Third Princess is Genji's pursuit, in Part I, of his cousin Asagao. Asagao is the daughter of a brother of Genji's father. Genji was courting her already in the Chapter 2 "Hahakigi"). She kept her distance, but at times thereafter he continued to pursue her, even at the risk of scandal. Years later, in Chapter 20 "Asagao," he lays siege to her again. The chapter begins:

> Genji, whose peculiarity [*kuse*] it was as usual never to break off
> a courtship that he had once started, sent her frequent notes, but
> she remembered the trouble she had had with him before, and
> she kept her answers strictly correct. (t366)

In her case, too, Genji's motivation has been attributed to erotic nostalgia for the late Fujitsubo, although it is unclear where that element might lie.[12] Later in the chapter one reads, "Genji did not exactly burn for [Asagao], but her coolness maddened him, and he hated to admit

---

10. Shirane, *The Bridge of Dreams*, p. 39; Field, *The Splendor of Longing*, p. 25; Bargen, *A Woman's Weapon*, p. 128; d'Etcheverry, *Love after "The Tale of Genji,"* p. 95.
11. Ōasa, "Onna Sannomiya no kōka," pp. 85, 88.
12. Shimizu, *Genji no onnagimi*, pp. 43–49.

defeat" (t372). Some have therefore invoked Genji's love of risk, as in the case of Oborozukiyo, or simply his refusal to lose a contest once begun.[13] However, these ideas are not helpful, considering that by the time of the "Asagao" chapter Genji is mature and established. In Murasaki he already has his personal treasure, and he has recently been offered the office of chancellor.

Early in Chapter 21 "Otome," an aunt of both Genji and Asagao makes it explicit that, even long ago, Asagao's father had wanted to marry his daughter to Genji and that he did not consider Genji's then-current marriage to Aoi an obstacle (t380). He and the aunt both took it for granted that Asagao outranked Aoi, even if the prestige of Aoi's mother and the power of Aoi's commoner father might have made the marriage politically tricky to achieve. The aunt ignores Murasaki, who for her does not count. Social "common sense" does not give Murasaki, a prince's unrecognized daughter, the weight to be taken seriously as Genji's wife. Later on, in relation to the Third Princess, she counts even less.

That is why Genji pursued Asagao in the chapter named for her, and no doubt also why he set out to court her in his youth. Even then he desired her imperial prestige. Now the problem is acute: Murasaki is publicly unworthy of him. Long ago he chose her without reference to social convention; he loves her deeply; and she is the emblem of the private autonomy on which he insists. However, he sees as he rises that autonomy outside the established social structure is not enough. He therefore seeks to conform to this structure in order to turn it to the ends of his own sovereignty. Asagao is not fascinating personally, but in a sense she is an old friend. His campaign to possess her has nothing erotic about it. He simply wants a princess worthy of him. With this one, however, he fails.

---

13. Field, *The Splendor of Longing*, p. 177.

Therefore he accepts in time Suzaku's incomparably more prestigious but far less interesting daughter. Perhaps her connection with Fujitsubo piques his curiosity, but he does nothing to find out whether her personal qualities correspond to those that he may casually imagine. They do not matter, as long as she is more or less what her birth and upbringing would lead one to expect. She is simply the culminating ornament to his glory.

No passage of the tale is more masterfully written, more difficult, or from the perspective of this essay more instructive than that in "Wakana I" between Suzaku's final choice of Genji and Genji's acquiescence. So exalted is the rank of both men, and so sensitive their dignity, that the matter is very delicate indeed. Suzaku cannot risk embarrassment by straightforwardly offering his daughter to Genji, because Genji might decline. He cannot safely approach Genji at all unless he already knows that Genji will say yes. Meanwhile Genji cannot just ask for her without lowering himself to the level of all the others, far beneath him, who have already done so. He must maneuver Suzaku into offering her to him.

Suzaku therefore requires reliable, discreet intelligence regarding Genji's feelings on the subject, and Genji needs a similarly discreet way to convey them to Suzaku. Two subordinates serve this purpose. On Suzaku's side there is the Third Princess's senior nurse and on Genji's one of his officials, the nurse's brother (t581). Genji has ample opportunity throughout to let Suzaku know that he would refuse if asked. Since he does not, the process continues. The weight and delicacy of the negotiations can be gauged from the way they end. By the time the two men meet to discuss the matter Suzaku knows Genji's position, yet he still dares not speak plainly. He only asks Genji to assume responsibility for finding his daughter a suitable husband, and on the surface that is all Genji agrees to do. However, the narrator confirms that each knows exactly what the other means. The passage ends, "With these words, Genji accepted" (t587).

If ever in the tale an educated English reader's natural understanding diverges from the one widely assumed in Japan, it is here, on the subject of what to make of this back-channel conversation. Speaking for herself and her brother, the nurse tells Suzaku that Genji's household recognizes the close relationship between Genji and Murasaki, but also takes for granted Murasaki's inadequacy as Genji's wife, and that all therefore hope to see him properly married. Similar people were saying similar things ("Those two would not go at all badly together" [t368]) when Genji courted Asagao. The nurse further assures Suzaku that Genji himself "deeply desires a lofty alliance and . . . has so little forgotten [Asagao] that he still corresponds with her" (t580). According to her brother, she reports, "[Genji] would undoubtedly welcome the idea [of the marriage], since it would mean the fulfillment of his own enduring hopes" (t581). Nowhere in these pages, in thought or speech, does Murasaki figure in Genji's calculations.

These calculations make sound, if heartless, social sense. They self-evidently illustrate the practical truth, often dramatized in English and other European languages, that underlings are privy to their masters' secrets. However, this truth is so incompatible with the view of Genji accepted in Japan that no writer on the tale in English even mentions the testimony of the nurse and her brother. Those who mention it in Japanese do so only to dismiss it. [14] According to one authority, the reader understands that Genji's courtship of Asagao sprang from a "retrospective passion," and the nurse's report is therefore a "petty, irresponsible assumption." "Ordinary people," he wrote, "are hardly capable of understanding Hikaru Genji's inner feelings."[15] Another doubted that the nurse could possibly believe what she says

14. A notable exception is Mitoma Kōsuke, a scholar of myth and folklore, who accepted the nurse's and her brother's testimony. See "Suzaku-in ron," p. 364.
15. Ōasa, "Onna Sannomiya no kōka," p. 76.

and refused to take her brother's testimony seriously.[16] No two readings of the same material could diverge more completely or cast the tale's hero in a more different light.[17]

THE FINAL CONFRONTATION

Genji's marriage moves the contest between the brothers into a final phase provoked by the suffering of the woman dearest to each.

In order to honor the Third Princess as her rank demands and her father expects, Genji must neglect Murasaki. However, he finds himself discharging that obligation less and less willingly, and when Murasaki falls ill he spends nearly all his time at her side. In his absence Kashiwagi, who in the past became infatuated with the Third Princess, gains access to her.[18] She conceives, Genji discovers the truth, and the terrified Kashiwagi dies just after the birth of her (Kashiwagi's) son. Genji's neglect of the Third Princess, in Murasaki's favor, is at fault. He has abysmally failed the brother who counted blindly on him and who in the meantime has become a monk at a mountain temple. The incident is a disaster for Genji, too, needless to say, but for the moment he expects to keep it hidden.

---

16. Akiyama, *Genji monogatari no sekai*, pp. 165, 183 n. 4.

17. Bitterly disappointed by the Third Princess, Genji eventually blames himself for having "allowed a wanton weakness to get the better of him" (t593). "Wanton" suggests an erotic motive, but whether the original (*adadashiku*) means just that is unclear. "Frivolous" might do better. While the note to the standard Shogakukan edition of *Genji monogatari* (g4/62–63, n. 2), states that Genji laments his excessive erotic susceptibility, the Iwanami edition (Yanai ed., *Shin Nihon koten bungaku taikei*, vol. 3, pp. 240–41, n. 9) explains that he regrets having been drawn by foolish curiosity to the idea of marrying a princess and then having been unable to refuse Suzaku's request. The idea of marrying her for her rank, too, might now look frivolous to him. In any case, Genji may be veiling his less worthy motives from even himself, and the narrator veiling them from the reader.

18. The Third Princess is hopeless at running her staff, who should never have left her alone or been allowed to do so. This lapse is typical of her.

The Third Princess is terrified of Genji, and desperately ashamed. After the birth she tells him "in a much more grownup manner than usual" that she is dying and that she intends to become a nun (t679). He replies that she greatly exaggerates the gravity of her condition and that she cannot possibly become a nun. Her doing so would make him look bad, and in any case, she is his. His constancy of interest in every woman he has once known (described as his "peculiarity" in connection with Asagao) is legendary, but the other side of it is that he cannot release a woman whom he has once claimed.

Privately, however, even Genji begins to reconsider.

> The poor thing is all too likely to come under a cloud again if she goes on with me this way. . . . People will note my indifference, and that will be unfortunate, because when [Suzaku] hears of it the fault will appear to be entirely mine. Her present indisposition makes a good excuse to let her do it—I might as well. (t679)

"The idea repelled him," the narrator says, but even Genji recognizes that he will be well rid of her, if only he can make it appear that impending death left her no choice but to renounce the world and that he therefore permitted her to do so. He assumes that Suzaku does not know and need not find out.

He is wrong. Suzaku has already blamed him repeatedly and has even taken countermeasures against Genji's neglect of his daughter by raising her even further in rank, thus increasing the pressure on Genji to treat her properly. He even suspects that her child is not Genji's, having worked this out when he learned that she was pregnant.

> [Suzaku], cloistered on his mountain, heard about her condition and thought of her with tender longing. People told him that Genji had been away for months and hardly visited her at all, at which he wondered despairingly what had happened and

resented more than ever the vagaries of conjugal life. He felt
uneasy when [Murasaki] was seriously ill and Genji, so he heard,
spent all his time looking after her. . . . *Did* something unfortunate occur while [Genji] was elsewhere? Did those hopeless
women of hers take some sort of initiative without her knowledge or consent? (t665)

Yes, he knows. Genji cannot escape his informed censure. It is already
upon him.

A few days after the birth, the Third Princess cries out in anguish
that she may never see her father again. Genji must inform Suzaku.
Devastated, Suzaku comes down from his temple under cover of
night and goes to straight to his daughter. This fatherly response is
disastrous.

Dazzling gifts have always so favored Genji that Suzaku has had
little reason to expect much good from him personally, but for the
sake of his daughter's future and his own peace of mind he still ven-
tured to pin all his hopes on him, at least as a husband for her. Genji
has now betrayed him in that, too. Having entered religion once the
marriage was settled, Suzaku should have renounced all profane
attachments, but his anxiety about her has haunted him repeatedly
ever since, disrupting his practice and turning his thoughts back to
worldly sorrows. Then her piteous call reaches him. His helpless
response compromises his religious vows, his dignity, his practice,
and even the character of his eventual death. It is one thing for a
father to bear his own trials patiently, but quite another for him to
suffer while a beloved daughter, whose future he has done everything to ensure, nonetheless suffers misery and humiliation. Not for
a moment can he doubt that Genji is responsible.

Suzaku's sudden arrival is a grave shock (t680). While his daughter implores him to make her a nun, the horrified Genji struggles in

vain to dissuade a once all but helpless pair now obstinately in league
to thwart him.

> [Suzaku] silently reflected that after accepting the daughter offered
> him with such boundless trust, Genji had failed in his devotion
> to her. . . . Why not take this opportunity to remove her from
> [Genji] . . . without exposing her to ridicule by leaving the impres-
> sion that she had merely despaired of him? (t680–81)

His dissatisfaction with Genji, however decorously phrased, is finally
explicit. He obliges his daughter. Genji, beside himself, can only weep.

Murasaki never recovers from the shock and the consequences of
Genji's marriage to the Third Princess. During four more years of crisis,
weakness, and reprieve, she begs Genji repeatedly, in vain, for permis-
sion to renounce the world. Then she dies. Lost without her, he can do
little thereafter but await his own death.

CONCLUSION

Suzaku dies before the beginning of Part III, during which the Third
Princess drops out of the narrative. The rivalry established in the tale's
opening chapter runs its course to the end of Part II and ruins the last
years of both brothers. However, a third of the tale remains unaccounted
for. What, then, of Part III?

The reception of this part is particularly diverse. Some readers
prefer it, some admire it for theoretical reasons, and others strive
to understand why it should differ so from what precedes it. Many
readings of it, in whole or in part, have been proposed. I have argued
elsewhere that the embittered Suzaku, who broke his religious vows
to save his daughter from Genji, lives on as a wrathful spirit intent on

destroying Genji's legacy[19] and that Suzaku's curse therefore hangs over Part III.[20] This idea extends the brothers' story to the last line of the tale. However, the narrative's ambiguities and inconsistencies make it, too, impossible to prove.

The foregoing reading of the "bones" of Parts I and II dismisses the widely accepted, insistently erotic approach to the hero—one that renders him all but unintelligible among figures of comparable stature in other literatures by effectively denying him political motives and ambitions. This emphasis on brilliantly evoked relations with women also leaves much about the tale unexplained and makes it seem entirely episodic in nature. It could have been that, of course: a series of romantic adventures and misadventures continuous only thanks to passing time. However, it is not. That is one of the most extraordinary things about it, and yet another testament to the genius of the writer who gave it to the world a thousand years ago.

REFLECTIONS ON PART III

Genji's death closes Part II of the tale. By the beginning of Part III, eight years later, Suzaku, too, is gone, and the Third Princess has vanished from the narrative. Even alone, Part III would be the masterpiece of Heian fiction, but its relationship to what precedes it is not entirely clear.

Part III principally concerns Kaoru, thought to be Genji's son but really Kashiwagi's; Prince Niou, Genji's grandson; two full sisters, the daughters of an impoverished prince; and their half-sister, Ukifune. Kaoru and Niou are friends and rivals, but interest has long focused

---

19. Many stories roughly of the time attest that this is exactly what happened to a monk who broke his religious vows.
20. See Tyler, "Genji and Suzaku: The Possibility of Ukifune."

especially on Kaoru and on Ukifune, whose story the tale's closing chapters tell.

The heroes of later Heian fiction recall Kaoru rather than Genji, whose creator evoked his character, career, and scope in a manner not emulated thereafter. Modern scholars (mainly male) have often called Genji an "ideal" hero, but the female author of *Mumyōzōshi* (ca. 1200) found in him much to criticize. Of Kaoru, however, she wrote, "There is nothing about him that one would wish to be different."[21] Current readers may agree, despite Genji's canonical prestige, either because as men they identify more easily with Kaoru or because as women they object to Genji's ways.[22]

Part III therefore differs significantly from the rest. Indeed, some scholars have noted a "feeling of mismatch" (*iwakan*) or an "epistemological disjunction" (*ninshikiteki setsudan*) between it and the rest.[23] One discerned in it "multidimensional fragmentation of the subject" and characters unable even to communicate among themselves.[24] Another, in a particularly influential essay, likewise found here a new approach to characterization that, in keeping with a "hollowed-out" world, undermines the "myth of unity" of character.[25] Indeed, he discussed the divergent character of Part III in terms startling enough to stir thoughts of different authorship. However, he made no such suggestion.

Single authorship has always been taken for granted, and in modern times the idea that someone else might have had a hand in the tale remains (in the absence of any evidence beyond the narrative itself)

---

21. Higuchi and Kuboki, *Mumyōzōshi*, p. 199.
22. The ways of the hero of *Sagoromo monogatari*, for example, are far from edifying, but he is still unlike Genji. For a discussion of Kaoru as a character, see Tyler, "Pity Poor Kaoru."
23. Kubo, "Zokuhen sakusha ibun," pp. 207–208 and ; and Kanda, *Monogatari bungaku, sono kaitai*, cited by Kobayashi, "Uji jūjō no genzai ni kaete: aku no zanshō," p. 352.
24. Takahashi, "Aishū no tsumi," pp. 153–54.
25. Mitani, "Genji monogatari daisanbu no hōhō," p. 94.

academically out of bounds. The possibility has been raised at times, especially regarding Part III's initial chapters, but only to meet silence or dismissal. Accepted effort has gone instead into arguing consistency of authorial purpose and, often, rising literary achievement.

Part III begins, "His light was gone, and none among his descendants could compare to what he had been" (t785). Discussion, too, begins with this sentence. Kaoru and Niou, Genji's successors, are lesser men in a diminished world. One critic saw in the tale as a whole a Hegelian dialectic of light and darkness.[26] Another wrote, "The atmosphere of *The Tale of Genji* turns dark and cold, as though one had stepped down into a cellar."[27] Chateaubriand (1768–1848) similarly described Napoleon's successors as "dubious, nocturnal creatures . . . in a world the great sun of which was gone."[28]

For centuries commentators have understood the serious Kaoru and the womanizing Niou to divide Genji's chief traits between them. This reading is natural, since the complementary pair is a ubiquitous motif in premodern Japan. However, the characterization of Genji in Parts I and II cannot explain the way these two are evoked in Part III, with its "multidimensional fragmentation of the subject."

Efforts to read Part III as consistent with the rest do not always succeed. For example, it has been proposed that Kaoru's discovery of the two Uji sisters in Chapter 45 "Hashihime" "echoes" Genji's discovery of Murasaki in Chapter 5 "Wakamurasaki."[29] Perhaps it does. In outline, however, it better matches the first episode of *Ise monogatari*, since it involves two marriageable sisters, not the one little girl of "Wakamurasaki." Moreover, the earlier scene is fresh and unassuming, the later one elaborate and theatrical. The reader may prefer

26. Kobayashi, "Uji jūjō no genzai ni kaete," p. 349.
27. Odagiri, "Uji jūjō: Chūsei bungaku e," p. 393.
28. Chateaubriand, *Mémoires d'outre-tombe*, pp. 3–4; author's translation.
29. Shirane, *The Bridge of Dreams*, p. 140.

either, but granted that both share the *kaimami* (peeping through a crack) motif, they still differ greatly in flavor. The "echo" may not be one.

Other suggested parallels, too, stand or fall according to the reader's perspective. Declaring that "[n]o understanding of Part Three is possible without an understanding of Part Two,"[30] one scholar cited, for example, the roles played by two "sisters" (*shimai*) in Part II (Murasaki and the Third Princess, cousins unrelated in life until Genji marries the latter) and the two full sisters and one half-sister of Part III; and the adulteries between Kashiwagi and the Third Princess (Part II), and Niou and Ukifune (Part III). However, these examples illustrate "epistemological disjunction" equally well. From the perspective of contextual circumstance and literary character they shed no particular light on each other.

The modern academic (not to mention the pop) reception of *The Tale of Genji* deserves study in itself. National pride, trends in political and social thought, and literary fashion are among the factors that have influenced it. The literary theorist Takeda Munetoshi wrote in the mid-1950s:

Part One was written from an idealistic perspective, although one cannot call the ideals in question very high. Part Two conveyed actual suffering from an objective perspective and so at last approached reality. Part Three can be said to have conveyed the times through individual experience and reflected human universality beyond time, and thus to have achieved symbolic truth in the deepest sense. With Part Three, *The Tale of Genji* comes at last to deserve being called a masterpiece.[31]

30. Ishida, "Seihen kara zokuhen e," p. 22.
31. Quoted by Akiyama, "Kanketsuteki na seishin hatten ron," p. 138. The passage is from Takeda's *Genji monogatari no kenkyū.*

Several decades later Konishi Jin'ichi defined for each part of the tale a pair of themes (reality and insight, karma and fated suffering, piety and spiritual blindness), each of which embraces the preceding ones, and read Part III as a supreme masterpiece that sums up in Kaoru's dilemma (eros or piety) the fundamental concerns of the whole work.[32]

Perhaps. Or perhaps not, depending on the reader. Ukifune illustrates the issue. She has been praised for freeing herself from men (especially Kaoru) and setting out bravely toward salvation. Some have even suggested that through her, the tale's last heroine, the author herself reached paradise. However, the narrative also suggests that Ukifune may mean only trouble for those around her and even for herself.[33] Such are the enigmas and ambiguities of the tale's remarkable Part III.

WORKS CITED

Akiyama Ken. *Genji monogatari no sekai*. Tokyo: Tōkyō Daigaku Shuppankai, 1964.

Akiyama Ken. "Kanketsuteki na seishin hatten ron." *Genji monogatari o dō yomu ka* (*Kokubungaku kaishaku to kanshō bessatsu*) (April 1986).

Bargen, Doris. *A Woman's Weapon: Spirit Possession in "The Tale of Genji."* Honolulu: University of Hawai'i Press, 1997.

Chateaubriand. *Mémoires d'outre-tombe*. In Gallimard, La Pléiade, vol. 2.

d'Etcheverry, Charo B. *Love after "The Tale of Genji": Rewriting the World of the Shining Prince*. Cambridge MA: Harvard University Asia Center, 2007.

Field, Norma. *The Splendor of Longing in the "Tale of Genji."* Princeton NJ: Princeton University Press, 1987.

Higuchi Yoshimaro and Kuboki Tetsuo, eds. *Matsura no Miya monogatari, Mumyōzōshi* (*Shin Nihon koten bungaku taikei*, vol. 40). Tokyo: Shogakukan, 1999.

Ishida Jōji. "Seihen kara zokuhen e." In *Genji monogatari kōza* (10 vols.), vol. 4 (*Kyō to Uji no monogatari, monogatari sakka no sekai*). Edited by Imai Takuya et al. Tokyo: Benseisha, 1992.

---

32. Konishi, *A History of Japanese Literature*, , vol. 3, p. 333.
33. See Tyler, Royall "Genji and Suzaku: The Possibility of Ukifune."

Ishikawa Tōru. "Hikaru Genji ryūtaku no kōsō no gensen." In his *Heian jidai monogatari bungaku ron*. Tokyo: Kasama Shoin, 1979.

Kachō yosei. Edited by Ii Haruki (Genji monogatari kochū shūsei, vol. 1). Tokyo: Ōfūsha, 1978.

Kakaishō. Edited by Tamagami Takuya. In *Shimeishō, Kakaishō*. Tokyo: Kadokawa, 1968.

Kanda Tatsumi. *Monogatari bungaku, sono kaitai: Genji monogatari Uji jūjō ikō*. Tokyo: Yūseidō, 1992.

Kobayashi Masaaki. "Uji jūjō no genzai ni kaete: Aku no zanshō." In *Genji monogatari: Uji jūjō no kuwadate*. Edited by Sekine Kenji. Tokyo: Ōfūsha 2005.

Konishi, Jin'ichi. *A History of Japanese Literature*. 5 vols. Princeton NJ: Princeton University Press, 1986.

Kubo Tomotaka. "Zokuhen sakusha ibun: *Kachō yosei* kara keiryō bunkengaku e." In *Genji monogatari: Uji jūjō no kuwadate*. Edited by Sekine Kenji. Tokyo: Ōfūsha, 2005.

Mitani Kuniaki. "Genji monogatari daisanbu no hōhō: Chūshin no sōshitsu aruiwa fuzai no monogatari." *Bungaku* 50 (August 1982).

Mitoma Kōsuke. "Suzaku-in ron." In his *Genji monogatari no denshō to sōzō*. Ōfū, 1995.

Ōasa Yūji. "Onna Sannomiya no kōka." In his *Genji monogatari seihen no kenkyū*. Tokyo: Ōfūsha, 1975.

Odagiri Hideo. "Uji jūjō: chūsei bungaku e." In *Hihyō shūsei Genji monogatari*, vol. 3 (*Kindai no hihyō*). Edited by Akiyama Ken et al. Tokyo: Yumani Shobō, 1999.

Shimizu Yoshiko. *Genji no onnagimi*. Tokyo: Hanawa Shobō, 1967.

Shirane, Haruo. *The Bridge of Dreams: A Poetics of "The Tale of Genji."* Stanford, CA: Stanford University Press, 1987.

Takada Hirohiko. "Suma, à la croisée du lyrisme et du destin." In *Cipango* (Numéro Hors-série, *Autour du* Genji monogatari), 2008.

Takahashi Tōru. "Aishū no tsumi: Ukifune no genzoku to bukkyō." In Sekine Kenji, ed. *Genji monogatari: Uji jūjō no kuwadate*. Tokyo: Ōfūsha, 2005.

Tyler, Royall. "Pity Poor Kaoru." In *A Reading of "The Tale of Genji."*

Tyler, Royall. "The Possibility of Ukifune." In *A Reading of "The Tale of Genji."*

Tyler, Royall. *A Reading of "The Tale of Genji."* Blue-Tongue Books, 2016; slightly reformatted, under a new imprint, from the original edition published in 2014.

Tyler, Royall, tr., *The Tale of Genji*. New York: Viking, 2001 (hardback); Penguin, 2002 (paperback).

Yanai Shigeshi et al, eds. *Genji monogatari*, 5 vols. Tokyo: Tokyo: Iwanami Shoten: 1993–97.

Chapter 2

The Epistemology of Space
in *The Tale of Genji*

WIEBKE DENECKE

NAVIGATING *GENJI*

Although *The Tale of Genji* is a sprawling narrative in fifty-four chapters, populated by several hundred characters, featuring almost eight hundred *waka* poems, and running to thirteen hundred pages in the most recent English translation, the tale relies on a surprisingly small repertoire of narrative moves and temporal and spatial models. Plot is frequently developed along patterns of replacement, displacement, or alternative emplacement: protagonists like Genji are out to replace lost parents or lovers with closely resembling ersatz figures; or they "displace" the frustration of their desires by choosing a momentarily more attainable object of love; or new, parallel protagonists—of a next or displaced same generation—are suddenly "emplaced" into ever more complex stories, drawing on the power of previous plotlines. Temporally, the tale moves along repeating patterns—with stunning variations—of the life paths of the growing number of protagonists through romance, love, marriage, politics, court life, and Buddhist renunciation. And spatially, the tale operates on a limited number of models for describing and encoding space that often exceed their literal reference.

This chapter uncovers the "epistemology of space" inscribed in the tale, arguing that Murasaki Shikibu was keenly interested in philosophical questions of how humans, or in particular Heian Japanese, experience, describe, remember, value, and use space along the trajectory of their lives and of how spatial categories can be mobilized to great narrative effect. And it shows how China and continental culture played a pivotal role in formulating and engaging these questions throughout the tale.

Although today *The Tale of Genji* counts as a quintessentially Japanese classic, its engagement with China—as a geographical, political, social, textual, linguistic, literary, material, and aesthetic presence and entity—shapes the novel on virtually every page. The tale's elevation to a classic of "national literature" in the late nineteenth century just around the time that the militarily ascendant Japanese Empire started to invert the power balance in East Asia's Sinographic Sphere (the countries relying traditionally on the Chinese script and textual canons, including today's Korea, Japan, Vietnam) has blinded us to this overwhelming presence beyond the most obvious references to China and Chinese texts in the tale. "China" appears more often as a domestic cipher than as a foreign cultural space and, as I will show, it allowed Murasaki Shikibu to work through fundamental questions about spatial perception and representation: How does space create, structure, and "color" human experience and memory? How can representations of space shape literary characters, structure their psychology, and evoke larger narrative arcs and moods? Where should one place Japan or the Heian capital in the spatial and political cosmology of the greater Chinese world, East Asia's Sinographic Sphere? And, crucially, how could a female author living in a strongly gender-segregated society grasp and narrate male spaces that were physically or socially inaccessible to her? What role did forms of spatial duality, such as gender segregation, play in Heian society and how and to what effect does Murasaki Shikibu represent them, "translate" them into the aesthetic space of the tale's narrative?

This essay explores how philosophical questions about humans' experience of space, and writers' manipulation of spatial representation, inform the world of the *Genji*; how they drive the tale's plot, character portrayal, and stylistic texture; and how Murasaki Shikibu, by developing such a programmatic approach to space and spatial representation, helps us grasp the human condition with all its complexities, felicities, failures, and sufferings, small and large. To show this we will explore how the author's engagement with these questions is tinged by her experience as a Heian courtly female confined to writing in the vernacular language in the shadow of East Asia's authoritative lingua franca of Literary Chinese, of the Chinese literary tradition, and of the ambiguous cultural authority of the cipher of "China."

SPATIAL MODELS

What are the main models of spatial experience and representation in the *Genji*? How does the author deploy what we call here an "epistemology of space" and how does it structure and underwrite the tale's narrative? Where and how do these models surface and to what effects does Murasaki Shikibu use them?

Concentric Imperial Space and Foreign Authority

Much of the action in *Genji* happens in domestic spaces: the residences of the protagonists whose location, fittings and furniture, and attached retinue of ladies-in-waiting and servants mark social status and, thus, their inhabitants' political and romantic prospects over the course of the tale.[1] Permeable to the outside, with the light wooden architecture, movable screens for room structuring, and omnipresence of opportunities for spying, eavesdropping, and gossiping, this most intimate unit of space is framed in an expanding web of concentric circles partially modeled on Chinese political cosmology and mapmaking practices. It emanates from the emperor and his palace at the center, the aristocratic residences and gardens in the capital, and the more immediate outskirts of the capital, to the provinces, the Korean states and China, and, occasionally, India. On the Japanese version of this map, cosmological authority is suspended in a bipolar disjunction: political power rests with the Japanese emperor in the capital, the main stage of the tale, but cultural authority declines proportionally from the capital into the remote rustic provinces, to attain new levels of sophistication once reaching the greater Chinese world on the continent. Episodes and moments plotted on this map often use tokens of foreign authority to bestow legitimacy on domestic practices.

They can appear as foreign people with special skills and powers. In the hardly cosmopolitan Heian capital, encounters with actual foreigners were quite rare, and it is all the more significant that Murasaki Shikibu in the opening chapter of the tale features a physiognomist from Koma, probably pointing to the powerful Northeast Asian state of Parhae (698–926), with which the archipelago had close diplomatic and trade relations, rather than the contemporary Koryŏ Dynasty (918–1392).[2] He is startled by the young prince's facial features ostensibly destining him to become a ruler, which in turn precipitates the emperor's decision to make his son a commoner to avert power struggles.

---

1. On residential spaces and narrative in the *Genji* see Kim, *Genji monogatari no kūkan hyōgenron*.
2. Kawazoe, *Genji monogatari to Higashi Ajia sekai*, pp. 46–51.

Official missions to China had ceased, but the memory of the missions exchanged with Northeast Asian states like Parhae, providing treasured exchange with continental culture, was still vivid and trade with Koryŏ ongoing, although the Japanese court refused to acknowledge official relations with the Koryŏ court. Against this background Murasaki Shikibu introduces the Korean physiognomist as a figure of foreign authority who precipitated his father's decision to make Genji "a Genji" and bestowed the sobriquet of "Radiant Prince" on him (w21). Later in life, an adult Genji, hearing that his Akashi Lady had just given birth to a daughter, underwrites the Korean diviner's authority by gratefully recognizing the accuracy of his prophecy: that a son of his would become emperor (Reizei) and a daughter the mother of an emperor (the newborn later Akashi Empress) (w321). Though the Korean prophecy appears first, it becomes subsequently clear that the Emperor had previously consulted a Japanese physiognomist, who had made a similar prediction. The author thus has foreign authority cut both ways: she highlights the Korean physiognomist's authority, only to put him to a "domestic test," which in turn supports the authority of the Korean verdict (w15).

There are also foreign objects with special powers: "Karamono," 唐物, precious overseas imports from the Korean states, China, India, or other places on the continent. As Kawazoe Fusae has amply shown, they play a prominent role in the tale as "status symbols." They give a lavish exotic touch to courtly occasions, like the "Chinese silk," "Chinese brocade for scroll stands," and "Korean brocade" at the picture contest ceremony (w368f), or seduce in private, as when Genji ends up spending a momentous night with his Akashi Lady, whom he has recently moved to the capital. He is enthralled by an atmosphere pregnant with things Chinese, such as a seven-string Chinese-style *koto* placed on an embroidered pillow of Chinese silk, a calligraphed line about plum trees, and her appearance in the white formal robe he sent her with Chinese-style patterns of birds and butterflies in branches of plum. Genji cannot resist this potent lure of chinoiseries, although he is fully aware how furious Murasaki will be because he does not spend the first night of the year with her (w461).

Yet more powerfully, Murasaki Shikibu uses *karamono* to mark prominent points of plot inflection. Sick after Yūgao's spooky death, Genji seeks out a healing ascetic in Kitayama and gets a first glimpse of the young Murasaki, the love of his life, through the fence of a nearby villa owned by a bishop. The Bishop bestows on Genji a rosary made of embossed seeds from fruits of the Bodhi tree that Prince Shōtoku acquired from the Korean kingdom of Paekche and medicine jars of lapis lazuli. Not incidentally, this fated encounter happens when Genji for the first time sees the capital from a distance: attendants tell him of yet greater wonders like Mount Fuji and Akashi (where he will eventually find his Akashi Lady); and right before Genji leaves, when some older nuns remark on his surreal perfection, the Bishop laments that Genji was destined to be "born during the final period of the Dharma in this troubled realm of the rising sun" (w107). Gifting Genji with a superb *karamono*, crafted in Paekche and transmitted to Japan by Prince Shōtoku, the founding figure and transmitter also of Buddhism to Japan, and placing Genji's life into the broader context of rebirth during the decline of the Buddhist Law creates a spiritual, even transcendental aura around the protagonist: it endows Genji's fateful encounter with Murasaki with ultimate value and karmic significance.

Beyond the greater Chinese world, India appears occasionally as the origin of a powerful foreign script and textual world, embodied for example in the Sanskrit charms the ascetic writes for Genji in the Kitayama episode or the farewell letter the Akashi Lady's father leaves behind when he retreats to the mountains after his granddaughter has an heir and his dreams have been fulfilled. As a Buddhist novitiate, her father writes in what looks to her like a very strange style, almost "like Sanskrit" (w490). Murasaki Shikibu does not miss the opportunity to implicitly praise Genji's command of this exotic, Buddhistic style: his expert gaze finds the letter to be extremely well written.

Thus, while India is typically a source of Buddhist truth, whereas literary entertainment and appreciation often focus on the pleasing juxtaposition of "Japanese-style" (*wa*) and "Chinese-style" (*kan*) writing, Korea appears in courtly entertainment culture, especially in music, song, and dance. During the Autumn Foliage excursion two boats carry musicians of Chinese-style music (*Tōgaku*, associated, as in court politics and the structure of the capital, with the more powerful left side) and Korean-style music (*Komagaku*, right side) respectively, playing for the two different dance repertoires (w151). During a cherry blossom celebration, the victorious right side of a Go game gets the appropriate Korean-style fanfare (w912). Beyond music, Korea is associated with fine paper. In Chapter 32 "Umegae," Genji makes elaborate preparations for the initiation of his daughter by the Akashi Lady as crown princess, hosting competitions of mixing perfumes and incense, and collecting and copying calligraphy books and paintings for his daughter's quarters. He asks various young courtiers to draw a waterscape with reeds on a beautiful stock of Koma paper, with poetic lines in *kana* script worked into the composition. Genji, with his half-brother Prince Hotaru, appears here as central connoisseur of the art of calligraphy and its past and current practitioners; he praises Emperor Saga's (r. 809–23) calligraphy of Chinese characters, *Man 'yōgana*, in a copy of the eighth-century *Collection of Myriad Leaves* (*Man 'yōshū*). And he himself jots down cursive *Man 'yōgana* on Chinese paper and reserves the finer and more delicate lines of female-style full-blown *hiragana* calligraphy for the Koma paper. This episode features a complex interplay of various scripts, calligraphic styles, and writing materials, as the delicately blurred *wa-kan* juxtaposition of scripts, namely of cursive *kanji* (verging on *kana*) versus explicit *hiragana* calligraphy, plays out on two different sheets of paper, a stiffer, more formal Chinese one and the more feminine, softer Korean one (w616ff). The foreign "prestige object" of Korean paper becomes here a gift for the new Princess at this solemn moment of her induction to the palace; but it functions as the more clearly domestic signifier, carrying Japanese text in domestic *kana* script (rather than Japanese text in cursive forms of Chinese script, as with the Chinese paper).

Unlike foreigners who might satisfy domestic needs but remain "foreign bodies" in the fabric of Heian society, *karamono* in the form of objects, or even music, dance, and ultimately texts, are deeply embedded in domestic tastes and consumption. And while they might at times give a scene a whiff of the exotic, they can also become completely domesticated and function as domestic signifiers.

A good case in point is the portrayal of Genji's exile, brought on by his affair with Oborozukiyo, his archenemy's sister. Geographically Suma and Akashi were only about fifty to sixty miles away from the capital—some days of arduous travel. But narratively, Murasaki Shikibu pushes these locales far into foreign space: she has Genji go through scenes of farewell so lengthy that the arrival in Suma seems endlessly deferred; the "provinces" are unlike anything Genji has ever seen, outlandish and populated by brutish fishermen; a dominant image in the Suma chapter's poems is the burning of seaweed to extract salt, suggesting associations with uncouth local folk, with smoke, smoldering passions, tears, separation, and death, all things that are, like exile, out of control and transgressive. Also, Genji comes to speak in the voice of or with deep-felt sympathy for Chinese models of exile suffering—from Qu Yuan (trad. fourth to third centuries BCE), the Chinese exiled minister who committed suicide, to the great Chinese poet Bo Juyi (772–846) or even Wang Zhaojun, the Han Dynasty Princess sent off as a diplomatic bribe to marry the Xiongnu khan (as well as domestic exiles such as the poet-official Sugawara no Michizane, who died in exile, and Ariwara no Yukihira).

We can interpret the rich tapestry of Chinese references, modes, and moods during the exile and in its aftermath as, in some way, compensation for Genji's fall from favor. What Genji momentarily lacks in imperial favor is replaced by the projection of foreign—textual—authority onto domestic political space. The specific intertextual references have received much attention.[3] But it is important to put their nature and occurrence into broader narrative perspective and note that various types of China-inspired moods—artistic, elegiac, and even sarcastic ones—appear particularly often right before, during the exile, and during its aftermath: they show Genji in Sinitic light and might. Right before exile, in Chapter 10 "Sakaki" when his father has died and his factional enemy the Kokiden Consort is dominating court affairs, a diminished Genji is empowered, in extensive episodes, as a connoisseur of Chinese books, a scholar of Chinese learning, and an excellent writer of Chinese-style poetry. After Suma he moves to the less forlorn exile in Akashi, where he meets the Akashi Lady, who gives him the future Akashi Empress, his access to political success. The Akashi Lady is associated with Chinese-style pine trees[4] and, when Genji leaves Akashi, receives as a memento his Chinese seven-string koto (*kin no koto*), which he had brought along in imitation of Bo Juyi, although this instrument saw its heydays in the courts of Emperor Daigo and Murakami in the tenth century and had fallen out of fashion by Murasaki Shikibu's time.[5] In Chapter 15 "Yomogiu," Genji catches up with Suetsumuhana, his Safflower Princess, whose dilapidated residence and old-fashioned Chinese furniture objects reveal her hopeless decline. Only with Chapter 18 "Matsukaze," when Genji literally settles back into the capital by beginning to

---

3. See in particular Shinma, *Genji monogatari to Haku Kyoi no bungaku* and *Genji monogatari no kōsō to kanshibun*.

4. Shinma, *Genji monogatari no kōsō to kanshibun*, pp. 201–16.

5. Nelson, "*Genji monogatari* ni okeru gengakki," pp. 12–15.

remodel his Nijō villa, does the narrative move beyond exile and the dense intimation of Chinese modes and moods that still support him on his gradual way to rehabilitation and political power. A last crowning moment of compensating for domestic exile through reference to foreign textual authority appears in Chapter 17 "Eawase," where the scrolls of paintings and poems Genji produced in Suma are ultimately selected as the winner in an elaborate picture contest that keeps the court abuzz with excitement and evokes discussions about Chinese- and Japanese-style painting. Prince Hotaru celebrates Genji as a supreme Chinese-style poet and a newly discovered spectacular painter (w371). This is a final poignant closure to Genji's exile, where spectators of the scrolls relive Genji's sufferings on the shores of "foreign" Suma, safely in the capital, and Genji is branded a hero of Chinese-style poetry and scholarly erudition.

Temporal Space: Genji's Chronotope

The concentric imperial map includes on its periphery the presence of foreign authority, but foreign authority can variously be projected onto domestic spaces, as we saw with the chapter sequence around and during Genji's exile: this space–space blending has interesting parallels to the space–time blending used by Murasaki Shikibu to color the profiles and moods of protagonists and their spaces, enhancing the depth of her protagonists' and her readers' experience. Seasonal time often intersects with spatial arrangement in the *Genji*, as with the placing of women in Genji's Rokujō villa, each with their characteristic garden: Murasaki and Genji come to reside in the southeast quadrant, associated with spring; Akikonomu, the former High Priestess of Ise and later Umetsubo Empress, in the southwest—autumn; the Akashi Lady in the northwest—winter; and Hanachirusato in the northeast—summer. The ladies vie over the splendor of their residences and gardens by competing over their respective seasons: at the end of Chapter 21 "Otome" Akikonomu boasts to Murasaki in poetry about her gorgeous autumn foliage, a challenge that Murasaki in the adjacent quadrant finally responds to in Chapter 24 "Kochō" with her hosting of an opulent spring feast. This Chinese poetic topos was already popular at the court of Emperor Tenji in the seventh century, and the author was probably also inspired by the poems composed in mutual response between Bo Juyi, Yuan Zhen (779–831), and Liu Yuxi (772–842).[6]

On a more abstract level, important caesuras in plot progression are often symbolically marked through spatial rearrangement: Genji builds the Rokujō villa in the "Otome" chapter, when he is at the peak of his power, "arranging" his women in more stable circumstances, and when the narrative starts to move on to the next generation, including his own son. Comparably, after Genji's death Chapter 43 "Niou no miya" begins by discussing the locations of the survivors: who moved or stayed where and why. Similarly, after the death of the older Uji Princess, Kaoru tries to cope with his devastating loss by developing plans to remodel the Uji villa, including the construction of a temple to worship an effigy of his dead beloved (w1096).

In moments of time–space blending, things Chinese—such as *karamono* and the Academy, embodying Chinese learning—usually mark a chronotope of tasteless conservatism and an ominous promise of hopeless decline and pathetic misery.[7] Suetsumuhana and her panoply of old Chinese furniture and apparel exemplify this. She clings desperately to her old ways and the dilapidated mansion she

---

6. Shinma, *Genji monogatari no kōsō to kanshibun*, pp. 125–46.
7. It is important to note, though, that the "modern" and "contemporary," important aesthetic categories in the *Genji* for architecture, fashion, or personal bearing, are not necessarily always desirable. Consider for example the unfavorable contrast between the overly "modern" and inappropriately gaudy style of the Minister of the Left's residence (refurbished for the coming-of-age ceremony of his granddaughters, the children of the Kokiden Consort), and Fujitsubo's subtly subdued quarters (w 178).

inherited from her late father, Prince Hitachi. Among the female protagonists associated with *karamono*, Suetsumuhana's Chinese-style predilections embody a tasteless fixation on the past, whereas the Akashi Lady's Chinese-style elegance shows her humble gracefulness, and the Third Princess's association with *karamono* embodies the opposite chronotope of Suetsumuhana, namely shallow "modern" immaturity. Suetsumuhana seems trapped in a time capsule that is hard to penetrate from the outside: when her aunt, a "modern" woman, visits Suetsumuhana to persuade her to leave her father's residence and move with her to Kyushu, she finds the house in ruinous condition, can hardly open the sagging doors, and has to find "three paths to a hermit's hut," an allusion to a line by the Chinese poet Tao Qian (365–427) that indirectly compares the Princess's mansion to a Chinese hermit's hut (w346). That the Chinese heirlooms from her father were actually very precious in the author's time, in commercial and antiquarian terms,[8] but signal here an outlandish lack of taste and inability to face the present, is a paradox that heightens both our disdain and pity for Suetsumuhana's tragic fate. She is trapped in the past, caught in a wrong chronotope.

The chronotope of tasteless conservatism appears in less deplorable and more parodic guise in scenes involving the Confucian Academy. Famously, in Chapter 21 "Otome" when Genji decides against promoting his son Yūgiri to higher court rank but enrolls him instead in the Academy to have him acquire Chinese learning, the erudite academicians appear hopelessly outdated, awkward relics unable to cope in court life, formulaic in speech—and poor (since they even have to rent robes for the occasion). Poking fun at outmoded scholasticism is probably a perennial topic in any culture boasting esteemed scholarly institutions and traditions, but Murasaki Shikibu gives this topos a particular edge in

---

8. Kawazoe, *Genji monogatari to Higashi Ajia sekai*, pp. 143–66.

the eleventh-century world of Heian Japan: after the ninth century the Academy declined into an institution of professional training for scholarly family lineages,[9] while the Fujiwara regents cemented their power, and the disjunction between the Academy's cultural authority—endorsed by the authority of Chinese knowledge—and its political insignificance created an ambivalent profile that invited parody and schadenfreude. The Academy appears here as a faded institution beyond its heydays, retrojected by the author into an anachronistic chronotope; and it is intriguing that this happens exactly at the moment when in "Otome" the tale begins to "double up," with Genji well settled, and to move on to the next generation of protagonists, which will in turn hand over the stage to yet another generation in the final section of the tale, the "Uji chapters." Thus in this chapter generational change, "growing out of one's time," is not just a feature of the Academy, to comic effect. But it starts to affect the narrative arc of the tale, to somewhat elegiac effect, as the coming of age of Genji's son in "Otome" and the following sequence of chapters focusing on Tamakazura, Tō no Chūjō's lost daughter by Yūgao, parallels the height of Genji's power and already injects a sense of the passage of time and fated decline.

Spatial Imbalances

GENJI'S EMPTY CENTER: CHINESE-STYLE POETRY (KANSHI) AND ACADEMIC LEARNING

There are undoubtedly moments that parody Chinese knowledge as useless and redolent of stuffy scholasticism, such as Yūgiri's enrollment at the Academy and the episode about the erudite daughter of an academician, whom one of the interlocutors during the "Rainy Night Discussion" about preferable types of women courted and

---

9. See Steininger, "The Heian Academy."

who illustrates how ridiculous Chinese learning can look in a romantic relation when the woman is the scholar. But it is easy to forget that on a higher level Chinese knowledge and in particular the ability to compose Chinese-style poetry hold supreme authority in *Genji*. They constitute the *Genji*'s "empty center."

Throughout the tale Genji is celebrated as a hero of Chinese scholarship (as opposed to being an academician, a slave of Chinese scholasticism). Just to point to a few examples, in Chapter 10 "Sakaki," Genji expertly answers Emperor Suzaku's, his older half-brother's, questions about the Chinese classics, while Tō no Chūjō tries to impress the learned Genji with his collections of Chinese books and sponsors a poetry banquet, where the praises of Genji's scholarly and poetic talents are sung and Genji, suggestively, compares himself to the Duke of Zhou, a central figure in the pantheon of Confucian sages (w245ff). His unsurpassable mastery of Chinese-style literacy extends also to official prose genres: when he asks a doctor from the Academy to write a prayer text (*ganmon*) for the forty-nine-day funeral rites for the unfortunate Yūgao, the doctor has nothing to improve on the rough draft Genji dashes off in haste (w91). Characteristically, the academicians, the actual "professionals," in contrast to the uncannily flawless "amateur" Genji, have nothing but ultimate praise for Genji's Chinese-style compositions. No character in the tale can even get close to Genji's reputation as a brilliant Chinese-style poet. And it is significant that his career as the tale's hero of Chinese-style poetry starts when the young boy exchanges poems with the Korean mission members that include the physiognomist who bestowed the sobriquet of the "Radiant Prince" on him: the "cultural capital" that helps him launch his career is the foreign authority of the Korean physiognomist, who praises his poem, as well as the handsome gifts he receives as reward (w15). After that moment in the first chapter of the tale, occasions where Genji's Chinese-style poems receive unanimous praise abound.

Interestingly, the parody of Chinese scholasticism in the context of his son's studies at the Academy has received more attention than the pervasive authority that Murasaki Shikibu grants Chinese scholarship and literary composition throughout the tale. Given the voluminous Genji scholarship, why has this obvious fact been so little noticed and discussed? One obvious reason is that, while the tale features almost eight hundred *waka* poems, not a single original line from a Chinese or Chinese-style poem appears in it. After the ninth century, Heian women did not participate in the all-male sphere of Chinese-style composition. Murasaki Shikibu was (in)famous for her exceptional erudition in the Chinese textual tradition, as her father doted on her literary talent despite her being a woman, and tutored Empress Shōshi in Bo Juyi's poetry. Whether just a playful pose to hide the author's Chinese learning or a genuine expression of her discomfort with transgressing a male domain, moments where the narrator or a protagonist expresses the social disapproval that haunted women who presumptuously took on the "airs of a scholar" appear frequently throughout the tale. The narrator's typical disclaimer after Genji receives superlative praises for his Chinese-style verses composed at one or another poetry event—namely that she could not record the poems, as women were supposed to know nothing of this kind of poetry—hides the fact that Murasaki Shikibu strayed almost deeper than possible into the exclusively male sphere of Chinese-style composition: unlike with earlier tales such as *The Tale of the Hollow Tree* (*Utsubo monogatari*), Murasaki Shikibu often lets the reader appreciate Chinese texts as they were chanted at the time, in glossed *kakikudashi* renderings, often to dramatic effect.[10] After his first wife, Aoi, dies, Genji leaves behind two poems, prefaced by lines from Bo Juyi's "Song of Everlasting Sorrow," in *kakikudashi* gloss-translation: "With whom shall I share our old pillows, our

10. See Amano, "*Genji monogatari* ni okeru kanshiku rōshō no dokusōsei."

old bedding"; "The flowers are white and heavy with frost" (w208). When his father-in-law, the Minister of the Left, sees Genji's poems and these lines, singing of Emperor Xuanzong's and Yang Guifei's tragic fate and the possibility in this life of absolute love and absolute loss, he breaks down in uncontrollable grief over the double loss of his daughter and his son-in-law, whose calligraphy and choice of words from Bo Juyi capture his feelings of despair with such uncanny perfection. While Genji might *quote* Chinese texts in Japanese gloss-rendering, the reader is tantalizingly and systematically frustrated to see Genji *write* even a single of his so lavishly praised Sino-Japanese plain verse lines. The author teases our curiosity: for example in Chapter 8 "Hana no en," she makes a point of saying that the official lector of the poetry composed at the occasion could hardly get through Genji's Chinese-style poem, because the enthusiastic audience would interrupt him constantly, heaping praises on every single line (w173). Staging a recitation of a Chinese-style poem by Genji, savored line by line by the audience, makes the absence, *Genji*'s "empty center," more poignantly present. Intriguingly, Murasaki Shikibu compensates for that absence by inserting a *waka* poem that Fujitsubo composes in private to herself, ambivalently smitten by Genji's exceptional performance on this illustrious occasion. Withholding the "empty" lines of Genji's Chinese-style poem, inserting an intimate poem by Fujitsubo that had no place at this public event, the narrator slyly notes this strangely unequal replacement procedure: "Since Fujitsubo composed this privately, I wonder how it came to be known to the court?" (w173). This is one of the many examples where Murasaki Shikibu creatively plays with the linguistic, aesthetic, and narrative imbalances that a hero of Chinese-style verse inevitably introduces into a Japanese vernacular tale.

While these imbalances were rooted in Heian social customs, another reason for the neglect of Genji as a hero of Chinese-style learning and poetry is buried in our own historical moment: the

Genji's overdetermined stature as the quintessential classic of Japanese national literature has discouraged scholars from acknowledging the Chinese-style profile of Genji, although much valuable work has been done over the past decades to uncover intertextual relations between the *Genji* and specific Chinese texts and to reassess Murasaki Shikibu's understanding of the Chinese canon. The ideological framework of "national literature studies" has blinded us to the central position of *kanbun* literacy in traditional Japan, replacing it with the triumphal myth of Japanese vernacular literature as the defining factor of Japanese cultural identity; only if we transcend this anachronistic myth and recapture the traditional world of letters with its complex interplay between modes of Chinese-style and vernacular literacy, prosody, and stylistics can we grasp the pioneering boldness of Murasaki Shikibu's tale: putting a hero of Chinese-style literacy at the heart of a vernacular, female-authored tale.[11]

SPATIAL DUALITIES: THE AESTHETICS OF JUXTAPOSITION

While scholars have so far hardly noticed the imbalance that Murasaki Shikibu introduces with her Sino-Japanese hero at the "empty center" of the *Genji,* the "spatial imbalances" rooted in Heian gender inequality have received ample attention—women's exclusion from state affairs and from access to the buildings, events, and textual production associated with it; a lack of mobility of the female aristocracy beyond the women's quarters, with their screens and shutters, or beyond trailing kimonos hanging from blinded chariots when en route; exclusion from the world of Chinese learning and Chinese-style composition: all these social customs made for a deeply dualistic experience of Heian noblewomen. More broadly, the past decades have witnessed vivid debates about patterns of duality and binarism

---

11. For a recapturing of the traditional world of letters see Kōno et al. eds., *Nihon "bun" gakushi,* vols. 1 and 2.

in Japanese culture, from David Pollack's *The Fracture of Meaning* (1986) to Thomas LaMarre's *Uncovering Heian Japan: An Archaeology of Sensation and Inscription* (2000) or Kaori Chino's "Gender in Japanese Art" (2003) and Atsuko Sakaki's *Obsessions with the Sino-Japanese Polarity in Japanese Literature* (2005). Variously called "*wa-kan* dialectic" (Pollack), "Sino-Japanese polarity," (Sakaki), or "double binary structure" (Chino) (2003), these related approaches explore and problematize a set of correlative binaries that played out in traditional Japanese social and aesthetic practice: male versus female agency; "public" (*hare*) versus "private" (*ke*) spaces and occasions; *kanji* versus *kana* scripts and, relatedly, *otoko-de* versus *onna-de* (male and female calligraphic styles); Chinese-style texts and genres versus Japanese ones; *kara-e* versus *yamato-e* (Chinese- versus Japanese-style painting); among others. In particular LaMarre and Tomiko Yoda[12] have warned against associating any of these binaries with modern concepts of an ethnopolitical or ethnolinguistic difference between "China" and "Japan," and, indeed, Pollack, Sakaki, and Chino all deal with imaginary forms of "China within Japan": China as a catalyst of Japanese identity formation. Today persistent discomfort with these binaries has less to do with the categories per se—there is no doubt that all of these had some hard edge of reality that affected life in Heian Japan and were also intimately interconnected. Rather, the problem rests with the cognitive structure of the "binary" per se—the dangers of essentializing the categories—and the indomitable variety of their incarnation along the continuum ranging from cosmologies to social customs and aesthetic practices. Simply put, there are too many exceptions to the correlative scheme: *waka* poetry performed on public (*hare*) occasions; women knowledgeable in Chinese studies, like Murasaki Shikibu, Sei Shōnagon, and the "academician's daughter" from the "Rainy Night Discussion" in the

---

12. Yoda, *Gender and National Literature*, p. 244.

Genji; or Ki no Tsurayuki writing a vernacular diary in a female voice, presumably imitating the genre of male Sino-Japanese diaries; the long list could go on. As long as we focus on the cognitive structure of a "binary," we tend to think descriptively and essentialize; instead, once we focus on aesthetic "juxtaposition," a concept I choose here to get at the same set of issues, we vacate the categories of referential content and think operationally, so that "exceptions" disappear into the pleasure of ever new combinations, recombinations, permutations with variations: any Japanese or Chinese "essence" disappears into an ever moving kaleidoscope of possible recombinations and degrees of difference. To think through "juxtapositions" rather than "binaries" it is helpful to separate, as much as possible, social customs from aesthetic practices. Sure, there were some hard glass ceilings in Heian social life, where for example "gender," "writing and literacy," and *"hare"* spaces and institutions neatly map onto each other: no woman ever passed the exams at the Confucian Academy, nor did women in Murasaki Shikibu's time compose Sino-Japanese poetry. Beyond that, "juxtaposition" of variables (rather than binaries) was a pervasive source of aesthetic perception, practice, and consumption from literary texts to the arts of calligraphy, painting, and music, or architecture, fashion, perfumes, and incense, to name a few. Moving from the potentially essentializing, descriptive "binaries" to the mobilizing, permutational aesthetic operation of "juxtaposition" transforms the vexing "exceptions" to the correlative binary categories from a challenge to the rule into the very incarnation of the aesthetic rule of playful dualism.

Patterns of juxtaposition and spatial duality appear on many levels in the *Genji*, as elsewhere in Heian literature: from representations of spatial segregation of the sexes (and the related literary topoi of "fence-peeping," (unequal) female and male anxieties about females inadvertently exposed to the spying male gaze, and deathbed scenes as long-awaited moments for other men to see the beauty of a previously inaccessible woman) to the dualisms within the capital and its topographic and political structure, between the capital and the provinces, or the continent and Japan; aesthetic juxtapositions of Chinese-style and Japanese-style (and sometimes Korean-style) modes in the various arts, in architecture and performance; or, not the least, juxtapositions of characters and generational change.

More subtle but all the more interesting are patterns of juxtaposition and spatial duality on the narrative level. Take, for example, the sequence of Chapters 7–9 "Momiji no ga" to "Aoi" : these chapters juxtapose radiant descriptions of official court festivals with intimate plot twists in Genji's love life. "Momiji no ga" intertwines Genji's superlative dance (and poetry) performance at an imperial festival with Fujitsubo's and Genji's agony as she moves beyond his reach into the palace as empress and their son is born, and the dismay of Genji's wife, Aoi, over his increasing devotion to the maturing Murasaki; Chapter 8 "Hana no en" shows again Genji's supreme appearance at an imperial banquet for Fujitsubo and the new crown prince, his unrecognized son, while, backstage, Genji starts an affair with Oborozukiyo, the sister of his archenemy, the Kokiden Consort, which will eventually result in his exile; and Chapter 9 juxtaposes the Kamo festival celebrations with the offense of Lady Rokujō, resulting in the death of Genji's first wife, Aoi, and Genji's marriage to Murasaki. This intertwinement of "*hare*" and "*ke*" plot stages allows the author to magnify Genji's superlative talents and reputation, positioning him as the embodiment par excellence of courtly splendor (*miyabi*), while slipping in glimpses of the dark reverse of Genji's glamour and tormenting the reader with the troublesome effects of Genji's amorous habits, sufferings, and flaws.

While the juxtaposition of "*hare*" and "*ke*" plot stages in this chapter sequence that shows Genji at his highest and lowest before his exile is straightforward and easily analyzed through a combination of the correlative binaries mentioned above, looking for the operational aesthetic device of "juxtaposition" rather than content-defined "binaries" also opens our eyes to Murasaki Shikibu's narrative crafting of less obviously binary scenes that play in more complex ways with spatial duality. Take the memorable "Rainy Night Discussion" in Chapter 2 "Hahakigi" among Genji, Tō no Chūjō, and two other courtiers about grades of desirable women, which inspires Genji's future pursuits of mysterious "middle-grade" women in the tale. Intriguingly, the conversation takes place in a *hare* building, but a *ke* setting of sorts: Genji, at the time serving as middle captain in the Palace Guard, is forced by a directional taboo to stay on in his office at the palace—where we find him more rarely than in women's quarters—and has a casual off-duty conversation with his colleagues. The palace grounds are swept empty during the early evening hours, which allows the party to feel more relaxed. The original spark of the conversation emerges from a pivoting pun, merging *hare* and *ke*, male and female spaces of agency, as well as, presumably, Chinese-style and Japanese-style calligraphic and textual modes: *fumi*. While Genji peruses books (書 *fumi*), probably Chinese texts he would keep in his palace office, his friend Tō no Chūjō starts to poke around in a cabinet with Genji's love letters (文 *fumi*) (w23). Thus, the conversation materializes from a merging of the scholarly with the romantic, a theme that continues with the Warden considering himself an "expert/academician" (*hakase* 博士) on the subject and indulging in dilettante lectures drawing farfetched analogies between women and handicraft, painting, and calligraphy (w30); it appears most explicitly in the account by the Junior Secretary from the Ministry of Rites (which supervised the Academy and administered its exams) of the all too scholarly masculine "doctor's daughter," who scared him with her depth of Chinese knowledge, her Chinese-style habitus, still lecturing him on her medical regimen of *Allium sativum* (in short, stinky garlic), even as he was breaking up with her (w87).

From a more literal perspective one can interpret in particular this last episode as yet another parody of women with scholarly aspirations, as the roles of male and female spheres of agency are inverted, to the disadvantage of the eccentric "garlic lady." But if one considers the broader picture of novel juxtapositions and mergings of binaries operative in this passage, we can see this episode as an inverted, complementary version of the parody of the academicians during Yūgiri's studies at the Academy: in the episodes at the Academy the reader sees how ridiculous actual Confucian academicians look when juxtaposed with real-life courtiers, who are powerful by birth and courtly poise, not by learning or merit; in turn, in the episode of the "Rainy Night Discussion," held in an ambivalently "private" palace building and an atmosphere that blurs discourses of scholarship and romance, we see how ridiculous lesser court officials look when trying to pose as Confucian scholars. In this reading the sympathy of the scholarly female author would, wondrously, be with the odd "garlic lady" rather than the untalented lowly official who is too stupid to understand her worth. Murasaki Shikibu's skillful varying juxtaposition and superposition and partial travesty of male/female roles and *kan/wa* and *hare/ke* binaries is too complex to comprehend through a dialectic of binaries but perfectly analyzable through a dynamics of ever shifting juxtapositions playing off each other. Adopting the aesthetic operational category of "juxtaposition" rather than the more descriptive and potentially essentializing category of a "binary structure" brings out the much more complex and aesthetically sophisticated narrative art of Murasaki Shikibu (and Heian texts in general). It also implodes the notion of a "China in Japan" away from any temptation of ethnolinguistic or geopolitical reification: there are simply too many "Chinas" and too many "Japans" (mappable to and combinable with too many versions of the other polar binaries) to make this category meaningful as an analytic master tool for grasping the Heian cultural landscape.

Referential Space: Forms of Subtexts in the Genji

"Spatial dualities," horizontal modes of exclusion, juxtaposition, or superposition, appear in the *Genji* both as a reflection of Heian social reality and as a means of aesthetic appreciation, a mode of narrative intervention, and a subtle tool for social critique of the Heian court world and etiquette. In turn, the referential space of allusions, quotations, and intertextuality is vertical and often adds temporal and emotional depth to particular spaces or plot elements. Allusion in texts is what potential energy is in physics: a good part of the heavy lifting of meaning-making is already present in the subtext, and fitting the subtext's semantic and pragmatic potential into particular moments in the tale enhances the tale's narrative power and sophistication.

This is not the place to survey the rich intertextual tapestry of the *Genji*, a topic that has generated a body of specialized scholarship.[13] Instead, we should remind ourselves that what today is often clinically called "intertextuality," the engagement with previous texts, comes in many different varieties to different effects in the tale. What are some main forms in which the *Genji* engages its subtexts?

First, there are the resonant place names in *waka*: *utamakura* (poetic pillows). As place names (or otherwise idiomatic expressions, called *utamakura* in Murasaki Shikibu's time) with particular associations defined by previous poems, they already appear in the *Man'yōshū*. Manuals like the mid-Heian *utamakura* compendia by Nōin and, right around Murasaki Shikibu's time, by Fujiwara no Kintō (966–1041), suggest that they were increasingly codified and used independently of their specific textual origins. Thus, most often

---

13. For Chinese and Chinese-style texts in particular see Shinma Kazuyoshi's *Genji monogatari to Haku Kyoi no bungaku* and *Genji monogatari no kōsō to kanshibun*. For an intriguing approach to intertextuality through questioning of the network of mid-Heian poetic language, letter writing, and the agency of ladies-in-waiting see Jinno, *Genji monogatari ron: nyōbō, kakareta kotoba, in'yō.*

utamakura rely on an "intertopical" rather than intertextual rheto-ric.[14] *Utamakura* operate on a strong aural immediacy, frequently also functioning as "pivot words" or phonetic puns (*kakekotoba*). One example involving Prince Niou, Genji's grandson by the Akashi Empress, who is one of the characters in the tale who appreciates the power of *utamakura*, should suffice as illustration. Consider how the Prince is drawn into the romantic pursuit of his Uji Princess and, eventually, Ukifune. True, Kaoru first tells him about this opportunity (with some apprehension, knowing Niou's amorous nature), but what really seduces Niou into undertaking a first visit is the pun-ning place name: *Uji* 宇治 ("sorrowful" 憂し, as for example in the poem by Kisen, one of the "Six Poetry Immortals," about his hermit-age southeast of the capital at "Ujiyama," or "mountain of woes").[15] The narrator sharply criticizes Niou's seduction by this clichéd *uta-makura*: "The fact that Niou was romantically drawn to a place whose name calls forth feelings of sad regret suggests the insincerity of his motives" (w955). Niou continues to spin out his romantic fantasies, like a game, along the phonetic appeal of *utamakura*: during a foliage trip to Uji, where he had hoped to visit his Uji Princess, he is stuck at a poetry party on the other side of the river, thinking despondently of "Lake Ōmi," or the Biwa Lake (w1017). The name puns on "meet-ing" and also on saltwater seaweed (*mirume*). This *utamakura* tor-ments Niou: "Uji River" is an outlet of Biwa Lake, and thus a likely association, but the "meeting" Niou hopes for is just as unlikely as finding saltwater "seaweed" in a freshwater lake.

There are no comparably strongly codified poetics and reper-toire of place names in the Chinese literary tradition, although place names play obviously an important role in Chinese verse. Visiting

---

14. On intertopicality, see Denecke, "'Topic Poetry Is All Ours.'"
15. Anthologized in the canonical early tenth-century imperial waka collection *Kokinshū*, poem no. 983. Ki no Tsurayuki. *Kokinshū: a Collection of Poems Ancient and Modern.*

a site of previous splendor now in ruins, seeking the *genius loci* of a place associated with an important historical event or figure, charting the ever unruly northwestern frontier through generic exotic place names evoking harsh living conditions, forced labor, and warfare in "border poetry": all these occasions called for the composition of Chinese poetry with poignant references to place names. But they often drew continuing significance from specific historical incidents and textual precedents. In contrast, place names in Japanese *waka* poetry, were more conceptualized and "topicalized," drawing on phonetic punning, metaphorical associations, and a seasonal repertoire, which made them into genuinely artistic literary tools.[16] Perhaps also for that reason Murasaki Shikibu shows much less interest in place names in Chinese verse than in Japanese *waka*. In the case of Niou, Murasaki Shikibu uses *utamakura* critically, to show a *way of thinking*—in romantic clichés—that further highlights the Prince's emotional shallowness. Yet she masterfully evokes Chinese places associated with Chinese texts, especially in the exile chapters, thus dispensing with the place names but giving all the heavier weight to the palpable experiences of space and place in the Chinese poets' work and life. Bo Juyi can offer the Japanese protagonists a *way of being*—emulation for emotional comfort and aesthetic sublimation of suffering. Bo Juyi's exile at Xianglu Peak at Mount Lu is a prominent example. Although the place name is not explicitly mentioned in the tale—educated people at the time would presumably have known—Genji emulates Bo Juyi's exile experience, when in 815 the Chinese poet was demoted for a couple of years to a low-ranking post in Jiangzhou, down to the smallest detail: Genji takes a seven-string koto, like his model; builds his residence in Suma in the image of Bo Juyi's hut; and moves in on the twenty-seventh day of the third month, just like his exile hero. And the speech of the southerners

16. See Denecke, "The Power of Syntopism."

there appeared as incomprehensible as the chirping of birds, as Bo Juyi puts it, and Tō no Chūjō observes.[17] Mount Lu and the episode of Bo Juyi's exile can, thanks to its historical specificity and iconic protagonist, become a blueprint for "referential emulation," a role-play that helps the protagonist cope with the harsh realities of exile, giving him dignity and opportunities for aesthetic sublimation and reassuring him and the reader that exile would eventually end, quickly, as it did for Bo Juyi.

The deepest form of engagement with subtexts occurs of course with Murasaki Shikibu's pervasive reference to the "Song of Everlasting Sorrow," which appears as a quotation or plot reference in poems and paintings, and even as a sort of survival manual for those in dire straits. In the *Genji* the historically unique tragic romance of Emperor Xuanzong and Prized Consort Yang, whom the Emperor had to watch getting strangled in front of his own eyes when she was blamed for the An Lushan rebellion, becomes conceptualized into a story of (dangerously) absolute love, tragic loss, and supernatural quest for finding one's beloved again. This is not a text that the *Genji* simply "alludes" to, but its archetypal themes become a subplot of the *Genji*, going from one generation to the next:[18] it features as a cipher for the ultimate love and inevitable tragedy of Genji's parents, for Genji and Murasaki's ultimate fate, and for Kaoru's love affairs in Uji.

Earlier I briefly sketched different forms of the author's nature and degree of engagement with previous texts: the at times pun-enhanced, rather generic "intertopicality" of place names / *utamak-ura* in *waka*, Genji's real-life emulation of Bo Juyi's Jiangzhou exile,

---

17. Pollack, "The Informing Image," p. 370.
18. In her article "The Search for Things Past in the *Genji monogatari*," Doris Bargen considers archetypal elements from the "Song of Everlasting Sorrow" as a "myth" of sorts that launches protagonists onto a search for the past and substitution in the present. My reading here considers it more as a very specific, conceptualized case of the various types of intertextual engagements in the tale, thus a "subplot."

and the conceptualization of archetypal elements from the "Song of Everlasting Sorrow" as a multigenerational powerful subplot. They are all different incarnations of the use of "vertical depth," referential space, in *Genji*.

"EPISTEMOLOGY OF SPACE": PHILOSOPHICAL OVERKILL?

Is it not philosophical overkill to reveal an "epistemology of space" in the *Genji*? Even for China there have been heated debates about whether the early Chinese corpus of "masters literature" (*zhuzi baijia*) could or should actually be called "philosophy": the historical rooting of, intellectual concerns about, and forms of inquiry, debate, and persuasion in texts like the *Analects, Laozi*, and *Zhuangzi* seem too different from Greco-Roman philosophy and its European aftermath. We risk misunderstanding the true nature and significance of this body of texts in East Asian cultural history and, thanks to their divergence, their potential to inspire future philosophical debates.[19] Arguably, the Song Dynasty Neo-Confucian synthesis, not the least due to the impact of Buddhist metaphysical speculation, created forms of thetical, conceptual, and systematic inquiry that seem much more comparable and relatable to the Western philosophical tradition, and the impact of Zhu Xi's Neo-Confucianism in Edo Japan resulted in the development of political and ethical thought that can be matched with Western values of "philosophicality." But a proper "epistemology," a theoretical contemplation of what, how, and how truthfully we can know? Even for early China we need to scrape together the little we have from the short-lived Late Mohist school

---

19. See Denecke, "Masters (zi 子)."

and the "logicians" (or "school of names"; *mingjia*) such as Gongsun Long (third century B.C.E.) to be able to make any argument that the Chinese masters were interested in questions of logic, language, and cognition at all. Do we not risk egregious overinterpretation of the *Genji* and Japanese intellectual history, for the understandable but misleading sake of giving Japan a coveted share of the royal discipline of philosophy that matters so much to Western cultural history that we have trouble imagining that any serious civilization could do without it?

We should turn away from the question of what philosophy can do for the *Genji*—since the early twentieth century the tale has already succeeded as "world literature" and does not need a philosophical face lift to vie for global attention. Inversely, the question of what the *Genji* can do for philosophy is suggestive. In a recent *New York Times* editorial, Jay L. Garfield and Bryan W. Van Norden made a bold call to introduce greater diversity into a discipline that "as a whole remains resolutely Eurocentric." Under the battle cry "If Philosophy Won't Diversify, Let's Call It What It Really Is," they call on every philosophy department that does not offer courses on non-Western thought traditions to refer to itself as "Department of European and American Philosophy," in all honesty.[20] This sobering solution—perhaps strategically polemical—shows the degree of frustration over the fact that the mainstream of the discipline of philosophy, despite decades of activism by "comparative philosophers" to engage the discipline's Eurocentric ivory tower in a less unequal dialogue, holds onto the claim to an uppercase "P," as in "Philosophy," a claim to universality that no other discipline in the humanities has been able to maintain in the face of the historical forces of globalization.

I believe there is a third path, between sobering isolationism that would reify an undesirable status quo and the seeming impossibility

20. Garfield and Norden, *New York Times*, May 11, 2016.

of having academic philosophers seriously embrace the study of non-Western thought traditions and divergent ways of "philosophizing." And this is where the *Genji* comes into play. Looking for "philosophy" in the *Genji* or Heian Japan can only yield false correlatives that will make the Japanese cultural tradition look deficient. Looking for "philosophicality" can make us aware, as I aimed in this essay, that Murasaki Shikibu quite recognizably and systematically inscribed a number of spatial mappings into the scenery, character depiction, plot progression, and narrative art of her tale: concentric imperial space enhanced by foreign authority, space–time blending, spatial dualisms and juxtapositions, and, lastly, different rhetorical articulations of space implied in intertexts and subtexts, thus in the tale's "referential space." These are elements that give the *Genji* the power of "philosophizability": an opportunity for contemporary philosophers to produce new visions of how space "is," in particular how it conditions human experience and how we can, conceptually, verbalize and communicate those experiences. Suggestively, Murasaki Shibiku's "spatial epistemology" resonates with Nishida Kitarō's (1870–1945) rich and complex concept of "place," first thematized in his essay *Basho* (Place) in 1926 and continuously developed until his death. A central stimulus for Nishida was the epistemological dualism of Neo-Kantianism, which posited the transcendental distinction between a metaphysically "objective" object and a "subjectively" perceiving subject. *Basho* 場所, or "place," is what frames both subject and object and has them both entangled in a relation conditioned by their particular "emplacement" in space, the particularities of an always existing relation, or history—in short, what we commonly call "context." All of the spatial models highlighted in the *Genji* defy any absolute cognitive object, but instead operate through the entangled emplacement of subject and object in the yet greater frame of *basho*. Nishida is mainly read—more easily for sure—as a philosopher writing in the

Western philosophical tradition with some local color. It can easily look that way, because he often carefully references his borrowings and inspirations from Western philosophical literature, while using Chinese and Japanese texts intuitively without explicitly referencing them. For example, he defines *basho*, when he introduces the topic in his essay, through the Greek term *chōra*, "place," in Plato's *Timaeus*, rather than defining and enriching Plato's concept through a positing of *basho*.[21] That translators have sometimes cleaned up his stream-of-consciousness style of traditional Japanese essayistic writing and fashioned it into a more philosophically acceptable analytic treatise, as Rein Raud [22] reminds us, has been reinforcing that impression. Yet what Nishida tries to propose with *basho* has a new face and philosophical productivity if we do not see it primarily in reaction to Neo-Kantianism, but hear the voices of *Laozi, Zhuangzi,* Buddhist metaphysics, and the jarred epistemology of Zen in the work of a man with deep erudition in Chinese and Japanese textual traditions. These sources of Nishida's thought represent different textures of "nondualism" that played out in East Asia's thought traditions. And here is the third path, what a reading of Nishida for example through the *Genji* could help us and contemporary philosophers tread: because Nishida speaks the language of Western philosophy so well, he could serve as a doorway—more accessible than frontal cultural difference—to comprehending nondualistic epistemological traditions and the way they played out in ethics, political philosophy, and aesthetics. Nishida and the East Asian traditions in which he was writing have much to offer to philosophers looking for new models of relativism *without* subjectivism (or "psychologism" and other unsavory effects that appear when we give up epistemological dualism and seemingly abandon claims

21. Nishida, *Place and Dialectic,* p. 50.
22. Raud, " 'Place' and 'Being-Time,' " p. 29.

to universality and philosophical rigor). John W. M. Krummel and Shigenori Nagatomo, translators of Nishida's work, comment that the significance of Nishida lies precisely in the "philozophizability" for the future, in conceiving of the possibility of a nondualistic but also not subjectivist philosophy in a world that has grown challengingly multicultural and pluralistic.[23] If we flip Nishida's mirror image of a "Western philosopher" with local color into that of an East Asian thinker conceptualized through Western philosophical terminology, philosophers in collaboration with Japan scholars can discover a wonderfully productive "third path," an indirect and more accessible entry into the truly different thought world of traditional East Asia before the nineteenth century. And for philosophers, the *Genji* would add a yet more interesting twist: proposing, in its spatial epistemology, forms of nondualism that precisely allow for an ever more complex aestheticizing play with spatial dualities in Heian social reality and its artistic representation. But our detour through philosophy also ultimately aims to do something new for the, in part, overworked field of *Genji* studies: namely to show how Murasaki Shikibu's "epistemology of space" is predicated on the manifold presences of China, which, way beyond figuring mostly as a foreign realm or exotic ornament, sit, in often highly abstracted fashion such as the operational device of juxtaposition, at the heart of *Genji*'s brilliant narrative art and psychological depth, for which the novel became so appreciated in the modern period.

WORKS CITED

Amano Kiyoko. "*Genji monogatari* ni okeru kanshiku rōshō no dokusōsei." In Nihei Michiaki (ed.), *Genji monogatari to Higashi Ajia*. Tokyo: Shintensha, 2010.

23. Ibid., pp. 43–46.

Bargen, Doris G. "The Search for Things Past in the *Genji monogatari*." *Harvard Journal of Asiatic Studies* 51.1, 1991.

Chino, Kaori. "Gender in Japanese Art." In Joshua S. Mostow, Norman Bryson, and Maribeth Graybill (eds.), *Gender and Power in the Japanese Visual Field*. Honolulu: University of Hawai'i Press), 2003.

Denecke, Wiebke. "'Topic Poetry Is All Ours': Poetic Composition on Chinese Lines in Early Heian Japan." *Harvard Journal of Asiatic Studies*, 67.1, 2007.

Denecke, Wiebke. "The Power of Syntopism: Chinese Poetic Place Names on the Map of Early Japanese Poetry." *Asia Major* 26.2: 2013.

Denecke, Wiebke. "Masters (zi 子)." In *The Oxford Handbook of Classical Chinese Literature 1000 BCE–900 CE*. New York: Oxford University Press, 2017.

Garfield, Jay L., and Bryan W. Van Norden. "If Philosophy Won't Diversify, Let's Call It What It Really Is." *New York Times*, May 11, 2016. https://www.nytimes.com/2016/05/11/opinion/if-philosophy-wont-diversify-lets-call-it-what-it-really-is.html. Accessed October 28, 2018.

Jinno Hidenori. *Genji monogatari ron: nyōbō, kakareta kotoba, in'yō*. Tokyo: Bensei shuppan, 2016.

Kawazoe Fusae. *Genji monogatari jikūron*. Tokyo: Tokyo daigaku Shuppankai, 2005.

Kawazoe Fusae. *Genji monogatari to Higashi Ajia sekai*. Tokyo: Nihon Hōsō Shuppan Kyōkai, 2007.

Kim Sumi. *Genji monogatari no kūkan hyōgenron*. Tokyo: Musashino shoin, 2008.

Kōno Kimiko, Wiebke Denecke, Shinkawa Tokio, and Jinno Hidenori (eds.). *Nihon "bun"gakushi. A New History of Japanese "Letterature"*. Volume 1 & Volume 2. Bensei Shuppan, 2015–17.

LaMarre, Thomas. *Uncovering Heian Japan: An Archaeology of Sensation and Inscription*. Durham, NC: Duke University Press, 2000.

Nelson, Steven. "*Genji monogatari* ni okeru gengakki no kyokushū to chōgen nitsuite: Kogakufu kenkyūsha no tachiba kara." *Nihon bungaku shiyō* 92, 2015.

Nishida, Kitarō. *Place and Dialectic: Two Essays by Nishida Kitarō*. Trans. John W. M. Krummel and Shigenori Nagatomo. New York: Oxford University Press, 2012.

Pollack, David. "The Informing Image: 'China' in *Genji Monogatari*." *Monumenta Nipponica* 38.4, 1983.

Pollack, David. *The Fracture of Meaning: Japan's Synthesis of China from the Eighth through the Eighteenth Centuries*. Princeton, NJ: Princeton University Press, 1986.

Raud, Rein. "'Place' and 'Being-Time': Spatiotemporal Concepts in the Thought of Nishida Kitarō and Dōgen Kigen." *Philosophy East and West* 54.1, 2004.

Ki no Tsurayuki et al. (ed.). *Kokinshū: A Collection of Poems Ancient and Modern*. Trans. Laurel Rasplica Rodd with Mary Catherine Henkenius. Princeton, NJ: Princeton University Press, 1984.

Sakaki, Atsuko. *Obsessions with the Sino-Japanese Polarity in Japanese Literature*. Honolulu: University of Hawai'i Press, 2005.

Shinma Kazuyoshi. *Genji monogatari to Haku Kyoi no bungaku*. Osaka: Izumi shoin, 2003.

Shinma Kazuyoshi. *Genji monogatari no kōsō to kanshibun*. Osaka: Izumi shoin, 2009.

Steininger, Brian. "The Heian Academy: Literati Culture from Minamoto no Shitagō to Ōe no Masafusa." In Haruo Shirane, Tomi Suzuki, with David Lurie (eds.), *The Cambridge History of Japanese Literature*. Cambridge: Cambridge University Press, 2016.

Yoda, Tomiko. *Gender and National Literature: Heian Texts in the Constructions of Japanese Modernity*. Durham, NC: Duke University Press, 2004.

Chapter 3

Ritual, Moral Personhood, and Spirit Possession in *The Tale of Genji*

JAMES MCMULLEN

INTRODUCTION

Of all aspects of *The Tale of Genji*, the eponymous hero's moral conduct, and especially his promiscuity, have historically been most problematic within its reception history in Japan and beyond. This aspect of the work seems also most likely to cause concern or even seem incoherent to modern readers. As a teenager, Genji abducts a girl, causing her death, cuckolds his father, the Emperor, and sires a son by his father's favorite consort, soon to be empress. His offenses are seemingly compounded when he later gains ascendancy within the court politically and socially, but, cuckolded himself, is unforgiving of the young culprit, whose death he causes by a malevolent stare. Genji's persistently libidinous behavior, though reported in the text as expected of someone of his status, is also depicted by the narrator as reprehensible. Yet despite his numerous affairs, in a narrative informed by realistic characterization, Genji does not become roué but preserves his pristine charisma.

This essay supplements Royall Tyler's exploration in this volume of the political and mythical elements of Genji's life story through a discussion of the moral consciousness expressed in the text. It argues that the morality informing the *Genji* is complex, pluralistic, and evolving. The moral world of the *Genji* is formed from several elements. The first comprises the values of a courtly community informed by the norms of an "aesthetic order" centered on ritual. This provides the *basso ostinato* particularly strongly in Part I of the novel, but also subsists through the entire narrative. Personhood and morality are, however, complicated by the overlay of several other traditions, which are based on premises at variance with those of the "aesthetic order." A nebulous combination of cosmic forces, including Heaven or "the sky," the sea god Sumiyoshi, indigenous myth, and geomantic mechanisms mainly of continental origin, controls the natural order but especially directs the fate of high-ranking figures. Shamanic spirit possession, often in response to moral circumstances, intrudes, usually to destructive effect, at important points in the unfolding narrative. Finally and pervasively, the beliefs and institutions of Buddhism are featured throughout the work and color its mood.

The moral world of the novel is not static; Genji himself goes on a moral journey. What follows first sketches these themes; it then traces their playing out through three episodes from Parts I and II of the novel: first, Genji's youthful seduction of Yūgao; second, the double episode of his cuckolding of his father the Emperor and fatherhood of a future emperor and the reprise of that episode some twenty years later; and finally the spirit possession of Genji's secondary wife Murasaki and the Third Princess by the spirit of Rokujō culminating in Murasaki's death.

THE "AESTHETIC ORDER"

The essay borrows from philosophy to identify in the novel a social order based on the centrality of ritual in the formation of moral personhood. This model is adapted from Herbert Fingarette's seminal analysis of the pattern of Confucian thought as exemplified in the *Analects* of Confucius. Also influential in the pages that follow is the development of Fingarette's thinking on early Confucianism by David Hall and Roger Ames. The use of these analyses is not an endorsement of their historical accuracy; as interpretations of the *Analects*, they are controversial. Nor is it claimed that Confucian thought historically directly influenced the formation of personhood in the *Genji*. The model adapted from the work of these scholars, rather, is used heuristically to shed light on the moral consciousness that informs the *Genji*. Another influence on the analysis has been the ideas on European court societies of the historical sociologist Norbert Elias (1897–1990).

Fingarette's analysis of Confucius's construction of the human self privileges "ritual" (Chinese *li* 禮; Japanese *rei* 礼) as the key to person formation, and its mastery as the primary existential charge on individuals. Human normative behavior is sited externally in the performance of ritual rather than, as in later Confucian thinking, the realization of an inborn propensity or adherence to an abstract or transcendental structure of values or law. "Ritual" covers religious and cultural ceremonies and, more broadly, the etiquette and norms informing relationships of persons within organized society. At its broadest, ritual "works through spontaneous coordination [of all forms of social intercourse] rooted in reverent dignity." Its perfection "is esthetic as well as spiritual," and beauty of person and deportment are important aspects of its practice.[1] Personhood is

---

1. Fingarette, *Confucius: The Secular as Sacred*, pp. 8–9.

acquired, shaped, and controlled by ritual.[2] It must be learned, but is also personal and particular, for "beautiful and effective [rite] requires the personal 'presence' to be fused with learned ceremonial skill."[3] Most important for Fingarette, there is little sense of an inner self or substantiated moral personality subsisting across time. Transgressive acts do not permanently stain the character of the perpetrator. The chief sanction against transgression is external to the individual and social. It takes the form of shame and the accompanying threat of disgrace. As a result, secrecy is paramount; it protects the individual from damage to an essential aspect of selfhood.

Fingarette's thinking on ritual is developed by Hall and Ames as a theory of "aesthetic order." This term is philosophical but retains its vernacular nuance relating to art and beauty. "Aesthetic order" is contrasted with the "logical order" more familiar in the West, where actions are judged in relation to logically formulated and abstract norms. In the latter order, moral choice, moral responsibility, transgressive behavior, repentance, and punishment are judged internally. Transgression is often reflected in self-accusation and guilt. Ritual and the "aesthetic order," by contrast, address particular external social actions and situations. Transgression is not identified by reference to universal principles, but in the perception of discrete behavior.[4] It is perhaps better referred to by the less morally loaded term "offense." As a consequence, shame is a more serious sanction than guilt. "Guilt is law-oriented in that it signals a personal acknowledgement that one has committed a breach of established conduct. Shame, on the other hand, is ritual oriented in that it describes

2. Ibid., p. 21.
3. Ibid., p. 8.
4. Hall and Ames, *Thinking through Confucius*, p. 172; Eberhard, *Guilt and Sin*, p. 121.

a consciousness of how one's performance is perceived by others. Guilt tends to be individual as a condition of one's relationship to law; shame tends to be communal as a condition of one's relationship to others."[5] Shame is found historically particularly in courtly societies, a social context in which, as Elias remarks, it "takes its particular coloration from the fact that the person feeling it has done or is about to do something through which he comes into contradiction with people to whom he is bound in one form or another."[6] There is disagreement over the moral aspect of shame. For Fingarette, "The Confucian concept of shame is a genuinely moral concept, but it is oriented to morality as centered on *li*, traditionally ceremonially defined social comportment, rather than to an inner core of one's being, "the self."[7] In contrast, Wolfram Eberhard (1909–89), writing of traditional China, asserts, "Shame can be regarded as an amoral principle: everything is all right, as long as action running counter to the rules of "correct" behavior remains secret."[8] Empirically "shame" and "guilt" form a continuum, and in this essay the two concepts are used heuristically. It is not claimed that Genji feels no form of self-accusation or guilt; as his life draws to an end, he arguably does so increasingly. Both shame and guilt can be absolved, but shame, in many situations, more easily so. If moral responsibility is calibrated, shame is "exonerated," its external burden lifted from the offender. A more radical form of redemption, "exculpation," an internal absolution from the offender's moral responsibility or blame, is required of guilt.

---

5. Hall and Ames, *Thinking through Confucius*, p. 174.
6. Elias, *The Civilizing Process*, p. 492.
7. Fingarette, *Confucius: The Secular as Sacred*, p. 30
8. Eberhard, *Guilt and Sin*, p. 120.

RITUAL AND THE "AESTHETIC ORDER" IN THE *GENJI*

As touched on in the introduction, Heian court society differed from the Confucian model, particularly in privileging the hereditary principle. Nonetheless, as in Fingarette's analysis of the Confucian *Analects,* an "aesthetic order" based on ritual underpins the *Genji* narrative. Quotidian life in the *Genji* is choreographed by rituals. It is central to the lives of the characters and is encountered at every turn. The circumstances, patronage, lavishness, preparation, appurtenances, and performance of court rituals, concerts, and etiquette are described in detail. It is through their performance of ritual and their beauty as performers that the characters present themselves.

Genji himself is constantly depicted as a performer, gifted ritualist, surpassing musician, and artist. At his first, teenage public appearance at the rehearsal before his father's excursion to the Suzaku palace, his miraculous dancing of "Blue Sea Waves" had "an unearthly quality" (t135); it "sent a shiver through the gathering" (t137). Genji's talents were karmically preordained (t137). His beauty is a recurrent theme; the narrative is punctuated by epiphanies of Genji, bewitchingly dressed from a seemingly inexhaustible wardrobe on departure or return from an assignation or other mission, or in performance, much as he would have been glimpsed by admiring semi-incarcerated female observers. He sustains this luminous charisma into middle age, enabling him to dominate his world. He "made a sight too marvellous for one ever to tire of watching" (t553). His magnificence and ascendancy in his world are comparable to, and eventually exceed, that of a reigning emperor (t502).

Genji's exalted birth combines with his extraordinary talent and beauty to confer special privileges. He is entitled to freedom and license, to wealth, education, and, in accord also with prevailing notions of male privilege in the society of his time, access to women.[9] A program of gallantry is built early into the novel, in Chapter 2 "Hahakigi," when young courtiers banter over their quest for the ideal woman. This kindles a compulsive appetite for amorous adventure in Genji. However, even in a society permissive to males, gallantry beyond conventional limits is offensive and dangerous. As his father, the retired Kiritsubo Emperor, warns Genji, "[W]anton self-indulgence risks widespread censure" (t165). It invites shame, which, it is remarked even late in the Buddhist climate of the Uji chapters, "can sometimes actually be worse than death" (t1037).[10] Shame derives from the judgment of discrete acts and behavior from within the court community and among the women in service to the privileged. It may indeed be moral, but is also aesthetic in the vernacular sense concerning beauty of appearance. It also reinforces social hierarchy: rusticity, provinciality, low status, lack of manners, unrefined speech, a little like "boorish" in English, are censured. To expose a person of Genji's status to someone rustic or provincial was an "affront" (t248). Only uncharacteristically, but significantly in Chapter 12 "Suma," when Genji is in the consciously Chinese-style limbo of exile among fishermen, does recognition of a universal humanity flash briefly in his consciousness to counter this deep-rooted privileging of social hierarchy (t251).

Shame is feared because it threatens the personhood on which the hierarchical society of the *Genji* is built. In Raymond Mortimer's perspicacious words, "These people are always wondering what impressions they are making."[11] An outwardly oriented self is particularly vulnerable when the very elements constructing it are impugned. As Elias puts it referring to loss of the antonym of shame,

9. For Heian period attitudes legitimating "a strong inclination to amorous activities pursued with total abandon" associated with the terms *suki* and *irogonomi*, see Rajyashree Pandey, *Writing and Renunciation*, pp. 82–89.

10. In contrast, see a later Confucian view expressed in *Mencius* (372–289 BCE), pp. 411–14.

11. Mortimer, "A New Planet," p. 371.

honor, the individual has "lost a constitutive element of his personal identity, without which his life . . . [is] meaningless."[12] One is reminded of the claim already quoted that the Japanese state was a "liturgical community" in which ritual was "soteriological in and of itself."[13] Dishonored by shame but lacking any strong metaphysically based sense of inner worth, the self collapses on itself. Little inner core of self-respect remains; the individual is prey to overwhelming fear of censure and mockery, and falls into self-pity, lachrymosity, and morbid despair, as most dramatically illustrated by the fate of Kashiwagi in Chapter 35 "Wakana II." The important concomitant is that secrecy is the most powerful initial reflex in response to a subject's offense. Evasion through entry into Buddhist orders accepting the tonsure, a protection from the opprobrium of the world, may be seen as another response, exemplified by the Kiritsubo Emperor's adulterous consort (later empress) Fujitsubo.

At the same time, the externality and particularistic perception of offense and its association with shame meant that it did not permanently tarnish the individual's interior self. Early in his life in particular, Genji's sense of entitlement and special status permit him to ignore conventional boundaries; he moves insouciantly from one woman to another. His offenses against his own close imperial relatives, his father, the Kiritsubo Emperor himself (with Fujitsubo), and his half-brother, Suzaku (with Oborozukiyo), however, occasion an overriding fear of discovery stronger than any inward sense of guilt. Tarnishing there is, as in the case of Rokujō, Genji's wronged early lover discussed at length below, but it attaches more to social reputation than to an individual's inner person.

Two important subthemes emerge from this analysis: disprivileging of women and the linguistic difficulty confronting translators

---

12. Elias, *The Court Society*, p. 95.
13. Miller, "Ritsuryō Japan," p. 119.

of the *Genji* in conveying the very different sense of personhood in the *Genji*. If the "aesthetic order" valorized Genji's gallantry as a man, it had an inverse impact on the lives of the women of his world. True, women are empowered in the limited sense that they are a repository and vehicle of the opinion that matters so much in their community. Some Japanese critics have seen women's entry into Buddhist orders through tonsure positively as a liberation of the self, a view that in Buddhist terms has validity. In general, however, women are asymmetrically disprivileged. Denied dignity as autonomous subjects, they exist primarily as passive objects of male perception. Their potential political importance as pawns in marriage alliances lends itself to instrumental suppression of their individuality. They have very little control over their own lives. High-status and nubile women must be constantly vigilant and defensive; they should not be exposed to the view of those outside their immediate kin. In contrast to men, they must repress their sexuality; as Genji declares to Murasaki herself: "A woman should never make the slightest gesture that might arouse a man's interest" (t704). Polygamy and the special clandestine nature of Heian period courtship make them constantly vulnerable to intrusive access by competing males and to the dangers of pregnancy. All potential causes of shame must be avoided. Women spend much of their lives in secluded semi-darkness. As the narrative shows, they are often the victims of male spying or actual rape, for which they, rather than the men, suffer devastating shame. Their manners should be inhibited, guarded, passive, and repressed: loquacity, or forwardness, or even too broad a smile lacked dignity (t492). Their personalities are allowed only indirect expression though verse, music, and calligraphy. Aging damages them as objects of male perception and is not treated kindly in the novel.

The "aesthetic order" and its values also create problems in translating the moral vocabulary of the *Genji* into English. There is a misfit between the moral language of the novel and modern English. One particular problem is that, seen from the perspective of a "logical order," the Japanese noun *tsumi* 罪 is ambiguous. Frequently translated as "sin," it covers a moral offense, a legal crime, and their punishment, an ambiguity that resonates with the externality of moral offense.[14] To incur a *tsumi* does not necessarily imply commission of an offense. Thus Genji can both speak of his impending "punishment" (*tsumi*) of exile as "unforeseen" (t236) and plausibly protest that he is unjustly blamed of any offense meriting exile (t233). In English, the language around morality is also colored by a "logical order" predicated on an autonomous moral person who determines choices with reference to a moral code. The discussion that follows will argue from examples that translators have unintentionally imposed on the moral thinking of Genji and other characters the nuance of what Fingarette calls "our own rich background imagery" of "the inner world of the self, of guilt or . . . of conscience and of moral responsibility."[15] The intention is to draw attention to an important nuance of insouciance, if not innocence, in the original text threatened with loss in translation. Particularly in his youth, Genji is not conscious of the heavy psychological burden suggested by the use of "guilt" in English translations. He looks toward "exoneration" rather than "exculpation" or "redemption" for his bad behavior. His contraventions of morality are better thought of as "offenses" rather than "transgressions" or "sins." Rather than guilt, he feels a less moral "compunction." Only late in his moral journey does he begin to feel something more akin to guilt or a troubled moral conscience.

---

14. Williams, *"Tsumi": Offence and Retribution*, p. 117.
15. Fingarette, *Confucius: The Secular as Sacred*, p. 32.

SUPERNATURAL AGENCIES AND MYTHOLOGICAL JUSTICE

The values of the "aesthetic society" condition the lives and expectations of the characters of the *Genji*. Genji himself, however, enjoys a special status that transcends the natural order. This supernatural privilege is administered through nebulously articulated cosmic agencies, accessible by divination, geomancy, and ritual intervention, and through myth. This theme is established early in the *Genji* narrative by the prognostications of the Korean soothsayers who identify a glorious future for the boy Genji that defies the rational expectations of his father and of the court community. To borrow a cosmological simile, as in the General Theory of Relativity light is distorted around celestial bodies of a certain mass, so "radiant" Genji distorts the moral field around himself. How, in Genji's moral journey, this supernatural favor yields to forfeiture of his good fortune and moral retribution is a theme of Part II of the novel.

In Part I, however, despite his dangerous behavior, cosmic agencies supervene to protect Genji through the sea god Sumiyoshi and to promote him beyond the norms of the court community. A profound reason for this, only hinted at in the text but identified in commentaries since medieval times, is the narrative's use of indigenous myth. As Tyler shows, Genji's seaside exile and subsequent triumph draw on the myths of the exiled noble and the ascendancy of the younger brother. Specifically, it follows the divine protection given to the mythical figure of Hikohohodemi, a younger brother like Genji himself, who, following exile, is said to have prevailed against his elder brother to gain dynastic ascendancy and rule over Japan for 580 years.[16] The exiles of both Genji and Hikohohodemi are wrongs associated with their respective elder brothers, but subsequently

---

16. Aston, tr. *Nihongi: Chronicles of Japan*, pp. 148–58; Philippi, tr., *Kojiki*, pp. 148–58. The parallels and differences between the myth and the *Genji* retelling are explored in Tyler, "Genji and the Luck of the Sea."

righted. So Genji triumphs over his elder brother the Emperor Suzaku and his faction to gain political ascendancy in the capital. This story, in Tyler's words, "transposes the myth into a Heian setting."[17] In effect, the myth absolves Genji of moral responsibility as the cause of his exile.

SPIRIT POSSESSION

Along with the "aesthetic order" and the intervention of supernatural agencies and myth, shamanic spirit possession plays an important role in the *Genji*. Spirit possessions are the projection of an individual's frustration, moral victimhood, anger, or jealousy. They emanate from the living (*ikisudama*) or the dead (*mono no ke*) and cause potentially lethal illness. When addressed by exorcists, they may articulate their cause through mediums (often girl-children), who are subject to seizures during which they claim to speak on their originator's behalf. The spirit realm and its interventions in human society may appear at times anarchic, but one important function is clearly retribution for a moral wrong. Outside the novel, the best-known example in Genji's world is the spirit of Sugawara no Michizane (845–903), like Genji himself, unjustly exiled. Within the novel, Genji's enemy the Empress Mother Kokiden, who has maliciously contrived his exile, suffers from an "afflicting spirit," circumstantially surely in retribution (t271). Such cases of retributive spirit possession function in parallel with karma but, through the procedure of exorcism, are empirically more accessible. Consistent with the "aesthetic model," possession, though

---

17. Ibid., p. 170.

life threatening, did not permanently damage the inner person, but was, in theory, alienable. In this world of atomized, particularized transgressions, the moral past of an individual was easily elided; no act of cosmic intervention or radical conversion of the soul was required for redemption. As Genji himself remarks airily, "As they say, anything can be purified one way or another" (t503). There is little suggestion of the need for penitence or of punishment, nor is confession or reparation part of the procedure. Exorcisms were not rituals of redemption. It is tempting to suggest that exorcism can transfer and absolve pollution or anger to mediums precisely because offense is viewed as relatively superficial; it is in large part the consequence of external and even adventitious circumstances.

The chief exemplar of spirit possession among *Genji* characters in Parts I and II is Rokujō, Genji's early high-ranking lover, and it is argued below that her spirit, like that afflicting Kokiden, performs a moral and retributive function. This proud woman is one of the *Genji*'s most influential figures. In a narrative in which violence figures little, the role of her spirit will be seen as closest to nemesis. Her spirit is a spontaneous but mutated emanation, precipitated by her victimhood at Genji's hands, but independent of her will; its baleful interventions have a destructive character beyond the control of Rokujō herself.

BUDDHISM

The "aesthetic order," supernatural agencies, and spirit possession inform the thinking of *Genji* characters, determining their ambitions, choices, and actions. Competing with the norms and values of this "aesthetic order," but frequently discordant with them and founded on more clearly articulated assumptions and imperatives, is a force that belongs to a different religious realm. Buddhism provided a rich, colorful, and profound interpretation of human existence. Its influence on the *Genji* is pervasive and intensifies as the narrative proceeds until its pessimism and melancholy become the dominant mood.

The Mahayana Buddhism of the Heian court, however, was founded on paradoxes and had ambivalent potential. In one direction, it reinforced the "aesthetic" model of society; it purveyed a kind of predestination: the belief that karma *sukuse; sarubeki koto; mono no mukui)*, inheritance from former lives, accounted for hierarchical privilege and, with that, entitlement to polygamy and even sexual adventure. Karma is empirically inaccessible; karmic predestination exonerated individuals of immediate moral responsibility for transgression, though not necessarily shame. It can be understood as similar in some respects to genetic inheritance in the modern world. When negative, like a congenital mental or physical disability, both karma and genetic inheritance may cause offensive behavior. To the Western mind, such genetically determined disability may bring shame, but is less likely to cause guilt; similarly, in the *Genji*, karmically ordained transgression does not leave a stain of guilt. Genji's affair with Oborozukiyo is, as he would claim, decreed by his karma. Genji can reasonably subsume it into his posture of innocence with respect to the causes of his exile. When his father, the deceased Kiritsubo Emperor, appears to the exiled Genji in a dream during the storm at Suma, he trivializes any offense: "All this is simply a little [karmic] retribution" (t259). At the same time, the Buddha (or buddhas generically) and "gods" are apparently not rigid implementers of predestination. They are merciful and receptive to intercessionary rites and prayers from those of high status. This aspect of Buddhism, therefore, challenged the "aesthetic order" of the *Genji*, at most weakly.

In another direction, however, Buddhist soteriology posed a more direct challenge. Buddhism addressed the individual rather than his social context; it posited an inwardly oriented individual salvation attained through disciplined renunciation and warned of the dangers of an individual's emotional attachments. It taught that existence and sense perception are illusory and the self, properly understood, insubstantial; its fatalism underscored the ephemerality of life. It imposed transcendent imperatives and asceticism on the individual. Offense against Buddhist precepts and above all the attachment of parents to their children imperiled future rebirths and was a charge against the individual's internal self. It could be a source of guilt rather than shame. Buddhism, it must also be noted, disprivileged women; Buddhistic expressions of misogyny intensify as the *Genji* narrative proceeds.

The lives and consciousness of the characters in the novel are touched in various ways and differing degrees by Buddhism. For some, Buddhism is the occasion for sumptuous celebratory displays or apotropaic rituals. For others, the quest for Buddhist salvation and desire for a favorable rebirth take over their lives. A minority has a deeper understanding of Buddhism as a moral doctrine of self-transcendence. Indeed, the many-faceted *Genji* narrative might be seen as a testing of the Buddhist imperative to renunciation through the successive experiences of characters, from the youthful Genji himself, who piously toys with the notion, through the Novice of Akashi and others. Buddhist values penetrate the narrative ever more deeply from Part II; a case is to be made that the true exemplar of Buddhist selflessness is Murasaki herself. In Part III, Buddhism, together with the profound challenges that it poses, dominates. Prince Hachi inflicts misery on his daughters in the cause of his own salvation, and the love life of Kaoru, the secret son of Kashiwagi, is crippled by Buddhist ascetic imperatives.

THE YŪGAO INCIDENT

Chapter 4 "Yūgao" resembles the paradigmatic short stories that other great authors have used to rehearse the themes of longer works. Since the age of twelve, Genji has been unhappily married to Aoi, the emotionally cold daughter of the Minister of the Left. He looks elsewhere. The Yūgao incident reveals major themes that are to dominate the long narrative: the passive victimhood of women, the role of karma and of Buddhism and its rituals, death, shamanic possession by a spirit, self-pity, male and particularly Genji's self-centeredness, the search for secrecy. There is also political awareness, for Genji feels compelled to account for his absence from court to his father, the Emperor.

Genji is still only seventeen, but his affair with the high-ranking Rokujō, widow of a former crown prince, whom he was expected to marry, was languishing, to her public humiliation. His curiosity is aroused by Yūgao, a young woman living in reduced circumstances next door to his nurse's residence in a noisy part of the city. He abducts her to a nearby isolated property. A terrifying disaster follows: the girl is possessed by the wounded and angry spirit of Rokujō and dies. Foremost among the "thoughts whirling through his head" is Genji's concern for his own person and for his reputation. "What could really have led him to risk his life in such a catastrophe? His recklessness in these affairs now seemed to have made him an example forever. Never mind trying to hush this up—the truth will always out. His majesty would hear of it, it would soon be on everyone's lips. . . . All and sundry would only know him as a fool" (t69).

Genji is uncritically supported through this crisis by his right-hand man, Koremitsu. He manages to get home, where he takes to his bed in anguish. Later that evening, Koremitsu reports that he has arranged a secret Buddhist funeral. Genji again expresses self-concern: "I wonder what is to become of me." Koremitsu persuades him that "he need not brood," for this incident is karmically ordained. Genji agrees in principle. Successive English translations of his words expose the problem of reflecting the "aesthetic order" construction of personhood in conventional English. All impute a sense of moral responsibility to Genji. Arthur Waley's Genji agrees with Koremitsu that the incident is karmically determined, but himself assumes responsibility: "You are right," said Genji. "But in the pursuit of one's own wanton pleasures to have done harm and to have caused someone's death—that is a hideous crime; a terrible load of sin to bear with me through the world."[18] Edward Seidensticker, more simply, has Genji agree: "So I tell myself. But it is terrible to think that I have sent a lady to her death."[19] Tyler introduces guilt: "I have been trying to convince myself of that, too, but it is painful to be guilty of having foolishly caused someone's death" (t71). Dennis Washburn also makes Genji shoulder moral blame: "You may be right . . . but though I try to believe it's the working of karma, I'm still tormented by the knowledge that my own frivolous actions and fickle heart have brought calamity and death to a woman" (w83).

In fact, the Japanese text states that Genji's main worry is not so much his own moral responsibility as fear of public censure. The text says literally, "It is hard that I must bear the opprobrium (*kagoto*) of having sent someone to destruction for the indulgence of [my] frivolous heart" (g1/176). Genji is concerned mainly with secrecy; his own culpability is, at best, indirectly admitted. He sees his relationship with Yūgao as karmically determined and implicitly beyond his control; nor does he see a causal connection between his own neglect of Rokujō and her spirit's assault on Yūgao. Genji genuinely mourns Yūgao. But his personhood apparently allows him to assimilate Yūgao's death without profound trauma to his inner being. Perhaps

18. Waley, tr., *The Tale of Genji*, p. 72.
19. Seidensticker, tr., *The Tale of Genji*, p. 75.

psychological realism requires that he, a privileged teenager, be self-centered. Even before the closure of the rites of the forty-ninth day of her death, Genji has resumed libidinal interest in two other women, Utsusemi and Nokiba no Ogi. The narrator comments, "He had not yet learned his lesson and he seemed as susceptible as ever to the perils of temptation" (t78).

GENJI'S GREAT OFFENSE AND EXILE

Genji's greatest moral offense follows soon. Now aged eighteen, he secretly cuckolds his father, the Emperor, and sires a son by the latter's favorite consort, Fujitsubo, soon to be empress. The child is to become heir apparent and, while still a teenager, emperor. As with Yūgao, Genji's reflex is to preserve secrecy. Dread of discovery casts a deep shadow on both partners in adultery. A few years later, however, Genji again violates respect for imperial privilege by sleeping with Oborozukiyo, a girl who is a favorite of his half-brother, the new Suzaku Emperor, and a younger sister of his factional enemy, the malicious Empress Mother Kokiden. Genji's presence in the court has become provocative; he retreats to voluntary exile in Suma. The *Genji* imputes to him a response to these offenses similar to that in the Yūgao episode. Once more, he invokes karma as exoneration of the disgrace of exile (t230; 233).

Reflecting these serious offenses, the *Genji* adopts special vocabulary for the mindset among participants in secretive high-status adultery. They suffer from *kokoro no oni* (心の鬼; literally, a "demon of the heart").[20] This locution is defined by the great philologist Motoori Norinaga (1730–1800) as referring to "a person who has

20. For a discussion of this locution in *Genji* see Sugiura, "*Genji* monogatari ni okeru 'kokoro no oni,'" pp. 37–50.

erred unknown to others, being frightened in their own minds." He links it to a Song Dynasty Chinese commentary on the Daoist classic *Liehzi*, where it seems to refer to delusional mental agitation: "When there are doubts, the doubting mind produces all sorts of delusions."[21] Examination of this expression as applied to "secret adulteries" in *Genji* suggests that it usually relates to the imagined reaction of the "world" or of particular individuals. It is primarily an outwardly oriented fear. A possible translation, literal and close to Motoori's understanding, would be "the specter [of opprobrium] in the mind." For example, when Fujitsubo gives birth to Genji's son, the baby's resemblance to his natural father causes her great anxiety. The Japanese text refers to Fujitsubo as suffering great distress from *kokoro no oni*. It reads, "*miya wa ongokoro no oni ni ito kurushiku*" (literally, "The Princess was in great distress from the specter [of the world's opprobrium] in her mind"; g1/326). But translators again tend to moralize *kokoro no oni*. Seidensticker, Tyler (t141), and Washburn (w158) all refer to Fujitsubo's feeling of guilt, though Seidensticker also adds "apprehension."[22] Waley surely conveys the sense best with: "Always there lurked in her heart the torturing demon of fear."[23]

Fujitsubo is afraid that a glance at the baby will arouse public censure of what she calls *ayashikaritsuru hodo no ayamari*, an admittedly ambiguous locution, paraphrased in modern Japanese commentary as "the senseless [? inexplicable] blunder that she had committed at that time [in spite of herself]" (g1/326) or "[a] blunder so bad that she wondered at how senseless she had been."[24] Seidensticker paraphrases this as "the awful truth"; Tyler gives it a slightly less moral nuance as "a misdeed that she herself found repellent"

21. Quoted in Motoori, *Tamakatsuma*, p. 95.
22. Seidensticker, tr., *The Tale of Genji*, p. 139.
23. Waley, tr., *The Tale of Genji*, p. 136.
24. Abe et al., eds., *Genji monogatari*, vol. 1, p. 326 (modern paraphrase); Yamagishi, ed., *Genji monogatari*, vol. 1, p. 282 (headnote).

(t141); Washburn is most moralistic with "the sin she had committed with Genji (w158)." In the text itself, Genji's feeling is similar to
Fujitsubo's, a particularistic and personal terror of the "rebuke" from
his father "were he to learn the full impudence of his own inadmis-
sible passion" rather than guilt over the offense itself (t165). Genji
and Fujitsubo do indeed feel a Buddhistic concern over the birth of
their love child, as their exchange of verses after Fujitsubo takes the
tonsure indicates, but it is less guilt over the adultery itself than, as a
later exchange of verses in Chapter 10 "Sakaki" shows, compunction
over the attachment associated with parenthood, an impediment
to their own salvation (t212). The dominant fear of both Fujitsubo
and Genji remains fear of discovery. Nearly a decade and a half later
when, after her death, an angry phantom Fujitsubo appears to Genji,
her first reproach is that, as she sees it, he has brought her shame by
leaking their secret (t374).

Before leaving for exile, Genji has a fraught meeting with
Fujitsubo, now removed from society as a nun. They share their most
guarded secret. While claiming his exile to be undeserved, Genji
confesses, "It's just that with regard to my having received such an
unexpected punishment, there is one matter about which, when
I put things together, I feel frightened before the sky (*sora*)" (g2/
179). Once again, translators imply that Genji feels a guilty fear of
retributive justice from Heaven. Seidensticker translates: "I tremble
before the Heavens";[25] Tyler: "I still fear the Heavens above" (t236);
Washburn, again moralistic: "I fear the judgement of Heaven for that
sin" (w263).[26] But it seems questionable whether Genji is primarily
concerned with supernatural retribution. More consistent with the

25. Seidensticker, tr., *The Tale of Genji*, p. 139.
26. For another example of moralizing *kokoro no oni*, see Seidensticker, tr., *The Tale of Genji*,
    p. 263, Tyler (t270), and Washburn (w306), who all invoke Genji's conscience; here,
    Japanese commentaries suggest that fear of the response of Murasaki and others to his infi-
    delity is his dominant feeling.

aesthetic model, might not the "sky" (*sc.* Heaven) be a vague reference to an all-seeing agent that might expose his paternity to the shame, censure, and ridicule which terrify him and Fujitsubo? The crisis around Genji's secret son will recede during his exile, but re-erupt five years later. At that time, the context and use of the term "eye of Heaven" will suggest that it is indeed the all-seeing aspect of Heaven that is feared. Meanwhile in his exile, the locus of moral responsibility shifts significantly; far from punishing Genji, a supernatural agency (the sea god Sumiyoshi) supervenes to protect and even recompense him. In contrast, it is the Emperor who fears retribution if Genji is proved innocent. Indeed, his mother, Kokiden, Genji's persecutor, does suffer what circumstantially can only be retributive punishment from "an afflicting spirit" (t271).

THE CRISIS RE-ERUPTS

Genji's apprehensive reference to the "sky" is proleptic. When he is thirty-one, the problem of the parenthood of his love child, now the teenager Emperor Reizei, re-erupts. Once more the moral burden of the adultery shifts from Genji himself onto this boy. First, the natural order is disturbed. "The light of the sun, moon and stars shone strangely" (t353). Fujitsubo dies. An aged monk, in "fear of the eye of Heaven" and of Heaven's "disastrous warnings" (t355–56), informs the Emperor of the cause; the object of supernatural intervention is not Genji's adultery, but the "offense" of the Emperor in not honoring Genji as his father. Even here, moreover, Heaven's intervention is described as admonitory rather than retributive. The dismayed young Emperor, though hardly personally or morally responsible, wishes to abdicate in favor of Genji, who resists. He is rewarded with promotion, however, and some years later, aged forty, in the climax of his career, he is "granted a rank equivalent to retired emperor" (t570–71). Genji's supernatural protection remains effective and the crisis passes. His offense against his father will remain secret (t631).

The narrative, however, proceeds promptly to show that Genji, still unregenerate, remains sexually attracted by imperial women. Akikonomu, daughter of Rokujō, whose angry spirit had possessed and killed Yūgao, has become the "Ise Consort," a secondary spouse to Genji's secret son, Emperor Reizei. Genji is strongly drawn to this girl whose guardian he has been appointed by her jilted mother. He tries to seduce her. Rebuffed, he internalizes his rejection as salutary. At this stage, however, he is not overly burdened by his past, but attributes his failures to pardonable youthful imprudence. "My old, frightening deep offenses were worse than this, but the Buddhas and gods must have pardoned my old loves as the mistakes of a time when I lacked prudence" (g2/464; cf. t360). Neither Genji's inner nor public self has been tarnished. For Motoori, Genji's claim is proof that the author is concerned not with the morality of Genji's offenses, but with the pathos that the perils of love may generate.

Following these events, Genji triumphantly pursues his life within the framework of the "aesthetic order." His "slightest journey . . . assumes the grandeur of an imperial progress," and to the world he has "increasing radiance" (t502). His presence conveys authority (t579), but he is "universally held" in "high regard" (t586). He is a master ritualist and musician and bequeaths a heritage of outstanding ritual (t609). Politically, he is appointed honorary retired emperor; not only is his secret son emperor; his daughter has entered the palace, where in due course she will become pregnant with a future emperor. Within himself, Genji is given to self-satisfaction. (t433; 527; 553). He looks young for his age (t488) and is not without vanity: "He appeared pleased with the lasting youthfulness of his own face" (t491). He feels untarnished by his past. Soon after his failure to seduce Akikonomu, he attempts to seduce another princess "with bewitching charm," claiming, "The winds of Heaven have carried away all my misdeeds from those years" (t367).[27] That same Heaven, of whose all-seeing eye he had expressed fear at the time of his exile, had neither disclosed his secret nor requited his transgressions with retribution. Protected by supernatural agencies, Genji has, in Tyler's words, "achieve[d] power through transgression." [28]

KASHIWAGI

As Genji lives into his fifth decade, however, events combine to unsettle his self-satisfaction. Perhaps the typhoon of Chapter 28 "Nowaki," which, toward the end of Part I, damages Genji's great Rokujō garden, foreshadows the future. From Chapter 34 "Wakana I," several developments again reset the moral field, weakening Genji's supernatural protection. This hitherto singularly favored man suffers the vicissitudes associated with ageing and mortality. Now middle-aged, less libidinous, and perhaps more susceptible to Buddhist beliefs, since his mid-thirties he has begun reflecting over his "wantonly foolish behavior" (t451). He provides caringly for his paramours. At one point, preaching sententiously to his son, he even seems to grope toward a version of the golden rule in the context of marriage: "One should have the profound motivation to make things work out well in the end both for both oneself and the other person" (g3/425; cf. t556; w621). It may be noted, however, that his contrition over his own conduct remains self-concerned: "How the roving lover brings his own troubles on himself," he muses (t541). Nearly a decade later,

---

27. Genji has his earlier potentially blasphemous attempt to seduce this girl, then the Kamo vestal; but this was only one of several grounds for Kokiden's plot to remove him from court (see t218–19).

28. Tyler, "The Hidden *Tale of Genji*," p. 11; see also Motoori, *Shibun yōryō*, pp. 91–92. On this subject, see Harper, *Reading "The Tale of Genji*," pp. 411–506; McMullen, "The Pathos of Love: Motoori Norinaga and *The Tale of Genji*."

when Genji, now in his late forties, talks to Murasaki in a mood of self-pity, his wording suggests something more akin to a bad conscience: "With regard to my ignominious misconduct, I have been strangely troubled and dogged by feelings of chagrin in my heart" (g4/205–206; cf. t645).

Gallantry is largely replaced by political ambition. A woman observer reports that Genji "deeply desires a lofty alliance" (t580). Polygamy and weak notions of exogamy allow him to marry his half-niece, the Third Princess, the youngest and favorite daughter of his half-brother, the Retired Emperor Suzaku. This girl, however, more than twenty years Genji's junior, is uninteresting. Genji himself is dismayed at her immaturity, but the misjudged marriage more profoundly troubles Murasaki, his secondary but most loved wife. More immediately, it creates problems for a new character at court, Kashiwagi, the eldest son of Genji's lifelong friend and rival, Tō no Chūjō. This talented and ambitious young nobleman is a lower-ranking Genji figure. He is already married to another Suzaku daughter, the Second Princess, but becomes ungovernably infatuated with her younger sister, Genji's new wife. The resulting episode provides an opportunity for the narrative to revisit high-status adultery in a context similar to Genji's. However, unlike the youthful Genji, Kashiwagi is not protected by any supernatural agency.

At first, Kashiwagi attributes his infatuation to karma and even seems to anticipate supernatural indulgence; "it is no offense to unburden oneself to the gods and buddhas" (t650, modified). Exploiting Genji's neglect of the Third Princess, he repeats Genji's cuckolding of his own father. She becomes pregnant. Agitated, Kashiwagi fears not the law, but, true to "aesthetic order," the shame that he would feel before Genji should he know. "He would have faced death willingly enough if he had violated an emperor's woman and the thing had then come to life and cost him such agony as this, and even if his present crime was not that grave, dread and shame overcame him at

the thought that His Grace [sc. Genji] might look at him askance"
(t652).

Genji finds out, and Kashiwagi's residual confidence is shattered.
He knows that he will not be formally punished (t662). What tor-
ments him, rather, is precisely his sense that "the sky has eyes" (g4/
258; cf. t661) and that he will be exposed.[29] He abandons going to
court and is consumed by self-pity, but, incoherently, blames both
karma or destiny and himself. "When I consider that this is something that I did willingly, there is no one whom I should resent. That
there is no way to complain to the buddhas and gods is because it is
destined" (t675). Genji himself, victim of Kashiwagi's offense, experiences "conflicting feelings" of anger and empathy (t 660; 662). His
dominant response, typically, is less condemnation of the offense
itself than a combination of contempt for Kashiwagi's incompe-
tence in failing to keep the affair secret, resentment of his insolence,
and fear of his own shame as a "decrepit old fool" (t666–67). His
exquisite revenge perfectly reaffirms the "aesthetic order": it combines shame, secrecy, and particularism. Seating Kashiwagi next to
himself at a ritual rehearsal, he "directs a stare" at him so baleful that,
as Kashiwagi later recounted, his "soul fled in anguish" (t677). In a
combination of cruelty and a compassion perhaps partly intended
to anesthetize Kashiwagi's pain, Genji has him drink repeated toasts
(t669). Kashiwagi flees. The consequences of Genji's discovery
for the adulterers are dire. Kashiwagi sinks into a private, terminal
depression; Genji is misogynistically unforgiving of the childlike
Third Princess. But just as the Reizei Emperor was presumed the son
of Emperor Kiritsubo, so Kaoru, the male child born of Genji's cuckolding by Kashiwagi, remains publicly presumed the son of "Shining
Genji." He will become the troubled hero of Part III.

---

29. The headnote quotes the fourteenth-century commentary *Kakaishō* to the effect that
"Heaven is the first to know."

What is the meaning of this disturbing episode? First, Genji him-self remains protected by secrecy. His misogyny allows him mainly to blame the unfortunate Third Princess. Most important for the argument of this essay, however, the overriding value informing the response of Kashiwagi and the Third Princess is shame, Kashiwagi's in particular at having offended Genji, the highest person in the land.

MURASAKI

Outwardly, Genji has prospered. Retribution for injurious moral offense, however, is both occult and dilatory; spirit possession serves moral justice and will in due time strike close to the hero himself. A theme that has subsisted like mycelium through the narrative bursts out to undermine Genji's later life. It strikes not Genji him-self, but Murasaki, his favorite but secondary wife, the girl-child he had abducted and reared to be his ideal mate. They are now middle aged, he in his forty-seventh year, and she the geomantically unlucky age of thirty-seven. Murasaki is Genji's creature; he has molded her in his own image, a female alter ego. Genji congratulates himself on the success of this project (t596). But Murasaki is also Genji's victim, solely dependent on him and insecure. As the narrator remarks early on, "Genji was all she had" (t233); only her place in Genji's volatile affections validates her position. A further poignant vulnerability is that, infertile, she cannot fulfill for Genji the most important female role, provision of an heir. He, however, while genuinely devoted, is frequently tactless concerning his other attachments. Murasaki struggles watchfully against jealousy; she also worries about her age (t636). Yet at her core, she claims an *amour propre*. In early adult-hood, hurt by Genji's recounting of his relationship with the Akashi Lady on his return from exile, she had turned away from him with the words "I am I" and composed a passive-aggressive verse wishing that she was dead (t286).[30] As Tyler comments, she "sharply affirms the distinctness of her existence."[31]

Genji is sensitive to social rank in his harem (t581); Murasaki's relatively low hereditary status and want of political usefulness compound her vulnerability. She reacts badly to Genji's marriage to the Third Princess. Genji does not understand how deeply he has hurt the woman whom, within the limits of his own self-satisfaction, his wandering eye, and his political ambitions, he genuinely loves. Where previously there has merely been tension between them, a "palpable estrangement" has opened.[32] Surveying his relationship with other women, the older, more prudent Genji professes to Murasaki some penitence over previous offences (t644–47). As this review ends, however, he becomes insensitive. "You are not without your dark recesses," he declares (t647). He leaves to spend the night with his new wife, tactlessly telling Murasaki that he will congratulate his new bride on her progress under his own tutelage in music.

ROKUJŌ'S POSSESSION

Murasaki is pitched into depression: "[A]m I to end my days burdened with those miseries that other women, too, find miserable and hateful?" (t647). That same night, she falls perilously ill with "chest pains." Genji hurries from the Third Princess to her side. She recovers temporarily in response to ritual intercession from Genji.

---

30. Tyler, "Genji and Murasaki," p. 23. Whether or not coincidentally, this self-protective "I am I" is found, albeit in a different context and nuance, in conjunction with "You are you" as a "saying" in a canonical Confucian source, the *Mencius* (p. 207) as *erh wei erh, wo wei wo* 爾為爾、我為我. For the balancing "You are you" applied to Genji, see the verse by Rokujō's posthumous angry spirit below, note 40.

31. Tyler, "Genji and Murasaki," p. 23.

32. Tyler, "The Disaster of the Third Princess," p. 95.

However, during a relapse, the cause of her illness is revealed to be the malevolent spirit of the long-dead Rokujō. The immediate trigger is the spirit's overhearing of a slighting reference to Rokujō in Genji's tactless review of his mistresses the previous day (t655). Genji confessed to Murasaki that he had found Rokujō "painfully trying company" (t646) and accuses her of overreaction to their affair. "[T]he way she brooded interminably over the matter and with such bitter rancor, made things very unpleasant." These accusations, the spirit claims, has "quickened feelings from long ago." Ranting through the girl medium, Rokujō's spirit angrily berates Genji for misrepresenting herself as a "disagreeable woman" (t654).

Critics, however, have looked for further reasons for this long delayed intervention of Rokujō's angry spirit. Tyler sees it as "the ghost of "Genji's past," "an agent of karma," and the "precipitating agent" of Murasaki's fate, motivated, he suggests, by "Genji's past misdeeds and enduring failings."[33] Surely, this is right. Genji's early unhappy affair with Rokujō seems to establish proleptically the moral rationale for his later decline. Its denouement represents a retributive principle analogous to karma but empirically accessible through the spirit's disclosure. It may plausibly be argued that the spirit's assault confers moral coherence on the *Genji* story.

Has the young Genji sufficiently wronged Rokujō to attract such retribution in his middle age, or is she rather, as some see, mainly an admonitory example of destructive jealousy?[34] Analysis of the early Genji–Rokujō affair, combined with the principle that angry spirits

33. Ibid., p. 104; Tyler's view of Rokujō's role is usefully summarized in his article "The Hidden *Tale of Genji*" pp. 17–22. Others take a similar line. Shirane, *The Bridge of Dreams*, p. 114, writes of Rokujō's possession as a "dramatic means of expressing a woman's repressed emotions, particularly jealousy and resentment caused by polygamy." Bargen, *A Woman's Secret Weapon*, p. 121, cites Rokujō's "resistance to male domination." Field, *The Splendor of Longing*, similarly writes of Rokujō's possession of Genji's women as "in a perverse fashion ... speaking for them" (p. 62).

34. On this theme, see Morris, *The World of the Shining Prince*, p. 260.

may redress moral wrongs, confirms the former to be plausible. There is no doubt that Genji deeply humiliated the proud Rokujō, refusing to accord her the public recognition of marriage, neglecting her, but, faced with losing her altogether, pestering her to perpetuate their relationship for his own gratification (t196). Significantly, many years previously, the retired Kiritsubo Emperor, identified in Japanese critical literature as a figure of sagely authority, had warned Genji specifically about his treatment of Rokujō: "never cause a woman to suffer humiliation" (t165).[35] The failure of their relationship haunts Genji through his life, though he vacillates over his own culpability. In his early thirties in conversation with her daughter, whom he has adopted, he apologizes for damaging her name (t359). Talking to Murasaki nearly a decade later, he again admits harming her, but defends himself, adding that "though she stuck to her mortification, it was not that bad" (*sashimo arazarikeri*, an elliptical utterance that a modern commentary takes to minimize his responsibility (g3/415–16; cf. t552).[36] But finally, reviewing his mistresses to Murasaki on the night before her possession, after criticizing Rokujō as tiresome, he is willing, with the greater compunction of his middle age, to concede that "in the end I was to blame" for their estrangement. But there are limits: he still feels that he has made sufficient amends to exonerate himself (t646).

For the proud Rokujō, by contrast, Genji's betrayal, reflecting her greater vulnerability and dependence as a woman, is traumatic, life-changing, and more complex. Genji's inconsiderate treatment left her bitter and "utterly destroyed" (t173). She ends the relationship and leaves the capital, in effect in voluntary exile, to accompany her daughter, the High Princess of Ise, to her provincial post, where

---

35. For this view of the Kiritsubo Emperor, see Sasakawa Isao, "*Honchō reisō* no sekiten shi," p. 56.

36. Compare Yamagishi ed., *Genji monogatari*, vol. 3, p. 170 (*furigana* gloss on text).

she stays some six years. At the same time, however, Rokujō remains dependent on Genji, in due course to become the most powerful man in the land. On her deathbed, she solicits his protection of her daughter, Akikonomu. Further to complicate the mutual dependence of Genji and Rokujō, through this arrangement Rokujō bequeaths to Genji the land on which he will build his great quasi-imperial Rokujō palace and garden.[37] Four times over their long relationship her spirit intervenes to afflict his women: during her lifetime first with Yūgao and then with Aoi; after her death with first Murasaki and then the Third Princess. But it is important for the moral balance of their relationship that the real-life Rokujō harbored no conscious vindictive or personal desire to punish Genji. She tells Genji that she had "no desire at all to see the lady harmed" (t173). "I did not want to come at all, but you see, it really is true that the soul of someone in anguish may wander away" (t174). She sees herself as a victim; "hers was the greatest of misfortunes" (t180).

Rokujō's spirit, in accordance with belief at the time, survives her own death as an "angry ghost." Claiming to speak on her behalf through a medium,[38] it rampantly weaponizes Rokujō's bitterness. It declares a wish to punish Genji himself, but has been frustrated by the supernatural "protection" still provided by his special status in the natural order. Instead, provoked by his jibe, Rokujō's spirit assaults his loved secondary wife. The medium's blistering poem expresses profound resentment against a culpable, still unregenerate Genji:

I indeed appear in a different guise, but, feigning innocence, you are wholly you. (*kimi wa kimi* nari; g4/236; cf. t655)[39]

---

37. Tyler, "The Disaster of the Third Princess," p. 95.
38. On this topic, see Blacker, "The Angry Ghost in Japan."
39. This balances Murasaki's much earlier claim "I am I." See note 31.

The spirit, however, also addresses a broader social wrong, reflecting Rokujō's own bitter experience of womanhood. On her deathbed some decade and a half earlier, Rokujō had told Genji, "My own life has taught me that a woman is born to many sorrows." She had enlisted his help to spare her daughter, Akikonomu, this fate (t294). Through the medium, the spirit now again charges Genji to ensure that her daughter "never participates in jealous rivalries with other women" (t655). The spirit's intervention, it seems, reaches beyond Rokujō's own unhappiness to address the suffering caused by antagonisms among what Genji himself calls the "exalted company" of elite women, where "the spirit of rivalry is a constant torment" (t645).

Genji will have none of this. He reacts with "amazement" to the medium. As ever concerned for appearances, he "took the girl's hand and held her down lest she embarrass him" (t654). The narrator reports that he "detested conversing with a spirit" (t655). Finally, he "quietly moved [Murasaki] elsewhere." Genji later does "all he could to conceal the way [Akikonomu's] mother had announced her by now detested presence." Discussing the matter with Akikonomu herself, he is evasive about the cause of her visitation, while stating that he is praying for Rokujō's salvation (t715).

In the short term, Genji's ritual expertise secures Murasaki's recovery. Frustrated, Rokujō's spirit turns to possess the Third Princess, whom she causes to take the tonsure. Genji is humiliatingly deprived of control over his trophy bride and his standing with her father, the Retired Emperor Suzaku, is damaged. Meanwhile, Murasaki's health declines. Though she survives for a while, the harm is irreversible. Murasaki's possession marks the beginning of the disintegration of Genji's fortunes. Supernatural agencies and myth no longer guard him. He loses his appetite for life. The arc of Genji's love life returns to near its beginning, with Rokujō.

SUMMARY: PROTEST, MORAL COHERENCE, AND THE *GENJI*

Implied in both the attack by the angry spirit of Rokujō on Murasaki and its request for the protection of her daughter is the principle that women are entitled to moral respect and that offenses against them ultimately incur retributive justice. A wider view of the *Genji* shows protest on behalf of women to be a recurrent motif. Generic sentiments concerning womanhood start early with the introductory banter among Genji and his male friends that sets the parameters for Genji's own quest. The question is framed as a rhetorical subordinate clause: *nado ka, onna to iwamu kara ni.* "Why just because they may be called women should they be utterly ignorant of the world, public and private?" (g1/89; cf. t35). Expressions of discontent on behalf of women recur. One of the most bitter will in due course come from Murasaki herself: "Ah, she reflected, there is nothing so pitifully confined and constricted as a woman. What will reward her passage through the world if she remains sunk in herself, blind to life's joys and sorrows and to every delight?" (t741). From the male side, the mirror image of such sentiments is a strident misogyny. Buddhist misogyny becomes increasingly salient: a master of discipline speaks of "birth in an evil female body" (t727). Genji's own misogyny is expressed in exasperated condemnation of the merely careless Third Princess, a girl young enough to be his daughter: "all women are a source of dire sin; every dealing with them [is] hateful" (t656).

Set in this broader context, the late intervention of Rokujō's angry spirit and its shattering denouement in Murasaki's illness and death confer both an element of protest and a moral coherence on the narrative. Genji is grievously punished for his promiscuity; unprotected by supernatural agency, he loses his most beloved and is plunged into despair. But there is a final irony. Murasaki, a woman, is allowed a death that is in some sense redemptive, true to the best spirit of the Buddhism that has become an increasing preoccupation over the long narrative.

The manner of her death, as Tyler poignantly shows, is "inspiring." She "rises above her situation" and "achieves the independence" that she had claimed long ago in a fit of pique as a twenty-year-old.[40] She wins what Genji fails to achieve: liberation from the world and a true denial of self; it is with her, rather than Genji, that the moral story of Part II comes home. His political ambitions, role as ritualist, and quest for the ideal woman abandoned, Genji loses his raison d'être, his ritually constructed self, and becomes a mere shell. True, the narrator observes that following Murasaki's death, he conceives "a pure and lasting" desire for Buddhist salvation. But even then, pointedly, he cannot free himself from the "aesthetic order," the precondition for his public triumph; he "also still dreaded what people might feel like saying about him" (t663). From a Buddhist point of view, Murasaki rather than Genji is the true hero of *The Tale of Genji*. She confers ultimate moral coherence on the story. Its *basso ostinato* remains "aesthetic order," but Part II ends in the major moral key of Buddhist self-transcendence.

ACKNOWEDGEMENTS

I am grateful to Nicholas Bunnin, Jenny Guest, Phillip Harries, and Rajyshree Pandey for reading drafts of this essay and offering helpful advice. The essay also owes much to the seminal critical essays on *Genji* of Royall Tyler.

WORKS CITED

Aston, W. G., tr. *Nihongi: Chronicles of Japan from the Earliest Times to A.D. 697.* London: George Allen & Unwin, 1956 (reprint of 1896 ed.).

40. Tyler, "Between Love and Pride," pp. 68–70.

Bargen, Doris G. *A Woman's Secret Weapon: Spirit Possession in "The Tale of Genji."* Honolulu: University of Hawai'i Press, 1997.

Blacker, Carmen. "The Angry Ghost in Japan." In H. R. E. Davidson and W .M. S. Russell, eds., *The Folklore of Ghosts.* Cambridge: D. S. Brewer for the Folklore Society, 1981.

Eberhard, Wolfram. *Guilt and Sin in Traditional China.* Berkeley: University of California Press, 1967.

Elias, Norbert. *The Civilizing Process.* Tr. Edmund Jephcott. Oxford: Blackwell, 1994.

Elias, Norbert. *The Court Society.* Tr. Edmund Jephcott. Oxford: Basil Blackwell, 1983.

Field, Norma. *The Splendor of Longing in "The Tale of Genji."* Princeton, NJ: Princeton University Press, 1987.

Fingarette, Herbert. *Confucius: The Secular as Sacred.* New York: Harper Torchbooks, 1972.

Hall, David L. and Roger T Ames. *Thinking through Confucius.* Albany: State University of New York Press, 1987.

Harper, Thomas, and Haruo Shirane, eds. *Reading "The Tale of Genji": Sources from the First Millennium.* New York: Columbia University Press, 2015.

McMullen, James. "The Pathos of Love: Motoori Norinaga and *The Tale of Genji.*" In Ii Haruki, ed., *Kaigai ni okeru Genji monogatari no kenkyū,* pp. 205–227. Tokyo: Kazama Shobō, 2004.

Mencius. The Works of Mencius tr. James Legge. *The Chinese Classics,* Vol. 2. Hong Kong: Hong Kong University Press, 1960. Reprint of Shanghai edtn, 1935.

Miller, Alan L. "Ritsuryō Japan: the State as Liturgical Community." *History of Religion,* vol. 11, no. 1 (Aug. 1971).

Morris, Ivan. *The World of the Shining Prince.* Harmondsworth: Penguin, 1964.

Mortimer, Raymond. "A New Planet." *The Nation & the Atheneum,* June 20, 1925.

Motoori Norinaga. *Shibun yōryō.* In Ōno Susumu, ed., *Motoori Norinaga zenshū,* vol. 4. Tokyo: Chikuma Shobō, 1969.

Motoori Norinaga. *Tamakatsuma.* In Yoshikawa Kōjirō et al., eds., *Motoori Norinaga. Nihon Shisō taikei,* vol. 40. Tokyo: Iwanami Shoten, 1978.

Pandey, Rajyashree. *Writing and Renunciation in Medieval Japan: The Works of the Poet-Priest Kamo no Chōmei.* Ann Arbor: University of Michigan, Center for Japanese Studies, 1998.

Philippi, Donald H., tr. *Kojiki.* Princeton, NJ: Princeton University Press, 1969.

Sasakawa Isao. "*Honchō reisō* no sekiten shi to "*Genji monogatari.*" *Higashi Ajia Hikaku Bunka Kenkyū* 13 (2014), pp. 47–59.

Seidensticker, Edward G., tr., *The Tale of Genji,* 2 vols. London: Secker & Warburg, 1976.

Shirane, Haruo. *The Bridge of Dreams: A Poetics of "The Tale of Genji."* Stanford, CA: Stanford University Press, 1987.

Sugiura Kazuko. "*Genji* monogatari ni okeru 'kokoro no oni'—'hito wo semeru oni' kara 'onore wo semeru oni' no monongartari e -" *Jōchi Daigaku bunka kōshōgaku kenkyū* (March 2013), pp. 37–50.

Tyler, Royall. *A Reading of "The Tale of Genji."* Blue-Tongue Books, 2016; slightly reformatted, under a new imprint, from the original edition published in 2014.

Tyler, Royall. "Genji and the Luck of the Sea." In *A Reading of "The Tale of Genji."*

Tyler, Royall, "Genji and Murasaki: Between Love and Pride." In *A Reading of "The Tale of Genji."*

Tyler, Royall, "The Disaster of the Third Princess." In *A Reading of "The Tale of Genji."*

Tyler, Royall. "The Hidden *Tale of Genji.*" Occasional Papers in Japanese Studies no. 2002-02. Cambridge, MA: Harvard University, Edwin O. Reischauer Institute of Japanese Studies, May 2002.

Tyler, Royall, tr. *Murasaki Shikibu: The Tale of Genji.* 2 vols. New York: Viking Penguin, 2001.

Waley, Arthur, tr. *The Tale of Genji* (one volume edition). London: George Allen & Unwin, 1935.

Williams, Yoko. *"Tsumi": Offence and Retribution in Early Japan.* London: RoutledgeCurzon, 2003.

Yamagishi Tokuhei, ed. *Genji monogatari.* 5 vols. Tokyo: Iwanami Shoten,1958–63.

Chapter 4

Flares in the Garden, Darkness in the Heart

Exteriority, Interiority, and the Role of Poems in The Tale of Genji

EDWARD KAMENS

Dyads are everywhere—in nature, in cognition, in politics, and in discourse, philosophical and other kinds—sometimes oppressively so, in that they may short-circuit our perception of nuance, subtlety, shades of difference, and the shifting, slippery character and significance of all things that are not fixed. One such dyad, "exteriority and interiority," is ubiquitous and perhaps inevitable in discussions of most all things cultural (also physical, metaphysical, and social), not only because it so neatly delineates spaces that would appear to be distinctive (even when they are not) but also because it is widely understood as the dynamic by way of which the human experience of phenomena, our responses in inward emotion, and their release in various forms of expression interrelate in a kind of causal chain.

In their introductory essay in *Rethinking Emotion: Interiority and Exteriority in Premodern, Modern and Contemporary Thought*, Campe and Weber state, "The notion of interiority and its central role in our understanding of emotional life and individuality are phenomena that belong to classical Western modernity."[1] Here, I will try to show that this notion does not "belong" only to "classical Western modernity." The idea that interiority is the space or site in which human individuals sustain the impact of their experience with the exterior world and, as a result, *express* their emotions through language, thus propelling them into the exterior world, is and has long been the cardinal tenet of East Asian poetics and traditional literary theory. But to say that things are not nearly so simple as that only begins to get at the challenge of grasping and then troubling these ideas. In this essay I will embrace and then retreat from, by complicating, any singular, one-dimensional account of what "interiority and exteriority" might mean for a reader of *The Tale of Genji*—who confronts its many manifestations at almost every turn of the page.

That claim is not meant to suggest that *The Tale of Genji* is unique in this regard. As readers, we oscillate between our positions outside the text before us and inside it, or *toward* it, because the text's maker or its language in whatever way it may be inscribed for cognitive perception does everything possible to capture our attention, direct that perception, or, in some cases, toy with us, or repel us back toward a less intimate, perhaps even alienated, "exteriority," or to leave us hovering in some unsettled state. Of course, the same can be said of what happens when we "read" a drawing, a painting or a sculpture, a building, a film, or interact with artifacts and other constructs in other media, with other senses, as we may do with music or other kinds of sound.

Here, however, I am concerned with the reading of texts, and one in particular and, especially, the poems *in* it and *of* it and their "interior" and "exterior" features, manifestations, and dynamics; but

1. Campe and Weber, eds., *Rethinking Emotion*, p. 1.

I will avail myself of the analogy to readings of other media that must be experienced visually—especially paintings, works in the medium that is literature's (and especially poetry's) sister art, particularly so in the Japanese tradition, and that offers us other kinds of *readings* of texts such as the *Tale*. In our engagements with both the visual and the textual, I believe, we need to allow ourselves, and teach ourselves, to take our place both outside these visible, communicating entities, in order to remain aware of ourselves as readers, viewers, receivers; but we also need to strive to read, or see, from *within* these entities and thus to yield, willingly or otherwise, and submit to their charms (the transporting magic that they may work), to let them speak to us as they will, and to speak back to them and of them about this experience, which always changes us, and to do so with a constant awareness that this oscillating exchange of sensations and sensibilities—the text's and the reader's—can have no endpoint, no single, fixed outcome or stasis.

When I conceptualize and seek analogies for interiorities and exteriorities of artifacts and phenomena and structures of many kinds in Japanese culture and, in particular, in the text and the world of *The Tale of Genji*, my thoughts turn to a very particular dyadic form, the "inside-and-outside of the Capital" painted screens (*rakuchū rakugai zu*), or "capitalscapes," as the art historian Matthew McKelway has called them.[2] (See figure 4.1a-b) These relatively large-scale multi-panel images, which, being *byōbu*, or standing, folding screens, are also a kind of furniture, which came into their own as a pictorial genre in the sixteenth century and flourished especially in the seventeenth, offer the viewer a panoramic—and utterly imaginary—scanning of the vast metropolis of Kyoto (one of the largest and grandest of

2. McKelway also refers to these works as "Kyoto screens," citing a passage dated to the year 1502 in Sanjōnishi Sanetaka's diary as the earliest mention of paintings of this kind and the use of that term. McKelway, *Capitalscapes*, pp. 1–2.

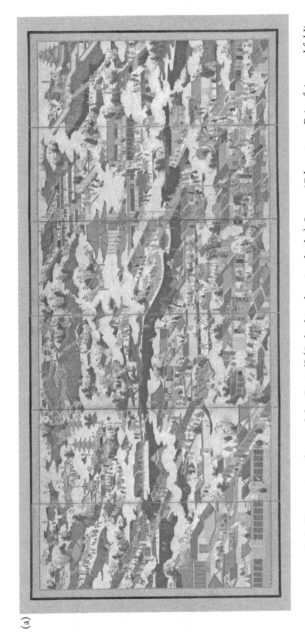

(a)

Figures 4.1a and 1b "Scenes in and around the Capital" (*Rakuchū rakugai zu byōbu*). Japan; 17th century. Pair of six-panel folding screens; ink, color, gold, and gold leaf on paper. Metropolitan Museum of Art, New York City: Mary Griggs Burke Collection, Gift of the Mary and Jackson Burke Foundation, 2015.

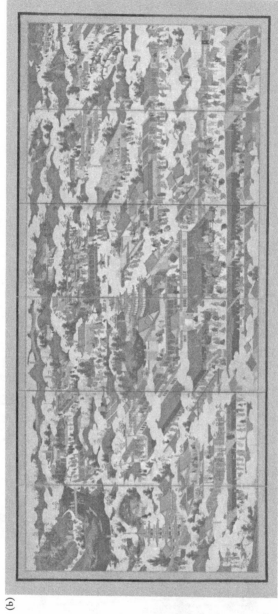

Figures 4.1a and 1b Continued

cities in the world at that time): no one could stand in (or fly to!) the artificially constructed position in which the posited observer would need to be placed in order to capture this view, and that includes the painter.[3] Spatial relationships, geographical realities, accurate scale—these were not the painters' aims in the crafting of these images; rather, these images give a sense of how the city was filled to excess with notable sites through the depiction of as many recognizable locations, buildings, and public and private spaces of importance as the surfaces of the screens could contain. Also, whether with just a few or with hundreds of human figures, they suggest movement, activity, and even the unheard but imaginable hum and buzz of life in a populous, self-important urban space—wafting music of pipes and drums, the shouts of out-runners and hawkers, groans of palanquin-bearers, the scraping of ox-driven carriage wheels on packed dirt or gravel, weavers' looms and fulling blocks on silk, birdsong and cock-crow, barking dogs.

This genre term, *rakuchū rakugai (zu)*—literally, "pictures of the interior and the exterior of the capital"—is, of course, a dyad, and its orthographic configuration, like many such neologisms introduced at various stages of Japan's adaptation of Chinese linguistic and graphic forms, shows this as well: in the phrase 洛中洛外図, the repeated graph is one that stands for "capital" through its derivation from the name of the ancient but paradigmatic Chinese capital, Loyang (洛陽), which served as one of the templates for the very concept of the capital city and the physical design and enduring plan (to this day) of its Japanese remake.[4] That city, founded as Heian-kyō in the eighth century, then later and still known as Kyoto, was the

---

3. See ibid., pp. 22–23, for McKelway's description of this "aerial perspective" as a "parallel orthogonal perspectival system."

4. Ibid., pp. 12–13, explains the derivation in some detail and notes that the nomenclature *rakuchū rakugai (zu)* does not appear in documents until the mid-seventeenth century.

seat of the imperial court establishment and thus Japan's political and cultural hub until late in the nineteenth century—and, of course, the setting, along with some of its most poetically charged peripheries, of the imaginary events and world that take shape in *The Tale of Genji*. It was also the place of its origin and the setting for most of its early history of reception. Indeed, it is virtually impossible to separate the history of the city and its cultural manifestations from the history, reception, and the very content and worldview and aura of the *Tale* itself: they are a bound pair.

But, as McKelway has shown, an inflexible notion of the spatial referents of *rakuchū rakugai* as a dyadic "inner and outer" may be misleading:

> Because the early Kyoto screens provide no sharp compositional delineation between Kyoto's urban and rural spaces . . . I interpret *"rakuchū rakugai"* as inclusive, emphasizing the integration of a total vision of the city. The earliest terms used to describe Kyoto screens, *"Kyōchū"* and *"rakuchūga,"* furthermore, relate closely to contemporary usage of these terms to speak about "all of" or "throughout" Kyoto . . . . The totalizing and all-encompassing visions of the sixteenth-century Kyoto screens more closely parallel the nuance of *Kyōchū* than the implicit distinctions attributed to *"rakuchū"* and *"rakugai."*[5]

It is this idea and structure, of a "totalizing and all-encompassing vision" composed of disparate, noncontiguous, but carefully chosen elements that I want to work with here in thinking about the "inside(s)" and "outside(s)," the parts and wholes—especially the parts that are poems—and the "all-of" *The Tale of Genji*, not to suggest a "totalizing vision" of it in a reductive way, but to consider what

5. Ibid., p. 14.

it means to move or be moved between and through its interior(s) and exteriors, as embodied in the textual elements that bring them into being for us as readers.

Here again I am aided by a wealth of artifacts in the visual realm, for quite a few visual renderings and representations of *The Tale of Genji* itself, in a variety of formats including but not limited to *byōbu*, and likewise dating from the same period as that in which the panoramic city screens flourished (as well as in earlier works), share some of the same uses of visual language and composition, despite their very different subject matters. In one way or another, the multiple divisions of the *Tale* (its chapters and clusters of chapters) are represented in these works as parts that not only "make up" but can stand for the whole. There are screens composed of images on fanlike shapes (actually, the modified semicircular papers that would be used to make folding fans) of all fifty-four chapters (a format also used in some Kyoto screens);[6] there are others that show only selected scenes from disparate points along the chronological spectrum of the text's unfolding plots, as though transpiring in a single blended or blurred time and in seemingly adjacent or contiguous spaces, both "indoor" and "outdoor."

One screen of this type that I know particularly well is a seventeenth-century pair (by an unknown artist of the Tosa school) in the Yale University Art Gallery, which show just four scene-episodes on their twelve panels.[7] (See figure 4.2a-b.) On the right screen we see the adolescent Genji's presentation to the Korean physiognomer/soothsayer in the Kōrokan reception hall, as told in Chapter 1 "Kiritsubo," followed to its immediate left by an even more elaborate interior scene from Genji's middle age—the final

6. Ibid., pp. 37–43, fig. 2.13, etc.
7. YUAG 1984.9.1-.2, accessible at http://artgallery.yale.edu/collections/objects/25532. See also Kamens, " 'The Tale of Genji' and 'Yashima' Screens," and Ohki, "Japanese Art at Yale."

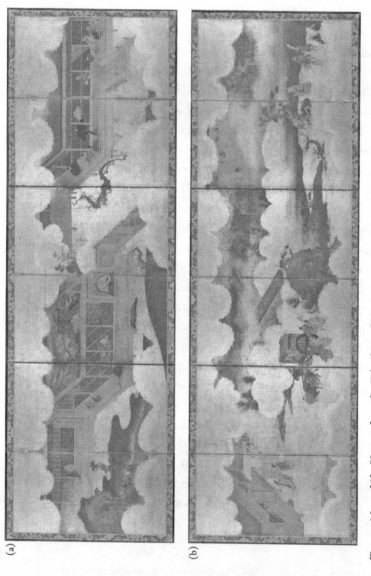

Figures 4.2a and 2b "Scenes from the *Tale of Genji*." Kyoto Kano School: 1625–60. Pair of six-panel folding screens: ink, color, gold pigment, gold flecks, and gold foils on paper. Yale University Art Gallery, Edward H. Dunlap, B.A. 1934, Fund. Right screen: interior scenes; left screen; exteriors.

(a)

(b)

rehearsal for a formal musical performance (which, for various reasons, never takes place) in which the most important women of his grand mansion, the Rokujō-in, and his son Yūgiri all take part on the various types of zithers and lutes (*koto, biwa*) on which they have been practicing under his direction; on the left screen, the artist has rendered (on the far right panels) the moment in the penultimate Chapter 53 "Tenarai," at which the venerable Bishop of Yokawa examines the bedraggled and barely living figure of a young woman (who turns out to be Ukifune) lying at the foot of a tree on a bank of the Uji River, lit by torches held by his wary and suspicious acolytes; and then, beyond a transitional area occupied by both buildings and gardens that may represent the spacious elevated platform or veranda on the exterior of Hasedera (which Ukifune visits in a prior chapter) or possibly Kiyomizudera, and their environs (in a manner that suggests a blurring with the geographically noncontiguous but plot-associated Uji),[8] and a diagonally skewed portion of a covered wall of the kind that would encircle a Heian aristocrat's urban mansion, the eye arrives at a depiction of another utterly disparate moment from a chapter near the beginning of the *Tale*: Genji's aide Koremitsu's encounter with a somewhat forward young woman who emerges from a relatively modest dwelling in "the wrong part of town" to offer a fan bearing a single white *yūgao* (Evening Face) flower and a coyly provocative message for Genji, who waits nearby but unseen and incognito inside the ox-drawn carriage surrounded by his men (in the eponymous Chapter 4, "Yūgao").

---

8. Ukifune, like the earlier heroine Tamakazura a generation prior to her in the timeline of the *Tale*, finds her way back into contact with her erstwhile kindred after making a pilgrimage to Hasedera to pray to its presiding Kannon for intervention; one might say that, down the line across several chapters and their plot turns and twists, she ends up at Uji as an indirect result of those forces at work, which in this case deliver her, against her will, back into her lover Kaoru's sphere, despite her subsequent effort to escape him, and to evade eros, by taking Buddhist vows.

In this composition, the chronology of the *Tale* would seem to be reversed or rearranged—although, as McKelway reminds us, the trajectory of time is not always to be read from right to left (if at all) in screens of this period and kind, and, perhaps more important than narrative sequence, other factors may be what prompted this choice of scenes and their spatial arrangement. In the right screen, the two grand interior scenes depict plot events that shape Genji's destiny as protagonist: never emperor but in many ways quasi-emperor, as the prognosticator foretold; master orchestrator and stage manager of his domestic domain, but never able to secure or stabilize the peaceful, emotionally fulfilled lives of its denizens, including his own. (This is indirectly suggested by, among other things, the fact that the antici-pated visit to the Rokujō'in by the reigning emperor, Genji's brother, for which this concert is a rehearsal, is eventually canceled.) In the left screen, conversely, we see two turning points in the unfolding sto-rylines of, first, Ukifune, whose seemingly inexorable lurch toward death has been forestalled, along with her passive (or maybe passive-aggressive) effort to remove herself from the erotic trap in which she, Kaoru, and Niou have found themselves, and then of Yūgao (not herself seen, but "present" somewhere farther inside the rooms from which her curious attendants peer toward Koremitsu, Genji, and the city street), whose own retreat from "the world" (after bearing a child with her onetime lover, "Tō no Chujo," and being hounded into separation and hiding from him by his powerful in-laws) will now be undone—as will she, as the recipient of Genji's consuming, destruc-tive love. On the right, the official courtly/governmental space of the Kōroden (the designated site within the city for encounters with the "foreign" and with foreigners) appears to give way and merge into Genji's Rokujō-in, a utopian/dystopian private/public residential compound that epitomizes, in fantasy, the ultimate in royal/aristo-cratic domestic luxury, perfection in both interior (living spaces) and exterior (garden landscaping) design, and their harmonization, coordination, and materialization (however imperfect) of an equilibrium of personal taste, cosmic order, and masterful management of nature.

Also, in the right screen, the viewer is given open access into the interior of both structures—the "official" Kōrokan (its historical location was at the intersection of Shichijō [the seventh east–west boulevard, counting north to south] and Suzaku, the city's central ceremonial north–south corridor) and the "private" Rokujō'in (fictionally close by, as it were, on the sixth east–west boulevard), from the well-established aerial angle. Here, too, there are strong suggestions of masterfully orchestrated and harmonized sounds—the music that we cannot "hear" but can, in a way, "see" or at least imagine, reverberating from the various instruments that Murasaki, the Akashi Lady, and the Third Princess as well as Yūgiri (on the veranda) all pluck. This man-made but nigh-celestial music is mirrored, as it were, in the first panels on the left, but there it is a natural, uncontrollable noise—the rushing waters of the Uji River, the crash of an unnamed cascade—almost but not quite drowning out the (unheard) words of the Bishop as he explains to his crew that this is not a trickster fox or a demon that they see before them, but a human being obviously in distress and in need of special care. Figures kneeling, praying, and moving about on the intervening temple veranda also suggest not only motion but rustling sound, beyond which (still moving visually leftward) we come to the unheard dialogue between Koremitsu and Yūgao's messenger, overheard, perhaps, by those inside the house and also, perhaps, by Genji inside that carriage parked nearby. Notably, however, at this edge of the screen the viewer, like Genji, is as yet denied access to the charms and temptations that await inside this inviting, if déclassé, dwelling, marked by those eye-catching, if inelegant, white flowers on its flourishing gourd vines.

It is likely to occur to an astute viewer that the configuration in the right panel, with its two representations of Genji's "turning points,"

both of which point, in different ways, to limitations, disappoint-
ments, and "falls" despite the scenic veneer of consummate splendor,
is mirrored (not without distortion) on the left in the relationship
between the outcomes of Ukifune's and Yūgao's stories. These culmi-
nate, on the one hand, in a mysterious disappearance that turns out
to be a literal (if inexplicable) "near-death experience," countered by
an attempt at quasi-death in Ukifune's taking of vows that is, in turn,
negated by an imposed return to "the world" and its erotic demands,
and, on the other hand, the abrupt and traumatic (also not wholly
explicable) but irreversible death of Yūgao, in the very midst of her
ill-fated erotic adventure with Genji. At the same time, the viewer/
reader might note, both of their stories leave residues and traces for
further plot development, though Yūgao's are more than fully developed (in the later story of her daughter Tamakazura, which unfolds
across several pages) while Ukifune's are left in an embryonic state
when the narrative trails off in its final lines, while she anxiously
awaits Kaoru's next move on her place of refuge and he contemplates
whether or not to make that move.

In this rendering of space, suggestions of sights, sites, and sounds,
and the construction of parallel as well as contrasting, divergent conditions, are the guiding principles— rather than faithfulness to linear
temporal sequence or more transparent, obvious references to plot
connections and suggested cause-and-effect nexuses (of which there
are plenty in the *Tale* that could have been used to compose such a
parts-into-whole, piecemeal-into-integration visual program). We
can read these internal, outward-"speaking" hints from the surface
of the painting—guided, to a great extent, by our knowledge of the
referent text, *if we have that knowledge*—and perhaps it can even be
read structurally, in this way, *if we do not*. Either way, as we sit or stand
before these screens, we are aware of being simultaneously held outside the world that they create, yet drawn, by means of memory, recognition, or perhaps just the act of mindful *seeing*, into that world and

beyond these individual but blended episodic scenes into the imaginary that the *Tale, as a whole,* creates and opens up to us. We yield to its charms and temptations, its stimuli of memory and fantasy, as we do to those of the *Tale* itself.

Jacques Derrida declared, "*Il n'y a pas de hors-texte*" and "*Il n'ya a pas rien hors du texte,*"[9] by which he has been understood to assert that meaning cannot reliably be sought through recourse to anything *outside* a text (such as "context"). But in the foregoing description of ways of reading a *Genji* screen like the one at Yale, I have suggested that there are both "insiders" and "outsiders" as readers—those "in the know" about the *Tale* at a level of considerable detail and those who have far less or no knowledge of it whatsoever. For the latter hypothetical reader/viewer, the screen might be the window through which a first, engaging, charming encounter with it takes place, leading to others of greater depth and intimacy. This is another oscillating relationship: the text informs the creation of the image as it comes into being, the image informs or alters its reader/viewer's perception of the text, and so on, ad infinitum. At a stage of dissemination well beyond the time of the coming-into-being of both text and its visual re-presentation (for example, in the present), the image (the Yale *Genji* screen, for example) can also aid, or determine, the ways in which the reader of the text "visualizes" its content—especially its architectural (interior and exterior) and outdoor (open-air) spaces.

That oscillating regime of spatial interiority and exteriority in the text of the *Tale* is also its most obvious manifestation of this dyad—again, even if the reader does not "know the territory." Most of its action takes place "indoors": in palaces, mansions, and sanctuaries ranging from the vast Sumiyoshi Shrine to the Ise Priestess's

---

9. Derrida, *De la grammatologie,* pp. 227, 233. He also labels two sections of this discourse "*Le dehors et le dedan*" and "*Le dehor est le dedans*" (with the copula X-ed out), but does not disentangle these gnomic phrases as such.

purification site at the "Shrine in the Fields" (Nonomiya) and the Eighth Prince's private chapel (*butsuma*) at his Uji villa, later remodeled by Kaoru, and, finally, the convent at Ono in which Ukifune finds refuge; and yet more singular structures such as the humble house in which Genji and Yūgao are distracted from their intimacy by "plebian voices" piercing its thin walls and the deserted villa to which Genji absconds with Yūgao, where she suddenly dies; or Genji's rustic but elegant dwelling in exile in Suma and the yet more elegant but still relatively exotic establishment of the Akashi Monk and his family, farther down the western coastline; and many, many more. Some of these sites, like the Kōroden, have cognates in historical reality (for example, the "haunted house" in which Yūgao succumbs to an evil spirit's attack is thought to have been modeled on the storied Kawara no in the villa of Minamoto no Tōru, an earlier Heian period courtier); others, like the Rokujō-in mansion, are imaginary variants or wholly fabricated. This oscillation between recognizable and more fuzzily fictionalized spaces is another cause for the reader to hover between a sense of recognition and a sense of disorientation in the space that this work of fiction (like all others) conjures, furnishes, and orchestrates (as is, for example, the opening line of the entire narrative: "*izure no ohontoki ni ka . . .*": "In whose reign was it . . . ?" [g1/ 17; w3]).[10]

Once in that space, the attentive reader of the *Tale* will be acutely aware of shifts in its narrative perspective as it observes and recounts the events and encounters that transpire therein, in imitation of its own frequent recourse to the trope of *kaimami*—voyeuristic peering into private interiors. This is often accompanied by eavesdropping as well, both explicitly and implicitly, and frequently, and markedly, the tellers of the tale carry this intrusive penetration to a further degree

---

10. See Coates, "Building and Gardens"; Coaldrake, *Architecture and Authority*; and Sarra, *Unreal Houses*.

in probings and exposures that lay bare the often torturous musings and internal psychic self-debates in which its characters engage, often at considerable length (and often, at one point or another, shifting into or wrapping up in one or more poems). This narrative trope of "interior monologue" (*shinnaigo*, or "private discourse within the heart/mind," as it was termed fairly early in medieval *Genji* commentary),[11] is just as important in shaping the reader's sense of variation in pace, ambience, and novelistic mise-en-scène as is the constructed geographical movement that the reader follows, or is drawn ineluctably along with, as the loci of action shift from one part of Heian-kyō to another and to its peripheries. In the *Tale's* final scenes, the locus shifts to Ono, a transitional point between the city, Uji, and Enryakuji, the Tendai complex atop Mount Hiei and the ultimate Buddhist monastic retreat.

The attentive reader of recent and contemporary *Tale of Genji* commentary and criticism will also be more than well aware of these spatial dynamics, for which reason I will not say much more about them here, except in considering the "interior" and "exterior" placement or presence of poems, some of which are themselves *shinnaigo* while many more are "out there" in the world of the *Tale*—in letters, in conversations, in utterances overheard—and still others drift in a space of memory and a fragmented state, half-remembered, partially quoted, gestured to obliquely as if in a passing thought on the part of a character or a narrator . . . and in the reader's memory as well. Like references to "known," historically recognizable and verifiable locations, these allusive moments, in particular, are orientation points that, momentarily and illusorily, situate the reader in what can seem, if only briefly, to be a familiar node in the vast network of literary materiality and spatiality that we often call "the intertext"—another

11. See Stinchecum, "Who Tells the Tale?"; Noguchi, "The Substratum Constituting *Monogatari.*"

entity that is of course not singular, never static, and never susceptible to complete embrace.

But first—because it is a topic also closely related to the role of
poetry in the *Tale*—I want to consider yet another aspect of it that
is both "inside" and "outside" but that is less often commented upon
or described in such terms: this is the intertwined issue of characters' names (as presented to us or created for us either within the text
itself, by various means, or outside it, in its ever-expanding clusters
of paratext) and of its chapter titles—some of which are also characters' names, some of which thereby "give" those characters those
"names," and others that derive from episodes, from loci of action,
and (like many of those characters' names or sobriquets) from poetic
figures linked to them, again by various means. These names (appellations, circumlocutions, labels, indices) are paratextual phenomena
that, over time, have come to act as if organic, "original," and inherent
to the text: they do inhere, but they have not always been there—or
rather, they are both there and not there.

Anyone who has taken the time to read a translator's notes about
the strategies adopted in one version of the *Tale* or another to address
the problem of characters' names and the language used in "the original," in modes at times deictic or oblique and (to some) maddeningly
mercurial, to identify subjects and referents who are *persons*, will
have had at least a glimpse of this challenge. Though this style would
have posed little if any such problem for the text's first readers, it has
long since become one of the most notorious among the linguistic
and rhetorical distinctions that, unavoidably, divide a Heian period
or Kamakura period version of the text and its conventions, as they
have been handed down to us, from any version in almost any other
language, including modern Japanese.

But where, after all, do any of the so-called names of the scores of
personae a reader encounters in the *Tale*, in any one of its versions—
or, perhaps more important, in discourse *about* it—come from? The

answer is that they "come from" both inside and outside the text. The protagonist acquires one of his names (such as it is) soon after that moment in Chapter 1, "Kiritsubo," that is depicted in the Yale screen: he is formally passing from early to late adolescence and quasi-adulthood in that he is married (at age twelve) to a woman we will come to know as "Aoi" while also obsessed with desire for his stepmother, "Fujitsubo," so "named" by the quarters assigned to her in the palace, as a consort (as was indeed the historical practice for high-ranking women of the court).[12] In this key passage, in which the narrator praises both the boy and his surrogate mother (and eventual paramour) from the point of view of "the world"—those who knew them or knew of them and their extraordinary beauty and talents— she receives the appellation "Princess of the Radiant Sun" in pairing with his (that is, Genji's) nickname, "Radiant Prince" (she, *Kagayaku hi no miya*; he, *Hikaru kimi* [g1:44]). In fact, the text has already given him the name Genji in a previous passage, when his father decides (acting in part on the advice of that Korean soothsayer) to designate him a commoner and assign to him (as emperors often did in history when thus reclassifying their kin) the surname Minamoto—that is, depending upon shifts in the reading of Sino-Japanese script, the "*Gen*" of "*Genji*," "Minamoto house or clan." Names, which we sometimes think of as fixed locutions, are in fact quite persistent in their oscillations, just as are identities and our perceptions of them: in the text and the world of the *Tale*, names (and their equivalents) are as protean and fugitive as is that transient, unstable world itself.

There are plenty of characters that the narrative text itself names, in introducing and describing them: some are known throughout its lengthy course by just one appellation (if any), but many others

---

12. In the fictional court-world of the *Tale*, the reader encounters quite a number of women similarly yclept: Kiritsubo, Kokiden, Reikeiden, Umetsubo, and more than one Fujitsubo, among others.

acquire, drop, and substitute a series of monikers as their narrative time progresses. And only a limited number of the members of this "cast of hundreds" receive what we might think of as personal names. Early on, for example, there is Koremitsu, Genji's foster brother, groom, and man-of-all-work; he is one of these few, and, notably, he is not placed in the fiction's mirror image of the highest echelons of court society. Far more characters are identified with literally descriptive nomenclature: the "Eighth Prince" (*Hachi no miya*) is just that—his father's eighth male child—and is explicitly so called in the text, while "Blackbeard" (*Higekuro*), the gentleman who eventually weds Tamakazura, gains that nickname—the one by which he is best known *outside* the text, in formal and informal discourse about it—because that is his most distinguishing physical feature; but he is most frequently referred to *within* the text by one or another of the pseudo-military-cum-civil titles to which he rises as his part of the story unfolds. The most prominent example of this pattern, surely, is that of the gentleman referred to only very early on in the text as "Tō no Chūjō," "The Fujiwara Captain"—Genji's first cousin, brother-in-law, best friend, and chief rival—but subsequently, in succeeding chapters, by the progressively lofty titles that accompany the exalted ranks that he achieves; despite which, throughout external discourse, and again from very early phases of reception right through the present, he is familiarly—and affectionately—"Tō no Chūjō" to virtually one and all who "know" the *Tale*. This is perhaps, at least in part, because the appellation is so euphonious, but also due to the fact that this character makes his strongest impressions on us, as readers, at the stage at which that is his proper nomenclature.

Notably, as is true for "Hikaru kimi"/"Genji" and so many others, the reader never learns what this Tō no Chūjō's personal name (*Fujiwara no* what?) might have been, if he had one (in the fiction's world); the same is true for almost every other character across the entire expanse of the text. Many, like Aoi, Kashiwagi, and Tamakazura, are also, technically, "Fujiwara," but personal names for them never appear. Instead, within the text *and* outside it, as we speak and write about them, they bear these names that are not names: sobriquets, nicknames, and a variety of circumlocutions that stubbornly adhere to them, as it is the social positions and circumstances, aesthetic preferences, evocative linkages with certain toponyms (their places of origin or physical locations of their primary residence), or the colors or scents or the actual names of flowers or trees that stand out in those episodes in which they make their most memorable appearances, that differentiate them. Or, in addition or alternatively, these appellations come from (or are introduced into the narrative through) poems they make or that others make about them or in dialogue or correspondence with or about them.

In this sense, such names are often part of the "odor" that lingers about the men and women of the *Tale*, at length (for its duration and onward through the ongoing time of its transmission), like the natural perfume that always attends the physical person of Genji and also of his faux son, Kaoru, or the artificial scent with which Kaoru's own cousin, friend, and rival, Niou, adorns himself. Both their appellations—not personal names, of course—mean "to give off scent (and color)," and both names attach to them as an outcome of the narrative's description of these defining features. These particular appellations—"Kaoru kimi," "Niou hyōbukyō" —are thus fine examples of the dual insided-ness and outsided-ness of this naming regime in *Genji* discourse: neither locution gets much use in the text itself, except for the latter as one of the titles of the chapter in which both characters make their first appearance as adults, ready to take over and share the protagonist role that the late Genji (presumed father of Kaoru and true grandfather of Niou) has ceded to them; and yet we cannot think of them as anything other than "Kaoru" and "Niou," a bound pair, hero-twins who are so much alike (in this olfactory attribute, among other things) and at the same time wholly different, as the narrative proceeds to show over the course of its final chapters.

"Utsusemi," "Yūgao," "Asagao," "Aoi," "Hanachirusato," "Suetsumuhana," "Tamakazura," "Makibashira," "Ukifune": these female characters' appellations are also the titles of the chapters in which they are introduced or in which they are central figures, but, except through occasional oblique references, the narrative text never calls them by these names. Warping Derrida's claim, I might say that context *within* the text produces these chains of signifiers, almost all of which are initiated, or crystallized, in poems within these chapters—which, in turn, give them their titles. (We do not know exactly how, or by whom, these titles were bestowed, but they are fixed in the transmission of the text and in our discourse about it.) Furthermore, "Yūgao," "Asagao" "Aoi," "Suetsumuhana," "Tamakazura" and, of course, "Murasaki" are all names of flowers (or plants), and all are the resonant, evocative, and figurally fragrant and colorful emblems that attach to these characters.

"Oborozukiyo" and "Akikonomu" are "names" of a somewhat different type: neither are chapter titles, but both come from episodes that give definition to these female characters' enduring identities, even as the courses of their lives arc far beyond those defining moments. "Oborozukiyo," "a spring evening of a misty moon," is a figure from a poem that this young woman murmurs at her first appearance in the text, in circumstances that lead swiftly to her "one night stand" with Genji—an encounter that alters the course of both their lives, in different ways, long beyond the "Hana no en" chapter in which it occurs. "Akikonomu," on the other hand, is a character who has been "present" in the narrative since her early introduction as the daughter of Genji's paramour Rokujō, but it is only much later, once she is installed in Genji's Rokujō ménage as his ward following her service as High Priestess of Ise and her mother's death, that she acquires this moniker. It derives from a conversation (laced with poems) in which she asserts that she prefers the season of autumn and its flowers and foliage (*aki konomu*) over spring, the favorite and enduring emblem of Murasaki *no ue*, Genji's truest love and the mansion's presiding female presence. That lady is herself so named as a child, in poems, through a complicated figural linkage of flowers (gromwell and wisteria), their colors (shades of purple), their seasons (spring), and their specific erotic and other connotations that also link her to her paternal aunt, Fujitsubo, whom she so strongly resembles in the longing Genji's eyes.

Other names for some female characters are, essentially, place names: thus we have "Rokujō" (i.e., *Rokujō no miyasundokoro*, the widowed "Rokujō Consort" of a crown prince), and we have the Akashi Mother (that is, "Akashi no ue," the woman Genji falls in love with during his residence during exile in Akashi) and her daughter, usually referred to as the "Akashi Princess" and, later, the "Akashi Empress," all of whom get their names from their residences—one in the city, one on the distant shores of Harima province, and those appellations serve at least in part to shape their identities—the one a consummate capital lady who nevertheless falls outside of its inner circle, the others aware that they are looked down upon and must therefore overcome the taint of their rural roots but do so through the paramount prestige that Genji bestows on them (as the partner of one and the father of the other). Still other characters come to be known by names that are in other senses not names: Ōigimi and Nakanokimi, the two Uji sisters whose lives become intertwined with those of Kaoru and Niou, are simply the "Elder Princess" and the "Second Princess" (literally, the "big sister" and the "secondary sister within the house"). Dozens of characters at the next downward stratum of the *Tale's* social world—the sphere of attendants, governesses, aides, and maids, who often serve as messengers and go-betweens—are labeled with "names" that are, in origin, office titles: "Myōbu," "Ukon," "Chūjō" (like "Shikibu" in the putative author's name and "Shōnagon" in her contemporary and rival Sei's sobriquets) all derive from titles used in the civil and quasi-military ranks of the court, in many cases transferred to such women from their male kin or assigned to them in the creation of a mirroring all-female household staff hierarchy.

And then there is the "Ōmi girl" (*Ōmi no kimi*), Tō no Chūjō's illegitimate daughter, whom he "rediscovers" when searching for "lost seedlings" in competition with Genji's recovery of his, Tō no Chūjō's, other illegitimate child, who is first poem-named as a flower, *nadeshiko*, a wild carnation, but later rechristened, also in a poem, Tamakazura—"a wreath of jewel-like vine." Unlike Tamakazura, who, under Genji's auspices, quickly sheds any taint from the years she spent in far-off Higo (northern Kyūshū) and in the care of her déclassé foster family, Ōmi never rids herself of her provincial handicaps—her crass and breakneck-paced speech, her ignorance of decorum, her much too forward and lusty declarations of sexual availability—are all put down to her rural background. In her case, "Ōmi," the name of the province to which she was adopted out, is a moniker imbued with taints that define her while also being rede-fined by her: as a place name it has a distinguished history, but in the *Genji* world it becomes, thanks to her, a locus of comic (some say heartless) counterpoint. It is also notable that she acquires no other moniker, whereas Tamakazura, her foil, acquires prestige not only as Genji's ward and "Tō no Chūjō's" (i.e., the "Minister's") (other ille-gitimate) daughter, but also through her appointment as "Principal Handmaid" (*Naishi no kami* or *Kan no kimi*) to the Emperor Reizei, so that subsequently she is referred to by that title in the remainder of her appearances.

Ōmi's worst trait, one that she shares with another comic/pathetic foil, Suetsumuhana, is her inability to make a proper poem: her howlers are filled with malapropisms, poetic place names, and other trite figures that are literally out of place, ill-matched, and tumbled together with no regard for precedent, not to mention taste.[13] Both women's poems are placed in such a way as to come across as parodies of the *Tale's* own poetic protocols: this, then, is an intratextual dynamic that leaps off the page to the attention of the amused reader, but which thereby calls attention to other effects that poems exert upon and in it.

And so I arrive at the final topic that I want to treat here: the ways that poems are simultaneously and partially "outside" of the rest of the *Genji* text in that they depart from it in form, and rhythm and, in many written and printed versions, are visually differentiated (indented, offset, marked apart)—and, of course, if read aloud, distinctively rhythmic and thus a departure from that which surrounds them—and are yet inseparably and indispensably "inside" it and "of" it. This is true of those poems that were composed with and for the text itself—as elements of its dialogue, its interpolated letters, messages, and graffiti (as is Makibashira's pillar poem) or as parts and parcels of the narrators' omniscient recollection and reportage of its multiple and often cross-referencing stories—and also of those that are cited, mostly in fragmented phrases or "lines," or through even more indirect reference, usually by its internal personae but, on occasion, by its narrators as well. In Japanese analyses this class of allusive citations is known as *in'yō,* "deployed as quotation," but it is not limited to classical *waka*: it includes lines and other segments of *saibara* songs, *rōei*-chanted settings of couplets, Chinese verses of both Chinese and Japanese origin, and here and there a few lines (sometimes misquoted) from Buddhist scriptures, Chinese histories, and the like. But taken together with its hundreds of "original," organically interwoven whole poems (there are almost eight hundred of them) as a variegated corpus of intertexts, they are a huge presence in the text, demanding an alteration of readerly attention as they slow

13. For examples, see w537.

or halt or divert its forward movement (in prose) in pregnant pauses (like dramatically situated musical rests) that bring narrative sub-arcs to emotional peaks, or fermatas, or to a kind of open closure, in that they conclude certain phases of action, interaction, or contemplation but reach out, through their proffering of time-trusted or contextually resonant figures and sentiments, to the vast intertextual matrices of the entirety of the rest of the text and to the whole of Japanese poesy, Chinese poesy, Buddhist lore, and more.

Derrida's dictum might need yet further moderation here: poems in this text (and in many another in the *monogatari* genre, though in my view nowhere else so powerfully and definitively) take on meaning through their own recourse to a "context" that is a vast corpus of poem-texts and text-based memories of them (and of other texts, sometimes blurred, sometimes willfully distorted, always potent), and they in turn create, alter, and define the very nature *of* the text. They simultaneously draw the reader into its "internal" textual world while gesturing to its "exterior(s)," to world(s) textual, physical, and metaphysical to which it links itself and which it, in turn, alters and into which it projects itself, open to the possibility of infinite readings and rereadings.

I will limit myself to just three examples of the workings of poems and poetry in the *Tale*, which is, among other things and perhaps above all, a housing *for* and *of* poetry—a superstructure not just built to *contain* poems (as we sometimes think of certain forms of the Heian *monogatari*, of which *Genji* is the ultimate exemplar) but constructed *by* them and by their creative and re-creative plenipotentiary (intertextually charged) energies, or "charms."

Chapter 27 "Kakaribi" (or "Kagaribi," "Cresset Fires"), passes by in a flash—almost shockingly so, since chapters surrounding it are generally much, much longer. It takes place as Genji's desire for Tamakazura as a possible sexual conquest approaches its zenith. Its brief text (two and a half pages in Washburn's translation) features only two poems, a tart exchange between the two of them, and both work with the central poetic figure of the chapter, which is also its name: Genji has just had the lanterns illuminating the garden of the northeast wing of the Rokujō complex (where Tamakazura resides with the older Hanachirusato as a sort of chaperone or dueña) relit, the better to see his beloved's features in their glow. It is a night in the seventh month—early autumn—and the hour is late; he knows he should return to his proper place at Murasaki's side.

> [T]he garden was soon bathed in a chill, soft light that height-
> ened the beauty of Tamakazura's figure. Her hair was elegantly
> cool to the touch, and Genji found her proper, modest bearing
> most endearing. He was reluctant to go back. "You should always
> make sure that one of your servants keeps the fires lit. It is eerie
> and unsettling when the garden is dark on moonless nights in
> early autumn."
>
> *The smoke from my passionate heart smolders*
> *Rising from an eternal flame of love*
> *To mingle with the smoke from cresset fires.*
>
> "How long must my hidden love smolder inside me? It may not
> be apparent to you, but deep inside a painful fire burns."
>
> Tamakazura found his attitude rather queer.
>
> *If, as you say, the smoke of your smoldering love*
> *Rises together with the smoke from cresset fires*
> *It will surely dissipate in the boundless skies.*
>
> "People will likely be getting suspicious about us." She seemed
> anxious. (w540)

Any reader will pick up on the erotic vibes here; "insider" readers may do so in part through recognition of the figure of "smoldering desire" transferred to a burning flame of one kind or another as a time-tested *waka* trope (many editions, including Washburn's, cite a particular poem in the *Kokinshū* as a touchstone). But the whole vignette is itself a replay of such dialogues-in-verse between wooing males and resisting (often dismissive, or at least very guarded) women, which are ubiquitous in *monogatari*, in diaries that also work in and with poems, and in "love" (*koi*)-themed sections of topically categorized and sequenced anthologies. Furthermore, Genji's "eternal flame of love" is also a doubling, two-layered affair: he refers both to his unquenched passion for Tamakazura *and* for her long-dead mother, Yūgao, and summons into this flame-lit garden the remembered traces of her smoldering funeral pyre (which he did not see with his own eyes, but heard tell of in Koremitsu's eyewitness report). Tamakazura fires back with a prediction (and a wish) that his fickle passions may soon disperse into thin air. In short, this vignette is already overloaded and overdetermined by its intertext, which reaches back into as well as far outside the *Tale*'s text itself—all with one move, one sleight of hand, abracadabra, multivalent conjuring act—but it thereby gains in its poetic and (melo)dramatic vigor, bite, and gently parodic (or parasitic?) seriocomic stop-action momentousness—all of which quickly passes, like the chapter itself, leaving an ash-like or vaporous, bittersweet resonance and acrid odor in its wake.

I have suggested that one might read the *Tale* as a housing for poems, or for poetry itself. Within that construct, furthermore, there are certain poems, and particularly fragments, or "smoky, vaporous traces," or ghosts of poems that are brought into its space and the reader's sphere of attention, which then seem to refuse to leave, to resist exorcism, but rather insist upon reasserting themselves, thereby complicating and enriching the texture of the text in their particular ways, with their own lingering flavors—sweet, bitter, acrid, always fragrant. This is especially true of certain poetic traces that are introduced into the text's extended (fifty-four-chapter-long) orchestration through fragmentary quotation (*in'yō*). One might cite many examples: there are the recurring references to Bai Juyi's "Song of Unending Sorrow," beginning in the very first chapter ("Kiritsubo") in the account of Genji's father's grief over the boy's mother's devastating death, which mirrors—as does their whole love story—that of the Tang Chinese emperor and his consort who are the song's protagonists. There is also the morphed revivification, through poetic quotation and adroit rearrangement, of the theme and attendant figures of nostalgic longing associated with the scent of orange blossoms, which thoroughly imbues and around which the short but evocative Chapter 11 "Hanachirusato" is built and that gives the woman with whom Genji falls in love in it her lasting "name," "the lady of the house of scattering [orange] blossoms." But here I will dwell on what may be the most frequently recurrent and multivalent but consistently potent poetic trace of which the text avails itself, at a variety of moments, some interrelated across plotlines, some more remotely in dialogue with one another, all together comprising an intratextual and intertextual nexus that again and again induces in the reader something like vertigo, or a combined sensation of *déjà-vu, déjà-entendu,* and *déjà-lu* (for we can see, hear, and/or read this poem at so many points along the trajectory of this text, and in so many others, and beyond them).

What I refer to here is the figure of "darkness of the heart," *kokoro no yami,* associated since its inception or, at least, its introduction into the repertoire of *waka* tropes with parental love and, particularly, a father's concern for the welfare of a daughter in her future course. That is how it surfaces in the *waka* world in a poem by one Fujiwara no Kanesuke (?–933, who happens to have been the great-grandfather of Murasaki Shikibu). It is the context given the poem in its earliest anthologized setting, the *Gosen wakashū,* in its prose preface (*kotobagaki*) that binds it to that particular and enduring connotation: readers are told there that he composed it one day when, getting a bit into his cups while drinking with some companions after a *sumo* match at court, they all fell to musing about their parental feelings, and he said (and/or wrote):

Hito no oya no kokoro wa yami ni aranedomo
  ko wo omohu michi ni madohinuru ka na
The heart of a parent is not darkness as such, and yet
  I have lost my way in the paths of anxious thoughts about my child.[14]

This is unblinkingly sentimental and, as *waka* go, relatively straightforward—a seemingly unfettered outpouring of paternal concern. (Kanesuke's daughter had recently gone into court service, to succeed or not in winning the sovereign's affection and in the management of rivalries and jealousies of the sort that, in the fictional world of *Genji*, did in Genji's mother and many a "real" woman as well.) If anything, it is the strong figure of a "path" or "way" (*michi*) that will inevitably be trod by a parent in his (or her) thoughts about a child's welfare that may look and sound fairly original and adroit in this composition, along with the rhetorical negative proposition—that such a parent's heart *is not the same thing as* (nor is a place of) darkness (*yami*, a word that suggests some affinity between that anxious of-this-world condition *and* the state of illusion from which the enlightened Buddhist devotee seeks to be freed).

Perhaps it was these features, or simply the apparently sincere sentiment that it conveys, that so effectively set this poem up for the string of subsequent admiring allusive gestures that it would receive across the years. Within the *Tale of Genji* alone there are something like a dozen such, imbedded both in poems, in dialogue, and in the

---

14. *Gosen wakashū* (Book 15, "Miscellaneous poems" 1, poem no. 1102.) In romanized transliterations of poems from the Heian period I represent initial consonants of syllables in the "h" column (*hagyō*) of the syllabary with "h." Many scholars prefer "f."

prose narrative "ground" (the so-called *sōshiji*), and, to some readers, they may begin to have an effect that is something like those
metaphorical non-stop "anvil strikes" that plague the brains of the
principles who sing the famous *stretta* finale in Act One of Rossini's
Il Barbiere di Siviglia. That is the risk run in such allusive practices,
but when they work—as I feel they do in the *Tale*, at each and every
occurrence of the "darkness of the heart" figure and elsewhere—they
are much more like the leitmotifs that so move (most) listeners of
Richard Wagner's operatic works. They are moments and spaces
where attention peaks while, at the same time, they are agents of fleeting jogs of recognition, delivering a sense of being at home, as it were,
in a familiar place from which reorientation and heightened concen-
tration may lead to yet more intense absorption, appreciation, and
a kind of interiorization. The sounds, the words, the rhythms sink
into our being, grounding us but also transporting us to . . . some
other place. Thus, paradoxically, the familiar, the recognizable, that
which seems constant even while undergoing change, also changes
the world we see, hear, and feel and, with it, us.

This is at least part of what I understand to be happening even
at the first appearance of this trope, in Chapter 1 "Kiritsubo," where
Genji's grandmother uses the figure to begin a speech that she hopes
her visitor from court, the Emperor's female aide Myōbu, will convey to him more or less verbatim upon her return to the palace: "The
darkness that envelops the heart of a parent who has lost a child is
so hard to bear . . . that I long to speak with you to lift that darkness.
Please come again." (w10); and again, in Chapter 7 "Momiji no
ga," when another royal female aide, Ōmyōbu, serving this time as
Fujitsubo's messenger after the birth of the prince she has borne as a
result of her congress with Genji, replies, in verse, to a poem he has
just uttered while "on the verge of tears," rearranges the figure but still
lets it speak volumes for what she feels and what she believes both
members of the guilty, anxious couple must feel:

The one looking on the child suffers regret
The one who cannot see the child suffers grief...
Must all parents wander lost in such darkness (w159)

To clarify the work of the allusion in this instance, Washburn interpolates these lines prior to Ōmyōbu's poem: "She recalled the poem by Fujiwara no Kanesuke that evoked the 'hearts of parents lost in darkness,' and replied: ... " No such language appears in modern editions, but one might say that it is implicit, more than sufficiently invoked by the words *ko* (child), *madohu* (lose one's way) and *yami* (darkness) in Ōmyōbu's poem.

Later, in Chapter 10, "Sakaki," when the still young and beautiful Fujitsubo, now widowed, takes vows as a nun in the hope of counteracting at least some part of her burden of adulterous sin, Genji begs an audience with her and, distraught at finally losing her but also envious of the freedom and relative peace that she may gain, utters this poem in her hearing:

My heart is set on that Pure Land beyond the sky
A land where a clear moon glows... yet I must wander
Lost like a parent in the darkness of this world (w241)

While in its first iteration in Kanesuke's verse, the "heart of darkness" (or rather, "the parent's heart that is not but, in anxiety, surely does become darkness") trope originates in and maps a father–daughter tie, it shifts in Genji's grandmother's use to a mother–daughter setting, and then, as taken up by Ōmyōbu and then by Genji himself, it shifts again to a couple's shared anxiety for their son (and the secret of his true birth) and then to a father–son reference. So, it seems, its subjects and its referents can cross and trade genders, but its potency is sustained even as it undergoes these metamorphoses.

In addition to these variations of its gendered frame, this figure also surfaces in several of the various "strata" of the text—not only in poems and in spoken dialogue, but also in the narrator's own (prose storytelling) voice, sometimes from that narrator's perspective, sometimes from that of characters whose minds and hearts (darkened or otherwise) she peers into and reveals. For example, in Chapter 9 "Aoi," it is such a narrator (in *sōshiji*) who perceives and reports what she imagines Genji must have felt when he first called upon his elderly father-in-law (and uncle by marriage) after the death of his (Genji's) wife Aoi, in childbirth and by spirit-possession: "It had been terrible to have to see the Minister [her father] so distraught, lost in the darkness of parental grief" (w198). That same (or another?) narrator, who shares a similar voice and narrative stratum, probes Genji's mind in exile, in Chapter 12 "Suma," with musings about his worries about his little son (later, "Yūgiri") back in the capital and rhetorically asks, "[I]s there any parent who has not lost their way over love for a child?" (w271).[15] Another troubled father, Genji's brother, the Emperor Suzaku, admits to his own anxiety about his daughter, the Third Princess, in conversation with his favorite consort, Oborozukiyo, saying (in spoken prose, not poetry), "A parent may wander lost in the darkness of their love for a child, but even that worry has its limits. How hard it is," he continues, "to part from one who has loved me as deeply as you have!"—thus revealing the basis for his inner conflict as he prepares to "renounce the world" by taking a monk's vows and withdrawing (from court, from parenthood, and from marriage) to Mt. Hie (w653). Before long, however, he will be forced to discover that those worries have no such limits: after his

---

15. This instance is also striking for its punning turn (*kakekotoba*): in the phrase *nakanaka ko no michi ni madoharenu*, we can read both "in this path" (*kono michi*) and "the path of [having] children" (*ko no michi*). The use of such poetic devices in narrative prose is yet another way that the text pauses for a nanosecond to capture the reader's attention in an altered manner and then (literally) moves on (just as do poems with *kakekotoba*).

daughter, who becomes Genji's child-bride at his insistence, bears a child (whom the reader knows is not Genji's) in circumstances that he believes to be deeply troubling (she was in fact assaulted by the obsessively passionate Kashiwagi, who gives his name to Chapter 36 in which these phases of their story unfold), he consents to "come down from the mountain" to try to mend her broken marriage. The narrator reports:

> Because Suzaku showed up so suddenly with no advance letter announcing his visit, Genji was startled and humbled by the honor of this imperial visit.
>
> "I know that I should no longer be preoccupied with worldly matters, but it's difficult to free oneself of delusions when lost on the dark path of a father's attachment to his child," Suzaku said [to Genji]. (w768)

And this is not the only time that a father, in conflict with his own feelings and obligations, his self-interest, and his parental inclinations, will characterize parenthood as a worldly handicap or "fetter" that detains his progress on or toward the Buddhist path. Suzaku himself does so earlier in the text, in a letter he sends to Murasaki shortly after the Third Princess takes her place in the Rokujō household (challenging Murasaki's preeminence there if only by virtue of her royal rank). He writes, in part:

> *My lingering attachments to the world*
> *Have now become fetters that hobble me*
> *Along the mountain path I would follow*
> You may think me foolish, but I cannot dispel the darkness of a parent's heart. (w667)

Here, *michi*, "the way," has become Suzaku's chosen "mountain path" toward Buddhahood, but he must still grudgingly acknowledge—and thus reveal that he resents—the parental ties that are "hobbling" him, filling his heart (the vital organ that is within, and which controls its possessor's state, and from which such expressions as these—in the classic poetic model—must inevitably flow) with that dreaded darkness.

In these renderings, one can see how this figure itself can take a dark, even ugly turn; or rather, it is turned, in the latter stages of the *Genji* text, toward ironic, bitter depictions of more than one father's misogynist hypocrisy and egotism: claiming to seek spiritual betterment for their own sakes, they disparage and demonize their own daughters, utterly reversing the more generous, "fatherly" (and perhaps banal) sentiment of the figure as first deployed by Kanesuke. The ultimate such father, of course, is the Eighth Prince, and the figure cannot escape his recourse to it in this later, twisted shape. First, speaking (in prose) to Kaoru, who has sought him out in Uji as a kind of spiritual guide (and surrogate father), he says (in Chapter 46 "Shiigamoto"), "Women are unreliable in all respects, mere companions to bring one comfort and pleasure . . . but they also stir powerful emotions in men. That's why they are such deeply sinful creatures, is it not? Parents are always lost on the dark path that is the love for their children but sons are far less cause for concern" (w961). Notably, he has no sons: he has but two daughters, the aforementioned Ōigimi and Nakanokimi, and one additional illegitimate and unrecognized third child, Ukifune; and shortly after this exchange, this selfish, world-weary, and emotionally frigid man decides to shed his fetters—those same daughters, the last traces of what seems to have been his only truly loving relationship, with their long-dead mother—and withdraw once and for all to a private retreat atop a nearby mountain, where he will devote himself to nothing but prayer. In a chilling, heartless letter, he writes to them: "It's distressing to have to abandon you in your precarious situation, with no one to take care of you in my place, and yet it serves no purpose at all to let your situation become an impediment to my salvation that will leave me wandering in eternal darkness in the next world." As if that were not enough, he goes on, in this terrible missive, to suggest that they, too, should henceforth withhold themselves from the world, refusing love, declining marriage ("unless you can make a match with a man who is worthy of you" [w962–63] and thus he condemns them to a kind of death in life, something like nunhood—which neither of them will achieve. Instead, Ōigimi starves herself to death rather than accept a sexual union with Kaoru, and Nakanokimi drifts into affairs with both Kaoru and Niou and into a troubled marriage with the latter, for which reason she will never find happiness, let alone stability. In the *Tale*'s moral universe—and perhaps in the view of this fiction's maker, too—this father *should* have let his heart be darkened with real concern and care for them. He is, however, the last of a series of troubled and troubling fathers—Genji is one, too—who people the *Tale*, many of whom, as we have seen, become the subjects, or the recycling agents, of these renderings of the "darkness of the heart" figure as its makes its winding way across and through its pages.

In the final chapter of the *Tale*, "Yume no ukihashi" (The Floating Bridge of Dreams), the winding way of the entire text, as we have it, trails off, leaving the story of Ukifune, Kaoru, and Niou unresolved. That chapter contains only one poem: it is Kaoru's, in a letter of resentment and reproach that Ukifune receives from him while holed up in her precarious refuge in Ono. This final epistolary verse invokes once again the figure of pathways (*michi*), and once again, like his teacher, the Eighth Prince, Kaoru claims (as if it is her fault, not his) that his passion for Ukifune has caused him to stray from the spiritual goals that drew him to Uji, and her father, in the first place:

> *I thought to call upon a master of Buddha's Law*
> *To be my guide along the path I hoped to follow . . .*
> *How is it, then, that I lost my way on love's mountain.* (w1318)

Here, the verb corresponding to "losing my way" is *fumimagahu*, a variant, in a sense, of Kanesuke's *madohu*, with the addition of *fumi-*, "taking steps onto the path, only to be led astray (or blocked.)" Kaoru (who refers here to having sought to replace his lost Buddhist companion, the Eighth Prince, with the Bishop of Yokawa, who is both Ukifune's rescuer and the agent of her forced return to "the world," having nullified—in another terrible missive—the vows he administered to her, at her insistence) has learned his Buddhist-tinged misogyny quite well (from both men); the last poem in the *Tale* leaves a bitter aftertaste in the reader's memory and casts a pall over all that has come before it and all that may follow . . . which the reader will not learn from its pages.

Nor will the reader find the figure of "the floating bridge of dreams" anywhere in the chapter, or anywhere else in the text. Where has it come from, and how does it claim its place as title for this last phase of the *Tale* (as we have it)?[16] Has it come from outside it, from some more diffuse repertoire of images of the unstable, the unresolved, the illusory—that is, from that vocabulary of figures in the rhetorical space somewhat uneasily shared by the secular erotic and the Buddhist episteme of emptiness? Or does it emerge from the text itself and its own prevailing episteme of the uncertainties of perception, the folly of human desire for stasis, the travails that will always be encountered on "love's mountain"? And might it also stand for the text itself, a lengthy, untethered, unreliable, shifting dream (in this case, one that issues from someone else's psyche and then imposes itself upon or is invited into ours, when we read) that, like our dreams, tapers off or abruptly breaks off, without closure? Is this *yume* a dream, or a nightmare?

16. See Shirane, *Bridge of Dreams*, pp. 192ff.

Fujiwara no Teika, a master court poet of the late twelfth to the early thirteenth century who, among many other things, created one of the most canonical of the several versions of the *Genji* text, on the basis of which we access and experience it today, also created (among his vast *waka* oeuvres) a poem that speaks to these questions, and more. He did so for a fifty-poem compositional sequence (*gojūshu*) commissioned by an imperial prince, Shukaku, in or around the year 1198. Addressing the general topic of "spring"—something he had done myriads of times before and would do many, many more times again—on this occasion he conjured this:

> *Haru no yo no yume no ukihashi todae shite*
> *mine ni wakaruru yokogumo no sora*
> On this spring night the floating bridge of dreams breaks apart:
> the sky a bank of clouds, separating, drifting, rising from the
> mountain peak. [17]

No one in Teika's time or anyone today who "knows" the *Tale* can fail to see, hear, and sense its traces here: he has seen to that. As commentators have shown, the poem also gestures to another, in the classic tenth-century anthology *Kokin wakashū*, attributed there to Mibu no Tadamine:

> *Kaze fukeba mine ni wakaruru shiragumo no*
> *taete tsurenaki kimi no kokoro ka*
> White clouds break up and scatter,
> separating from the peak when the winds blow—
> and likewise your faithless, wandering heart!

17. The poem is best known through its inclusion in the first book of "Spring" poems in *Shin kokin wakashū* (no. 38).

This is a poem that differs utterly in structure, rhetoric, and mood from Teika's: its figures—wind, clouds, a mountain peak—are metaphors placed in service of the enactment of a scenario concerned with fickleness and faithlessness in love. (It need not be read as Tadamine's personal sentiment; it is far more likely a performance of this topos.) And, of course, it has nothing to do with *The Tale of Genji*, which it predates. But it is also readily apparent that its figures and, perhaps, at least some of its erotic ambience have made their way, transformed, into Teika's poem, just as those elements of it that resonate with the *Tale* have done. The result is a poem that is most certainly outside of and exterior to the *Tale*, yet deeply engaged with and *of* it, and that I read as a kind of staging ground from which to launch a return, or repeated returns, *into* it. Indeed, the poem reads the *Tale*, absorbs it, reproduces it, and, like its figure of drifting, rising clouds, thus propels the *Tale*, and itself, once more out into the world, where it drifts up and out into a universe of untold possibilities—which are all our future readings and rereadings yet to come.

ACKNOWLEDGMENT

I thank Loren Waller for bibliographic research that supported the writing of this essay and Jeffrey Niedermaier and Riley Soles for their critical reading and helpful suggestions.

WORKS CITED

Abe Akio, Akiyama Ken, Imai Gen'ei, and Suzuki Hideo, eds. *Genji monogatari*. Shin koten bungaku zenshū. 6 vols. Tokyo: Shōgakkan, 1994–98.
Campe, Rüdiger and Julia Weber, eds. *Rethinking Emotion: Interiority and Exteriority in Premodern, Modern and Contemporary Thought*. Berlin: De Gruyter, 2014.

Coaldrake, William Howard. *Architecture and Authority in Japan.* London: Routledge, 1996.

Coates, Bruce. "Building and Gardens in *The Tale of Genji.*" In Edward Kamens, ed., *Approaches to Teaching Murasaki Shikibu's "The Tale of Genji."* New York: Modern Language Association, 1993.

Derrida, Jacques. *De la grammatologie.* Collection "Critique." Paris: Les Éditions de la Minuit, 1967.

Gosen wakashū. Ed. Katagiri Yōichi, *Shin nihon koten bungaku taikei* 26. Tokyo: Iwanami Shoten, 1990.

Kamens, Edward. "'The Tale of Genji' and 'Yashima' Screens in Local and Global Contexts." *Yale University Art Gallery Bulletin* (2007).

McKelway, Matthew P. *Capitalscapes: Folding Screens and Political Imagination in Late Medieval Kyoto.* Honolulu: University of Hawai'i Press, 2006.

Noguchi, Takehiko. "The Substratum Constituting *Monogatari*: Prose Structure and Narrative in *The Tale of Genji.*" Ed. B. T. Wakabayashi. In Earl Miner, ed., *Principles of Classical Japanese Literature.* Princeton, NJ: Princeton University Press, 1985.

Sarra, Edith. *Unreal Houses: Character, Gender and Genealogy in* The Tale of Genji (forthcoming).

Shin kokin wakashū. Ed. Tanaka Yutaka and Akase Shingo, eds. *Shin nihon koten bungaku taikei.* Tokyo: Iwanami Shoten, 1992.

Shirane, Haruo. *The Bridge of Dreams: A Poetics of "The Tale of Genji."* Stanford, CA: Stanford University Press, 1987.

Stinchecum, Amanda Mayer. "Who Tells the Tale? 'Ukifune': A Study in Narrative Voice." *Monumenta Nipponica* 35, no. 4 (1980).

Washburn, Dennis, tr. *The Tale of Genji.* New York: W. W. Norton, 2016.

Chapter 5

Calligraphy, Aesthetics, and Character in *The Tale of Genji*

TOMOKO SAKOMURA

INTRODUCTION

Alongside poetry and music, calligraphy was fundamental to a proper upbringing at the imperial court, where Murasaki Shikibu served as lady-in-waiting to Second Empress Shōshi and wrote *The Tale of Genji*.[1] Calligraphy binds Murasaki Shikibu's world at Emperor Ichijō's court with the fictional one she created in its historical, cultural, and social relevance. Marks produced with a pliable brush and ink function practically as records of thought and intent but also perform aesthetically. In the world of *Genji*, which is fundamentally characterized by the "aestheticization of everyday life,"[2] the aesthetic

---

1. Calligraphy came *first* among what was expected of good education. See Yoshida, "'Genji monogatari' Umegaemaki ni kansuru ichikōsatsu" p. 258.
2. This phrase is taken from Haapala, "On the Aesthetics of the Everyday," p. 40. For a discussion of an "other-regarding nature of aesthetic choices" and significance of aesthetically communicating one's moral status in the Heian courtly context, see Saito, "The Moral Dimension of Japanese Aesthetics," pp. 164–65. I thank my colleague Richard Eldridge for generously sharing these and other key texts in philosophy for this essay and for his guidance through

aspect is expected from a character and accordingly judged. In Murasaki's world and in her tale, calligraphy is more than a means of communication; it is a means of cultivation of oneself and character evaluation of others. Calligraphy is recognized as encapsulating and manifesting one's moral experience, educational refinement, and aesthetic sensibility, and presented as a core cultivation fundamental to a meaningful existence in society.

Calligraphy in *Genji* demonstrates Stanley Bates's suggestion that literature "opens up the moral dimensions of life to readers"[3] and offers a useful lens to explore the idea of an aesthetics of existence,[4] especially in that calligraphy was an essential practice throughout premodern times and the extent in which *Genji* served as a guiding text for and beyond its immediate readership, again through the premodern period. From *Genji*, we learn how calligraphy revealed a sense of self and of others, how calligraphy was an object of aesthetic and moral judgment, and what role it served in intersubjective relations. All the same, care should be applied to recognizing that the link between calligraphy and character serves the moral universe and infrastructure of *Genji* and should not be taken as a direct reflection of historical realities of the time.

Calligraphy in *Genji* offers an example of "the multimodal, embodied forms of address," in Monique Roelofs's words, that "help shape social and material affiliations and disconnections we inhabit. [These affiliations and disconnections] suffuse the desirability of aesthetic experience, as well as the turmoil it provokes in the ethical, ecological, epistemic, and political planes."[5] Calligraphy as a form of address has potency in the Heian context, and by extension in *Genji*,

---

the writing process. I am indebted to Melissa McCormick and Ryūsawa Aya for their thoughtful comments.

3. Bates, "Character," p. 409.
4. Foucault, "An Aesthetics of Existence," p. 451.
5. Roelofs, *The Cultural Promise of the Aesthetic*, p. 1.

since upper-class women of the court typically remained rarely seen behind bamboo blinds (*misu* 御簾) and standing curtains (*kichō* 几帳). Handwriting was used to gauge an individual, leading to scrutiny and judgment of the morphological quality of one's brush-writing for any suggestion it might reveal of the person doing the writing.[6] Richard Bowring writes, "The 'hand' reveals sex, age, status, and taste. . . . Relationships often begin solely on the basis of hand-writing, and graphology becomes an essential talent, and integral part of sexual mores. So strong is the mystique of the written sign that it becomes *the* mark of certain identity."[7] It should also be noted that since everyday handwriting had the potential to be extraordinary, though "calligraphy" means beautiful writing in English, qualitative distinctions suggested by the English terms "handwriting" and "cal-ligraphy" mean less in discussion of *Genji*.[8]

SCRIPT AND STYLE

Although brush-writing has fallen out of daily practice in Japan today, throughout premodern times the pliable brush was the primary tool for writing. Furthermore, until the late nineteenth century, when the Western, or Renaissance, conception of art—painting, sculpture, and architecture—was introduced to Japan, calligraphy reigned supreme as a cultural practice and artifact. During the early eleventh century, when *The Tale of Genji* was written, brush-writing encompassed per-sonal correspondence (letters, poetry), government documentation

6. Komai, *Genji monogatari to kana*, pp. 254–55.
7. Bowring, "The Female Hand in Heian Japan," p. 53.
8. In tracking every reference to calligraphy in the tale, the scholar Sugioka Kason demonstrates the centrality of calligraphy in interactions among characters. See Sugioka, *Genji monogatari to shoseikatsu*, pp. 381–87, for calligraphy references in *Genji*. On calligraphy in *Genji*, see also the chapter "The Cult of Beauty" in Morris, *The World of the Shining Prince*, pp. 183–87.

(edicts, records), and religious writing (sutra copying), with each of these categories governed by stylistic and formal conventions and precedents, including paper format, script type, textual formatting, and phrasing. Awareness of and ability to distinguish such conventions and precedents were expected and adherence to them scrutinized and fodder for discussion.

The physical aspect of calligraphy is the sum of brushed traces, paper vehicle, type of script, and mode of writing. Brush traces encompass ink tonality and quality of line, and mode of writing includes attention to spacing and arrangement of text. Like typography, calligraphy simultaneously acts as a record of semantic content and mark of visual expression. W. J. T. Mitchell describes this presence of verbal and visual expression as a "double face" to the eye and the ear: "One face is that of an articulate sign in a language; the other is that of a formal visual or aural gestalt, an optical or acoustical image."[9] As a visual representation, calligraphy draws attention to the morphology of the text.

The Japanese writing system was adapted from the Chinese one, in a gradual process over the mid-fifth to early sixth century. Although grammatically distinct from Chinese, Japanese adopted Chinese characters. Chinese characters are known as *kanji* 漢字 (Han letters) today, but in Heian times they were called *mana* 真名 (true name). Furthermore, there are three established script types, denoting *how* a character is written (in technical language, its "ductus"), also adopted from the Chinese system: standard script (*kaisho* 楷書) retains all strokes of a given character, running script (*gyōsho* 行書; also called semi-cursive script) abbreviates some of the strokes, and cursive script (*sōsho* 草書; also called grass script) drastically reduces the number of strokes in writing out a character. *Sho* 書, the common term in all three, stands for "script" as well as "writing" and "calligraphy."

9. Mitchell, "Word and Image," p. 51.

The Japanese syllabary, or *kana* 仮名 (provisional name), emerged in distinction to and out of *mana*. In the Japanese hybrid writing system, *kana* employs Chinese characters for phonetic value. The Chinese character 和, for example, does not denote "harmony" in *kana* but is used solely for its phonetic value, "wa." The *kana* syllabic system developed in stages and contains variations. In its initial phase, in the fifth to ninth centuries, it was variously termed *man'yōgana* 万葉仮名 (after the *Man'yōshū* 万葉集, an eighth-century anthology of Japanese poetry that was written using this method) and *onokode* 男手 (*otokode*), or "masculine hand," since it was used primarily by men in official settings. The style called *sōgana* 草仮名, or "grass *kana*," gives a special distinction to the way the characters are written in cursive script; the strokes are abbreviated within individual characters, but the characters do not connect with one another.

Further cursiveness gradually developed into a style known as *onnade* 女手 (feminine hand), translated as "women's style" in Royall Tyler's *The Tale of Genji*. This is the fully fledged form of *kana* (*hiragana* 平仮名), with the form abbreviated and simplified to the point that only a hint of the original Chinese character is discernible. A petition of 867 to change a surname illustrates the mixture of Chinese text, grass *kana*, and *onnade* (Figure 5.1). Chinese text inscribed in Chinese characters, *mana*, served as the official mode of writing in the male realm of government, whereas personal communication was primarily conducted in *kana*. It was used when women wrote to men and other women, and when men wrote to women. Compared with blockish *mana*, *onnade* is fluid in form. The continuous ligatures that connect the syllables in the mode of writing called *renmen* 連綿 (literally, continuation) facilitate the impression of downward movement and enhance fluidity. A fragment of a dedication record of 1018 for a calligraphy screen illustrates this formal distinction, with two lines of Chinese poetry written in *mana* with each character rendered within its own rectangular boundary and one line

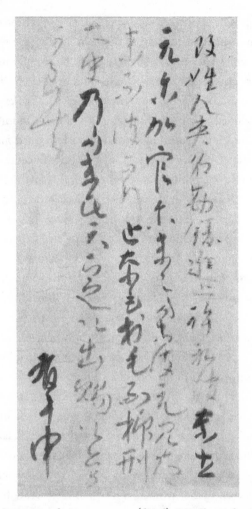

Figure 5.1 Petition to change a surname (detail). 867. Sheet of paper mounted as a handscroll, H. 30.0 cm. Tokyo National Museum. National Treasure. Image: TNM Image Archives.

of Japanese poetry written in *onnade* with ligatures connecting several syllables (Figure 5.2).

In Chapter 32 "Umegae," Genji masterfully uses these varied modes of writing. Genji is preparing a residence and a respectable dowry for his daughter, Akashi no Himegimi, who is eleven years old. A book chest was an essential part of the furnishings, and to fill it Genji "chose books that could serve her straight off as calligraphy models. They contained a great many examples that had made the best masters of the past famous in later generations" (t552). In addition, he sends blank books, brushes, and ink of the highest caliber to people in his circle, with the expectations that they will fill them with model-worthy calligraphy to serve as a model book (*tehon* 手本).[10] He himself brushes calligraphy for her:

> The cherry blossoms were over, the sky was a tranquil blue, and he wrote out the old poems as he pleased, just as they came to him in astonishing numbers, some in running script, some in plain, and some in the woman's style. He had a few gentlewomen with him, just two or three to grind his ink—women worth talking to when weighing one poem or another from some old and noble collection. All the blinds were up, and lost in thought that way near the veranda, with the book on an armrest before him and the tip of the brush in his mouth, he made a sight too marvelous for one ever to tire of watching. For anyone with a discerning eye it was a wonder simply to see the way he addressed himself to the sharply contrasting red or white of the paper, adjusted his hold on the brush, and applied himself to the task. (t553–54)

10. Historically, a good proportion of calligraphy heirlooms was *fragments* of calligraphy from books, scrolls, and letters, further illustrating the point that brush traces held significance over recorded textual content.

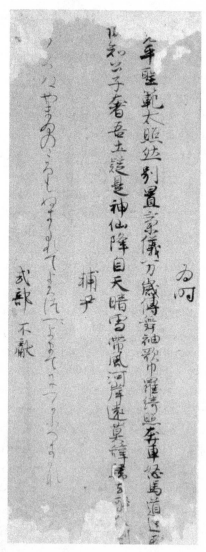

Figure 5.2 Calligraphy by Fujiwara no Yukinari (972–1027). Fragment of a 1018 dedication record of a calligraphy screen, included in the calligraphy album *Kanbokujō*. MOA Museum of Art, Shizuoka. National Treasure.

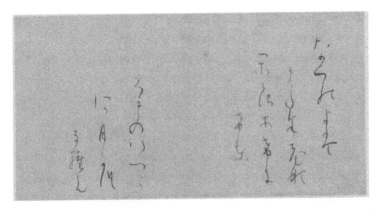

Figure 5.3 Calligraphy attributed to Ono no Tōfū (894–964). Inscription of poem. Heian period, tenth to eleventh c. Poem sheet mounted as a hanging scroll, 12.8 × 25.6 cm. Tokyo National Museum. Important Cultural Property. Image: TNM Image Archives.

This passage celebrates Genji's effortless ability to recite and inscribe poetry with due sensitivity. The tale positions Genji as the aesthetic standard, his cultivation and understanding of beauty unmatched to the point that his very act of writing becomes an aesthetic experience.

Premodern Japanese is written vertically, from top to bottom, with the text read from right to left. A work of calligraphy would be appreciated on the character/letter level, in how individual strokes form the character or letter; on the column level, in how characters and letters interact with one another; and on the level of the sheet or page, in how the overall text is laid out. Like a musical performance, this final point involves spatial pacing of brush traces. When written in *renmen* mode, ligatures connect multiple graphs and add a visual sense of flow. Scattered writing (*chirashigaki* 散らし書き) is an art of spatially arranging columns of text (Figure 5.3).[11] Whereas prose text is written

11. Nagoya Akira makes an important point that "scattered writing does not make the start flush, the space between lines also differs—it is a structure based on irregularity; it may

with columns of equal lengths, poetic text is often executed in elegant *chirashigaki*, manipulating column breaks and indentations.

Soon after the previous passage, Genji receives a visit from his brother His Highness of War (Hotaru Hyōbukyō no Miya), delivering his finished book. Here is Genji's reaction as he looked through it:

> His visitor's hand was not inspiring, but it was his little accomplishment, and he had written very cleanly indeed. The poems he had chosen from the old anthologies were distinctly unusual ones, and he had given them just three lines each, with pleasantly few Chinese characters. Genji was surprised. "I never imagined such wonders from you!" he exclaimed ruefully. "I shall have to throw all my brushes away!"
>
> "I thought I might as well do my best, as long as I was shamelessly to introduce my writing into such company," His Highness lightly replied. (t554)

In Genji's judgment, though the calligraphy was done "cleanly," it lacked inspiration, akin to a piece of music performed without flaw but lacking musicality. In Genji's assessment, His Highness makes up for that in content with his unusual selection of poems and in the orchestration of calligraphy in breaking the poem into three lines and inscribing mostly in *kana*.

In turn, His Highness of War's reactions to Genji's calligraphy pay close attention to style and script and the relations between paper and hand:

> Genji could not very well hide the books he had been filling, so he took them out. They examined them together. His running

---

appear to be irregular, but as a whole it needs to possess a balanced beauty." Nagoya, *Nihon no sho, Bessatsu Taiyo* 191, p. 5.

script on stiff Chinese paper struck His Highness as a miracle, while his quiet, perfectly self-possessed woman's style on soft, fine-grained Koma paper, lovely yet unassertive in color, was beyond anything. His Highness felt his tears gathering to join the flow of these supple lines that he knew would never pall, and the poems in expansively free running script, on magnificently colored papers from Japan's own court workshop, gave endless pleasure. (t554)

This assessment illuminates the idea of calligraphy as an object of admiration and connoisseurship. The three styles executed by Genji—running script, women's style, and free running script—were miraculous, "beyond anything," and the source of "endless pleasure." It is clear that Genji's calligraphy possessed the "inspiration" that was dearly lacking in His Highness's example, moving him to tears. Furthermore, due attention is given to the discussion of paper, such as color, types of media—thin paper (*usuyō* 薄様), poem sheet (*shikishi* 色紙), and fans (*ōgi* 扇)—and places of origin—China (Kara 唐), Korea (Kōrai 高麗), and Japan, specifically referencing high-quality paper made in Michinoku 陸奥 (an area in northern Japan encompassing Aomori, Iwate, Miyagi, Fukushima, and a section of Akita prefectures today).[12] Keen attention to morphological and material aspects of expression and meaning were important for the calligrapher and viewer (and sender and recipient, in the case of letters), informing a holistic idea of calligraphy in *The Tale of Genji*.[13]

The significance of connoisseurship in judging calligraphy appears further in the chapter:

12. The China–Japan dialectic appears also in discussions of paper. Kawazoe Fusae discusses paper–calligraphy relationships connected to appreciation of *karamono*. See Kawazoe, *Genji monogatari jikūron*, pp. 45–48.

13. Sugioka, *Genji monogatari to shoseikatsu*, p. 387.

Genji also immersed himself then in connoisseurship of *kana* writing, and he sought out everyone at all known for that skill— high, middle, or low—so as to have each write out whatever might be most congenial. He placed nothing of base origin in his daughter's book box, and he carefully distinguished the rank of each writer when he asked for a book or a scroll. Among all her wondrous treasures, some unknown even in the realm across the sea, it was these books that most aroused young people's interest. (t555)

This passage introduces social hierarchy into value judgment. On the one hand it shows that *kana* writing was a valued skill that had the potential of being recognized notwithstanding rank at the imperial court (high, middle, or low), but on the other hand the calligrapher's rank mattered when works of calligraphy were commissioned and assembled. Such careful attention to rank and deference to the system of rank permeated all aspects of life at the imperial court. Family rank played an immense role in status, promotion, and courtship, and it is evoked frequently by Murasaki Shikibu when establishing a character and assessing his or her calligraphy in *Genji*.

The passage also illustrates the practice of treasuring excellent calligraphy, often as family heirlooms. This is explicated further as conversations continue between Genji and His Highness of War:

They spent the rest of the day talking about calligraphy, and when Genji brought out a selection of poetry scrolls pieced together from different papers, His Highness sent his son, the Adviser, back to his residence for some of his own. There were four scrolls of the *Man'yōshū*, chosen and written by Emperor Saga, and a *Kokin wakashū* by His Engi Majesty on lengths of light blue Chinese paper pasted together, with a mounting paper strongly patterned in darker blue, rollers of dark green jade, and flat cords woven in a Chinese ripple pattern, all to lovely effect. His Engi Majesty had wielded marvelous skill to change his hand for each *Kokin wakashū* scroll, and they brought a lamp close to examine them. "They never disappoint one, do they," Genji remarked in praise. "People now can manage only a contrived approximation."

His Highness presented them to Genji on the spot. "Even if I had a daughter, I would not want them to go to someone who hardly knew what to see in them, and as it is, they would just go to waste," he said. (t554–55)

Discussed here are manuscript copies of two significant anthologies: *Man'yōshū*, an eighth-century collection that gathers poetry from the late seventh to late eighth century, and *Kokin wakashū*, the first imperially commissioned anthology of *waka* poetry compiled around 905. Many manuscript copies of these anthologies were made, as heirlooms and valued possessions. In this passage, they are examining manuscript copies by Emperor Saga (52nd emperor; r. 809–23) and Emperor Daigo (60th emperor; r. 897–930), two emperors renowned for their calligraphic prowess. His Highness's reasoning for giving them to Genji shows that one needs a connoisseurial eye for appreciation *and* execution. The notion of discernment and beauty dependent on the eye of the beholder is made clear in his statement that without the skill to discern what is good about the calligraphic traces they would "go to waste." The passage also notes that His Highness "who so loved fine things and cultivated such elegance was extremely impressed" (t554), suggesting that though His Highness's calligraphy skill was wanting, he possessed connoisseurial talent. As for execution, Genji's comment that his contemporaries "can only manage a contrived approximation" illuminates further that mastering the ability to replicate external form was not sufficient to achieve artistry.

In *Genji*, discussion of standards—both in execution and in appreciation—is anchored in temporal terms of past and present. The evocation of past calligraphers establishes calligraphy as a form of cultivation that has been and will be celebrated as a critical character/characteristic in one's moral existence. Looking closer at the past–present dialectic in *Genji*, two somewhat contradictory frames emerge. First is the idea of upholding works by calligraphers of several centuries prior, those comfortably of the distant past. For example, the text mentions four historical figures famed for their calligraphy: Emperors Saga and Daigo and courtiers Ono no Michikaze (894–966) and Ki no Tsurayuki (866?–945?) in another chapter.[14] Furthermore, mention of these historical figures in the context of a fictional tale effectively lends weight and validity to the discussion of calligraphic standards in *Genji*.

On the other hand, while having the eye to appreciate the old, one was expected to possess the ability to be of the present, exposing a tension between established and emergent standards of beauty. This is illustrated in the more short-term past–present dialectic that manifests in a binary of things in fashion and things passé. As the *Genji* scholar Kawazoe Fusae notes, there is great emphasis on the concept of *imamekashi* (fashionable, up-to-date, modern) in *Genji*.[15] A devastating example of a character lacking in fashion appears in Chapter 6 "Suetsumuhana." We are introduced to Her Highness (Suetsumuhana), the daughter of the Hitachi Prince, who, though of high birth, Genji learns is living in "sad circumstances now that her father was gone" (t114). Genji courts her with numerous letters, though with no response, much to his impatience. The effect of

---

14. Although no description is provided of their writing, Chapter 17 "Eawase" discusses narrative picture scrolls featuring calligraphy by courtiers Michikaze and Tsurayuki.

15. Kawazoe, *Genji monogatari hyōgenshi*, pp. 406–09.

Genji's letters in Suetsumuhana's dire circumstances is described as follows:

> The old place had been so antiquated even in her father's time that nobody went there, and now visitors struggled even less often through the garden's weeds, so that when, wonder of wonders, Genji's resplendent notes began to arrive, her pathetic gentlewomen broke into eager smiles and urged her, "Oh, my lady, do answer him, do!"
>
> Alas, their hopelessly timid mistress would not even read them. (t118)

A determined Genji finds his way to the residence, whereupon Suetsumuhana embarrassingly admits that she does "not know how to talk to people" (t118). To this, Taifu, who originally piqued Genji's interest in Suetsumuhana, says:

> "It pains me to see you behaving so much like a child, my lady. It is quite acceptable for the most exalted lady to retain a girlish innocence as long as she has her parents to look after her, but it simply is not right for you in your present unfortunate situation to remain shut up forever in yourself." (t119)

Following this, Suetsumuhana receives Genji, which leads to Genji unexpectedly breaking Taifu's trust in entering Suetsumuhana's room:

> Her Highness herself was numb with shame and wounded modesty, for which Genji did not blame her, since she still led so sheltered and so virtuous a life; yet he also found her comportment peculiar and somehow pathetic. What about her could possibly have attracted him? Groaning, he took his leave late in the night. (t121)

After this encounter, Genji writes the requisite morning-after letter, albeit delivered late in the evening, a delay that was painfully acknowledged by Suetsumuhana's ladies-in-waiting. Suetsumuhana responds with a poem:

> With the encouragement of all present, Her Highness wrote this poem out on *murasaki* paper so old that it had reverted to ash gray, in startlingly definite letters, antique in style and evenly balanced top and bottom. It did not deserve a glance, and Genji put it down. He did not like to speculate about what she thought of him. (t122)

In Genji's view, this letter fails on three counts: in the choice of paper, the style of calligraphy, and the manner of inscription. Suetsumuhana's writing in "definite letters, antique in style" meant that her strokes lacked cursiveness; "evenly balanced top and bottom" indicates that the letters and lines were not scattered in the manner fashionable of the day.[16] This is the moment in which Suetsumuhana finally writes to Genji, and the narrative describes her moral character and social circumstance as tragically out of date.[17] (Later in the tale, Suetsumuhana vindicates herself in her resolute commitment to her father's legacy and modes and manners that appear passé.)

Genji's critique of calligraphy is informed by his lived experience as a privileged member of the court aristocracy with access to excellent examples. His response to various calligraphy examples above displays that extra-calligraphic factors such as time, person, rank, and

---

16. For references to Suetsumuhana, see also Sugioka, *Genji monogatari to shoseikatsu*, pp. 63, 101, and Uehara, ed., *Suetsumuhana*.
17. It should also be noted that there are ladies in *Genji* who write in the old style *but* are still admired.

context critically inform aesthetic judgment. Judgment is also closely aligned with moral values in that the real-time decisions of the calligrapher are interpreted as corresponding to one's moral character.

HAND AND CHARACTER

That an individual's calligraphy style is called "hand" (*te* 手) demonstrates the close conflations between the person and his or her writing style. We see this conflation articulated in Chapter 2 "Hahakigi," which features a famous critique of women. Genji, who is seventeen years old at this point in the tale and a captain in the Palace Guards, listens to older men discuss the arts: first joinery, then painting, then handwriting. Their common theme supports not the obvious but the studied. For joinery, someone who makes things "nicely attuned to fashion so that they pleasantly catch the eye" can be distinguished easily "from the true master who works with success in recognized forms" (t27). For painting, someone who can paint "startling renderings of what no eye can see" may amaze, but the greater artist succeeds in conception and technique in rendering "commonplace mountains and streams" (t27). So there is praise for the commonplace. As for writing:

> "In the same way, handwriting without depth may display a lengthened stoke here and there and generally claim one's attention until at first glance it appears impressively skilled, but although truly fine writing may lack superficial appeal, a second look at the two together will show how much closer it is to what writing should be. That is the way it is in every field of endeavor, however minor. So you see, I have no faith in the obvious show of affection that a woman may sometimes put on." (t27)

This perspective echoes author Murasaki Shikibu's own reflections on calligraphy and moral life. In her diary, *Murasaki Shikibu nikki*, she reveals her rivalry with Sei Shōnagon (ca. 966–ca. 1025), the author of the *Pillow Book* (*Makura no sōshi*). The point of Murasaki Shikibu's critique is that she felt Sei Shōnagon was *showing off* her own talent.[18] She writes:

> Sei Shōnagon, for instance, was dreadfully conceited. She thought herself so clever and littered her writings with Chinese characters; but if you examined them closely, they left a great deal to be desired. Those who think of themselves as being superior to everyone else in this way will inevitably suffer and come to a bad end, and people who have become so precious that they go out of their way to try and be sensitive in the most unpromising situations, trying to capture every moment of interest, however slight, are bound to look ridiculous and superficial. How can the future turn out well for them?[19]

Murasaki's diary includes encounters with master calligraphers such as Fujiwara no Yukinari (972–1027). At the time of Murasaki Shikibu's writing of her diary and *Genji*, *Man'yōgana*, *sōgana*, and *hiragana* coexisted. Nanjō Kayo makes the key point that reference to calligraphy in Murasaki's diary is more about paper and manner of writing (*kakiburi*), due to the function of diaries as *factual* records. By comparison, *The Tale of Genji* has more descriptive characterization of calligraphy so that the reader will have a stronger sense and image of the characters.[20] She suggests that, though they are written

---

18. Nanjō, "Heian bungaku ni okeru kana shodō—'Makura no sōshi'," p. 189.
19. *The Diary of Lady Murasaki*, tr. Richard Bowring, p. 54.
20. Nanjō, "Heian bungaku ni okeru kana shodō—'Murasaki Shikibu nikki'," p. 23.

by the same individual, this is a key difference between the diary and the tale.

Genji's own critique of women and calligraphy appears in Chapter 32 "Umegae." The following passage represents a critical attitude toward contemporary calligraphy by Genji and, by extension, the author, Murasaki Shikibu. Here is Genji discussing the hand of various women he has had relations with to Murasaki, the love of his life:

> "Her Majesty's own writing has accomplished charm, but," he whispered, "it may lack a certain spark. Her Late Eminence's writing showed great depth and grace, but there was something weak about it, too, and it had little flair. His Eminence's Mistress of Staff is the one who stands out in our time, although hers has too many tricks and flourishes. Still," he concluded generously, "she, the former Kamo Priestess, and you yourself are the ones who really and truly write."
>
> "Surely I do not belong in such company!"
>
> "Do not be too modest! For warmth and sweetness, you know, there is no one like you." (t552–53)

He is discussing the calligraphy by Her Majesty (Akikonomu), Her Late Eminence (Fujitsubo), His Eminence's Mistress of Staff (Oborozukiyo), the former Kamo Priestess (Asagao), and Murasaki.

These judgments are impressionistic and subjective. As Thomas LaMarre notes, discussions of calligraphy in *Genji* "describe a range of quite heterogeneous styles and judgements without attempting to develop a single consistent thesis."[21] Akikonomu has "accomplished

---

21. LaMarre, *Uncovering Heian Japan*, p. 106. LaMarre continues on to describe "a grid of intelligibility for aesthetic judgment based on a loose competition between specific pairs," such as new versus old, *kana* versus *mana*, feminine style versus masculine style.

charm" but lacks "a certain spark." Fujitsubo shows "great depth and grace" but is "weak" and with "little flair." Yet in the next sentence, Oborozukiyo is praised as "standing out" in this time but with "too many tricks and flourishes." Murasaki's calligraphy is noted for "warmth and sweetness," and without qualification Genji states that Oborozukiyo, Asagao, and Murasaki are "the ones who really and truly write." In this elusive jumble of subjective evaluation, Genji confidently makes his aesthetic judgment, enabled by the fact that he is a "connoisseur," as described in the text. And here it is suggested to the reader that what makes a work good is clear to those in the know.

Another illustration of Genji's connoisseurship appears earlier in "Umegae," in a transformation from the ordinary to the extraordinary:

> "Everything is on the decline, compared to the old days," Genji confided to his love, "and this latter age of ours has lost all depth, but at least *kana* writing is superb now. The old writing certainly looks consistent, but it conveys no breadth or generosity and seems always to follow the same pattern. It is only later on that people began writing a truly fascinating hand, but among the many simple models that I collected when I myself was so keen on cultivating the 'woman's style,' a line quickly dashed off by the Haven, Her Majesty's mother—one she meant nothing by and that I acquired—struck me as particularly remarkable." (t552)

In this example by the Haven (Rokujō), something she wrote *in passing* captured Genji's attention. Genji does not reference the content of the missive, only that her hand was remarkable. In this case, judgment lies squarely with Genji, the connoisseur and ultimate arbiter of taste, who calls it good and worthy as a model for himself, notwithstanding the content or original intent. In this instance, an everyday letter (*fumi*) *becomes* a model by virtue of Genji's recognition. This distinction requires unpacking, because it means that Rokujō's calligraphy represents her mastery of the art and her accomplishment as a person. Mitani Eiichi interprets Rokujō's casual writing as "free" and "expressive of character."[22] Value is not absolute but resides in the discernment of the recipient.

Chapter 23 "Hatsune" offers another instance of a casual writing, this time by Akashi no Kimi, Akashi no Himegimi's mother, that captures Genji's attention:

> [I]t seemed to him that *this* was where true distinction was to be found. She herself was not to be seen. He looked about him, wondering where she might be, and noticed papers and notebooks scattered beside the inkstone. He picked them up and glanced at them.... The scattered practice sheets displayed a writing of great interest and originality. Not that she had pretentiously shown off her learning by mixing in a lot of cursive characters; no, she had simply written naturally and pleasingly. . . . He had just wetted a brush and begun to write when she slipped in, and he thought how very discreet she still was in her deportment, indeed how pleasantly so, and how unlike anyone else. (t433–34)

What Genji observes here are scattered *practice* sheets (*tenarai* 手習), so again brush-writing not for any *formal* purpose. Genji's focus is therefore not on content but script, which displays "writing of great interest" (*yue*) and "originality" (*suji kawari*). "Mixing in a lot of cursive characters" here means to include Chinese characters in the composition. The passage suggests that people did this to "show off learning" (*zaegaru*), and this was considered "pretentious" (*kotogotoshi*) in Genji's milieu. A discussion of how *discreet* she is in her *deportment* follows, offering a reading and interpretation

---

22. Mitani, "Ōcho bungaku ni arawareta shodōbi," p. 15.

of calligraphic traces as representative of a desirable or undesirable character.

Genji's first encounter with Akashi no Kimi occurs during Genji's exile in Chapter 13 "Akashi," and the episode illustrates how calligraphy as expression of cultivation could trump social status. In the province of Akashi, Genji becomes acquainted with the Akashi Novice and his daughter, Akashi no Kimi. Genji sends a letter:

> He was acutely aware that with her reputedly daunting standards
> the lady might be a startling rarity in these benighted wilds, and
> he did it very beautifully on tan Korean paper. (t266)

When Akashi no Kimi takes time to respond despite her father's urging, as "Genji's dazzling missive so awed her that she shrank from revealing herself to him," her father takes it on himself to write "on Michinokuni paper, in a style old-fashioned but not without its airs and graces" (t266). Genji is "mildly shocked" by his forwardness but follows with another letter:

> He had made his writing very beautiful. If it did not impress her, she
> must, young as she was, simply have been too shy; and if it did, she
> no doubt still despaired when she measured herself against him, so
> much so that the mere thought of his noticing her enough to court
> her only made her want to cry. She therefore remained unmoved,
> until at her father's desperate urging she at last wrote on heavily per-
> fumed purple paper, in ink now black, now vanishingly pale,
>
>> *"Your heart's true desire: hear me ask you its degree and just*
>> *how you feel.*
>> *Can you suffer as you say for someone you do not know?"*
>
> The hand, the diction, were worthy of the greatest lady in the
> land. (t266)

In this exchange, we do not get information on the style of the young lady's calligraphy, but the text remarks that she wrote with a lovely mastery of ink tonality, "now black, now vanishingly pale," conveying her aesthetic delicacy. Throughout *Genji*, quality of lines and ink tonality (*sumizuki*) are given due attention, akin to discussions of line and tonality in abstract paintings.[23] As Sugioka Kason suggests, Genji is intrigued by the fact that this lady, who lives far from the capital city, can match the abilities of those with the highest caliber at the imperial court.[24]

In the context of *Genji*, in most instances where assessment takes place, a person's character is closely related to his or her writing. This represents a different outlook from the notion of a constructed scribal or calligraphic personality, raised by John Carpenter. He notes, "Since calligraphy is the result of training and can be adjusted according to the needs of the occasion, it may be proposed that within courtly contexts that scribal personality is a construction closely related to social identity insofar as both are consciously created. A person can adopt different calligraphic personalities according to requirements of the function, and the models relied upon vary accordingly."[25] In *Genji*, the characters are not given a chance of this possibility.

CONCLUSION

Genji engages contemporary developments and fashions in handwriting—in *kana* and scattered writing—making clear to its readership what was considered stylish at the time. Whether one

---

23. Sugioka, *Genji monogatari to shoseikatsu*, p. 107. Sugioka also cites a passage in *Sagoromo monogatari* that discusses an example where letterforms were not particularly elegant but the beauty of ink tonality and *renmen* were superior.

24. Ibid., p. 99.

25. Carpenter, "Chinese Calligraphic Models," p. 157.

was stylish, like Rokujō, or not, like Suetsumuhana, led to consequences of greater magnitude. Readers do not see the characters
cultivating their calligraphic skills but rather learn the implications of the consequences of cultivation as described in their
characterization or in their actions. Calligraphy critique in *Genji*
conflates forms of brush-writing with a person's moral character,
framing calligraphy as direct manifestations of personhood and
cultivation. Readers are made aware of the power of calligraphy as
a means to lift oneself into meaningful existence. Values and suggestions conveyed through the actions of fictional characters no
doubt spurred Murasaki Shikibu's readers to raise their own calligraphy game and consider their own writing through the lens of
Genji. Indeed, standards and actions in the fictional world of *Genji*
became points of reference—morally and aesthetically—for centuries to follow, exerting their sociocultural influence on everyday
conduct in the real world. Stanley Bates's assertion resonates with
calligraphy in *Genji*:

> If it is the case that literature (or, more broadly, any art that rep-
> resents actions of characters in fictional narratives) is a histori-
> cally specific social practice that is related to the whole body of
> social practices, then it seems obvious that it will provide a major
> example of human self-understanding.[26]

The Tale of Genji came to be read as a guidebook for conduct
throughout premodern times, and therefore the ideals of calligraphy and character expressed in the tale had ramifications

---

26. Bates, "Character," p. 414.

outside the tale not only during Murasaki Shikibu's time but to the present day.

WORKS CITED

Bates, Stanley. "Character." In *The Oxford Handbook of Philosophy and Literature*, ed. Richard Eldridge. New York: Oxford University Press, 2009.

Bowring, Richard. "The Female Hand in Heian Japan: A First Reading." In *The Female Autograph*, ed. Domna C. Stanton and Jeanine Parisier Plottel. New York: New York Literary Forum, 1984.

Carpenter, John T. "Chinese Calligraphic Models in Heian Japan: Copying Practices and Stylistic Transmission." In *The Culture of Copying in Japan: Critical and Historical Perspectives*, ed. Rupert A. Cox. London: Routledge, 2008.

Foucault, Michel. "An Aesthetics of Existence." In *Foucault Live: Interviews, 1961–1984*, ed. Sylvère Lotringer. New York: Semiotext(e), 1996.

Haapala, Arto. "On the Aesthetics of the Everyday: Familiarity, Strangeness, and the Meaning of Place." In *The Aesthetics of Everyday Life*, ed. Andrew Light and Jonathan M. Smith. New York: Columbia University Press, 2005.

Kawazoe Fusae. *Genji monogatari hyōgenshi: Yu to ōken no isō*. Tokyo: Kanrin Shobō, 1998.

Kawazoe Fusae. *Genji monogatari jikūron*. Tokyo: Tōkyō Daigaku Shuppankai, 2005.

Komai Gasei. *Genji monogatari to kana shodō*. Tokyo: Yūzankaku, 1988.

LaMarre, Thomas. *Uncovering Heian Japan: An Archaeology of Sensation and Inscription*. Durham, NC: Duke University Press, 2000.

Mitani Eiichi. "Ōchō bungaku ni arawareta shodōbi." *Jissen bungaku* 41 (1970).

Mitchell, W. J. T. "Word and Image." In *Critical Terms for Art History*, ed. Robert S. Nelson and Richard Shiff. Chicago: University of Chicago Press, 2003.

Morris, Ivan. *The World of the Shining Prince: Court Life in Ancient Japan*. Tokyo: Kodansha International, 1994.

Murasaki Shikibu. *The Diary of Lady Murasaki*, translated by Richard Bowring. London: Penguin Books, 2005.

Nagoya Akira. "Nihon no sho." *Bessatsu Taiyō* 191 (2012).

Nanjō Kayo. "Heian bungaku ni okeru kana shodō—'Makura no sōshi' ni mirareru shodōkan to jidaisei." *Bukkyō Daigaku Daigakuin kiyō: Bungaku Kenkyūka hen* 40 (2012).

Nanjō Kayo. "Heian bungaku ni okeru kana shodō—'Murasaki Shikibu nikki' ni miru shodōkan." *Bukkyō Daigaku Sōgō Kenkyūjo kiyō* 20 (2013).

Roelofs, Monique. *The Cultural Promise of the Aesthetic*. London: Bloomsbury, 2014.

Saito, Yuriko. "The Moral Dimension of Japanese Aesthetics." In *Rethinking Aesthetics: The Role of Body and Design*, edited by Ritu Bhatt. New York: Routledge, 2013.

Sugioka Kason. *Genji monogatari to shoseikatsu.* Tokyo: Nihon Hōsō Shuppan Kyōkai, 2007.

Uehara Sakukazu, ed. *Suetsumuhana, Jinbutsu de yomu "Genji monogatari,"* vol. 9. Tokyo: Bensei Shuppan, 2005.

Yoshida Kieko. "'Genji monogatari' Umegaemaki ni kansuru ichikōsatsu—'Kana (onna-de)' no teagmi (shōsoku, fumi) to chōdo tehon ni tsuite." *Nihon Daigaku Daigakuin sōgo shakai jōhō kenkyūka kiyō* 11 (2010).

Chapter 6

Genji's Gardens

Negotiating Nature at the Heian Court

IVO SMITS

INTRODUCTION

Much time in *The Tale of Genji* is spent in, or looking at, gardens. Gardens amplify and prompt the emotions of the tale's protagonists. In Chapter 40 "Minori," for example, Genji's great love, Murasaki, lies dying, and as she is being visited by the Akashi Empress, Genji drops in. It is autumn.

> At dusk a dreary wind had just begun to blow, and she was leaning on an armrest looking out into the garden, when Genji came. "You managed to stay up very nicely today!" he said. "Her Majesty's visit seems to have done you so much good."
>
> With a pang she saw how happy her little reprieve had made him, and she grieved to imagine him soon in despair.
>
> *"Alas not for long will you see what you do now: any breath of wind*
> *may spill from a hagi frond the last trembling drop of dew."*

It was true, her image fitted all too well: no dew could linger on such tossing fronds. The thought was unbearable. He answered while he gazed out into the garden,

> *"When all life is dew and at any touch may go, one drop then*
> *the next,*
> *how I pray that you and I may leave together!"*
> He wiped the tears from his eyes. (t759)

This is in many ways a pivotal scene; little wonder that it was selected for representation in the twelfth-century *Tale of Genji Scrolls* (*Genji monogatari emaki*, ca. 1120–50), incidentally the oldest extant manuscript of the Genji text (Figure 6.1). The scrolls give us one of the earliest visual representations of a Heian garden, or more properly the *senzai* (var. *sezai*), the plantings in the part of the garden that is close to the house. Identifiable are bush clover (*hagi*), mentioned in the first poem, pampas grass (*susuki*, var. *obana*), and a plant variously identified as thoroughwort (*fujibakama*), maiden flower (*ominaeshi*),

Figure 6.1 Murasaki's deathbed scene, in the twelfth-century *Tale of Genji Scrolls*, which features one of the earliest visual representations of a Heian garden. Courtesy of The Gotoh Museum.

or bellflower (*kikyō*); there are traces of two other flowers as well, again thoroughwort or maiden flower and bellflower.[1] The colors have faded to the extent that a positive identification is difficult. All are autumn flowers that together with the pink (*nadeshiko*) and the kudzu vine (*kuzu*) make up the so-called seven plants (*nanakusa*) of autumn, a conceptual category already present in the eighth century. Autumn is the fitting season for imminent departure from life, as it calls forth the end of a cycle.

The garden is explicitly mentioned in Murasaki Shikibu's text, yet its depiction stresses certain rhetorical effects of the natural world. Just as the scrolls' so-called tangled writing (*midaregaki*, or *kasanegaki*), put to the paper as though in a spasm and used in the subsequent passage describing Murasaki's death, echoes and emphasizes the inner turmoil and emotional stress of the protagonists,[2] so does its illustration bring out their fragility of body and mind in this scene. The painted autumn grasses bend in the wind, visibly rippling the bamboo blind (*sudare*), which literally brings home life's parallels with the evanescent dew, mused upon in the poems, and underscore the wistful tone of this passage. Given the arrangement of the scrolls, in which each excerpt of the text ends with an illustration that both marks off the section and captures its essential qualities, one may infer that the autumnal plantings visually concluding Murasaki's deathbed scene highlight how nature can express the emotional states of literary characters.

This essay offers a series of readings of related gardens in *The Tale of Genji*. These readings are framed in a larger survey of garden design theory, practices, and uses in the Heian period (794–1185). Gardens

---

1. For reproductions of this scene and identification of the flowers in them, see for example *Kokuhō Genji monogatari emaki*, pp. 114–15; Shirane, *Japan and the Culture of the Four Seasons*, p. 3.
2. For this argument, see Jackson, "Scripting the Moribund," pp. 23–30; Shimizu, "The Rite of Writing," pp. 56–58; Okamoto-MacPhail, "Interacting Signs in the *Genji Scrolls*," pp. 277–79.

in this tale offer profound insights both into how Heian courtiers related to the natural world and into the structure of the tale's protagonists' relationships. In this sense, then, ideas of "nature" and basic structures in the tale are intimately connected.

"NATURALNESS" VERSUS "NATURE"

While one may safely assume that Heian gardens express some relationship with the natural world, it is debatable whether Heian court culture entertained any abstract concepts of "nature" as such, in the sense of the totality of objects and phenomena not created by man. The word used in Japan today to designate this notion of "nature," *shizen* 自然, is in essence a modern term, used from 1878 onward as a translation of the English concept. Although the term is listed as *jinen* (or *shizen*) in the twelfth-century vocabulary *Iroha jiruishō* (Dictionary, classified by pronunciation) and quite regularly appears in Sinitic (*kanbun*) texts of the Heian period, and sporadically in *The Tale of Genji* as well, it is normally used adverbially and means something like "spontaneously" or "unsurprisingly." Occasionally *jinen/shizen* is a noun, but in such cases, too, the word means "spontaneity" or even "unforeseen-ness"; maybe "natural-ness," but not "nature."[3]

The term *shizen*, then, is not helpful. However, *Iroha jiruishō* is instrumental in exploring the parameters of a more cultural-historical understanding of the worldview of the classical court. The dictionary does not provide definitions, but its internal organization makes it clear that the world was conceptualized through concrete objects and concepts. It classifies words first by pronunciation and then by a

---

3. For example when Yoshishige no Yasutane (?–1002) comments on the traumatic death of an acquaintance's daughter, he observes that her death "truly is the principle of naturalness [*jinen*], it is the tragedy of this-worldly limitations." *Honchō monzui*, pp. 421, 370.

standard set of twenty-one categories: heavenly phenomena (*tenshō* 天象), earthly forms (*chigi* 地儀), plants (*shokubutsu* 植物), animals (*dōbutsu* 動物), people (*jinrin* 人倫), the human body (*jintai* 人体), human affairs (*jinji* 人事), food and drink (*inshoku* 飲食), miscellaneous things (*zatsubutsu* 雑物), colors (*kōi* 光移), positions (*hōgaku* 方角), numbers (*fusū* 負数), single-character words (*jiji* 辞字), repeat-character words (*jūten* 重点),[4] compound-character words (*jōji* 畳字), Shinto shrines (*shosha* 諸社), Buddhist temples (*shoji* 諸寺), provinces and districts (*kokugun* 国郡), offices (*kanshoku* 官職), family and lineage names (*seishi* 姓氏), and personal names (*myōji* 名字). It is in the huge category of these assorted compound-character words that we find "*jinen/shizen*."[5] Yet where it concerns the natural world, as embodied in the first four categories, the dictionary as a whole places overwhelming emphasis on the concrete and the tangible. "Heavenly phenomena" are, for example, lightning, hail, rain, stars, and rainbows, and "earthly forms" consist of mountains, rocks, rivers, hot springs, ponds, woods, plains, and so on, but also man-made structures such as pavilions and gardens.[6]

In his recent discussion of aspects of nature in Heian court culture, Haruo Shirane draws a distinction between "primary nature" and "secondary nature" (*nijiteki shizen*),[7] a distinction between nature in the raw and nature cultivated or mediated by humans. In the latter case, one can argue that with Heian period nature one is dealing

---

4. *Jūten* are character compounds consisting of the same two characters in which the second character is indicated by a repeat graph (々).

5. It should be noted that different manuscripts of this dictionary can differ in content. For example, the *Iroha jiruishō* manuscript, copied out in 1838 and accessible through the Waseda University Library website, does not contain the word *jinen/shizen* (call. no. *ho* 02 00596).

6. In his recent treatment of "nature" (*shizen*) in the context of Genji's world, Kurata Minoru, too, focuses on natural phenomena such as mist and earthquakes. In other words, "nature" in relation to *The Tale of Genji* is conceived not as an abstract concept but as a set of concrete phenomena. See Kurata, "Shizen."

7. Shirane, *Japan and the Culture of the Four Seasons*, pp. 4, 9.

with culturally codified nature. In *The Tale of Genji*, as in Heian literature generally, one deals exclusively with represented "nature."[8] Furthermore, Heian texts do not offer a natural world that one could call "wilderness"; "nature" never seems to truly leave the confines of a human-inhabited world. Untouched primary nature was beyond conception, and consequently beyond description. Any depiction of what one may think of as nature in the raw becomes an instance of nature tamed, through the very act of representation.[9]

NATURE AND EMOTION: CULTURAL CODIFICATION OF NATURAL PHENOMENA

An important template by which to understand Heian domestication of natural phenomena is provided by the imperial anthologies of Japanese poetry (*waka*). The first of these is *Kokin wakashū* (A collection of poems ancient and modern [914]), usually abbreviated to *Kokinshū*, and it provided a norm for aesthetic appreciation of the natural world. The anthology established love and the progression of the four seasons as *waka*'s main themes, and often as connected categorical themes at that. Nature imagery was imbued with emotional projection, and, conversely, emotions could find expression in nature imagery. The first six of its twenty books are occupied with the four seasons; the poems in them are arranged in the sequence of progression throughout the year, from the first breeze of spring through the pine trees shimmering through the snow at year's end.

---

8. The same point is made by Takahashi in "Genji monogatari to shizen," p. 46.
9. The storm so central to Chapter 28 "Nowaki" is arguably a manifestation of nature in the raw, yet is described primarily through its aftermath. Its main narrative function is to allow Yūgiri to see his father's women during the survey of the damage the storm has done to the garden.

With this first royal collection, *waka* established itself as poetry that knew a substantial number of formal limitations yet would prove extremely creative in its explorations of established themes. As in traditional Chinese poetry,[10] "nature" in *waka* expressed itself through tangible objects, and there is relatively little variety in the species of trees and birds named. The repertoire of flora and fauna was not random; concrete nature imagery could and was grouped under specific headings in poetry collections such as *Wakan rōeishū* (Japanese and Chinese poems to sing [early eleventh century]) under specific headings, such as "Deer" or "Mountains and Waters." The images operated along the principle of categorical association (Ch. *lei*, Jp. *rui*), a symbolic correlation system made explicit in classical Chinese poetry and operative in Japan as well, which tied together a variety of phenomena into the same category.[11]

One result is that scenes of natural beauty correspond with the inner states of poets and fictional characters, and vice versa. When Genji's son Yūgiri visits his secret love Ochiba no Miya at her retreat in the hills at the foot of Mount Hiei, on a day in late autumn, he ventures into what seems unorchestrated nature. She is in mourning for her mother, who has just died, and the anxious and lovelorn Yūgiri, not quite knowing how to deal with this, passes through the hills; the scenery and the animals that inhabit it mediate his feelings for her.

It was a little past the tenth of the ninth month, and no one, however dull, could have failed to be stirred by the prospect of the moors and hills. Down a mountain wind that stripped the trees and swept a rushing storm of leaves from the kudzu

---

10. Smits, *The Pursuit of Loneliness*, pp. 24–25.
11. For examples of such categorical lists, see Shirane, *Japan and the Culture of the Four Seasons*, pp. 32–45.

vines on high came faint scripture chanting and the calling of the Name. The place was all but deserted beneath the gales; a stag stood by the garden fence, untroubled by clappers in the fields, while others belled plaintively amid the deep green rice, and the waterfall roared as though to rouse the stricken from their sorrows. Crickets among the grass sang forlornly, in failing voices, while tall, dewy gentians sprang from beneath withered weeds as though autumn were theirs alone. These were no more than the sights of the season, but perhaps the place and the moment made them unbearably poignant. (t737–38)

The description of the autumn scenery is full of poetic overtones: the reference to the wind sweeping leaves from kudzu vines carries an echo of an anxious love poem;[12] the lone deer is a stock image for the yearning lover; the waterfall is none other than the Otowa fall, with its powerful resonances of tears; concealed insects sighing without comfort call forth Yūgiri's lover in her hidden mountain village; and the purple gentians (*ryūtan* or *rindō*) were autumn flowers with a long pedigree in court poetry, of which Sei Shōnagon had observed,

---

12. Commentaries point to an older anonymous poem in a royal anthology that was compiled as Murasaki Shikibu was writing *The Tale of Genji*:

kaze hayami	The wind is swift,
mine no kuzuha no	so leaves from the kudzu vines on high
to mo sureba	are apt to shift
ayakari ya suki	their sides as easily as
hito no kokoro ka	someone has a change of heart.

Shūi wakashū 19.1251, "Miscellaneous, Love," "Topic unknown," "Poet unknown."

"I love how it appears brilliant in colour when all the other flowers have withered in the frost."[13]

While this passage counts in most commentaries as an instance of natural imagery employed in a sustained way to sketch the emotional state of a fictional protagonist, Heian literature also professed a sense that natural beauty was to be appreciated as a stimulus to the senses. "These were no more than the sights of the season, but perhaps the place and the moment made them unbearably poignant," Murasaki writes. Yūgiri's despondence is as much a reaction to the view he passes through as the scenery is an echo of his feelings. Takahashi Bunji points out how already in the tenth-century *Kagerō nikki* (The Kagerō diary) the woman known as Michitsuna's mother (936–95?) would use landscape scenes as a trigger for, rather than resonating with, emotional response.[14] On her way to Hase on a pilgrimage, she passes Uji and takes in the view in a series of observations interlaced with the explicit comment of how "moving" (*aware*) all the sights are.

> Gazing out, I see the surface of the water sparkling in between the trees and find it so moving.... In the direction of the river, when I roll up the blind and look out, I see the fishing weirs stretched across. As I have never seen lots of boats plying to and fro like that, it is all so moving and fascinating.... After eating lunch, the carriage is loaded on a boat, and as we go along smoothly from place to place, they say "Here's Nieno Pond" and "Here, Izumi River," where there are so many birds flocking together; the scene soaks into my heart; it is moving and enchanting. Having come secretly on my own like this, connecting with everything, I feel tears welling up.[15]

---

13. *Makura no sōshi* section 65, p. 120, translated in Sei Shōnagon, *The Pillow Book*, tr. McKinney, p. 58.
14. Takahashi, "Genji monogatari to shizen," pp. 51–52.
15. *Kagerō nikki*, pp.159–60, translated in *The Kagero Diary*, tr. Arntzen, p. 153.

Takahashi's point that Murasaki Shikibu's treatment of elements from the natural world operated both along normative lines of "secondary" nature codified in *Kokin wakashū* and in sync with the response-model provided by the *Kagerō nikki* is well taken. When one reads garden scenes in *The Tale of Genji*, it should therefore be with some caution that one invokes poetic schemata as the sole interpretative principle.

The idea that an emotional reaction to natural beauty is a very instinctive response also ties into a long-standing idea in East Asian poetics, the conviction that a poem is in essence "sincere" because it expresses a sincere emotion (Ch. *qing*, Jp. *jō*) in a given situation or scene before the poet (Ch. *jing*, Jp. *kei*). This explicit correlation of emotion and "scene" dates from the Song period (960–1279), but is implicit already in the classic formulation of this axiom in the Great or Mao Preface to the *Shijing* (Classic of poetry),[16] and it was echoed in the preface to *Kokin wakashū* as well.[17] Scenes of natural beauty were one important trigger of emotional response. Unsurprisingly then, a century or so after *The Tale of Genji* was written, a Heian poet voiced this idea in Sinitic verse that resonates quite strongly with Yūgiri's experience. On his way out of the capital, he passes a small shop at the city's outskirts and takes in the autumn view:

16. "The poem is that to which what is intently on the mind goes. In the mind it is 'being intent'; coming out in language, it is a poem. The affections are stirred within and take form in words." *Maoshi xu* (preface to the Mao Poems, ca. second century B.C.E.), in Owen, *Readings in Chinese Literary Thought*, pp. 40, 41.

17. "The seeds of Japanese poetry lie in the human heart and grow into leaves of ten thousand words. Many things happen to the people of this world, and all that they think and feel is given expression in description of things they see and hear." *Kokin wakashū*, p. 17, translated in Rodd and Henkenius, *Kokinshū: A Collection of Poems Ancient and Modern*, p. 35.

野店秋興	***Autumn inspiration at a vending stall in the fields***
釈蓮禅	Priest Renzen [1082?–after1149?]
郊西秋興触望多	In the western suburbs autumn provides an inspired view;
児店柴穿夕日斜	a rural stand in need of repair, the evening sun shines through.
林戸紅深桑梓影	Deep crimson its forest door: the light through mulberry and catalpa trees;
水畦雪冷稲梁花	frozen snow on paddies: the blossoming of rice and corn.
虫糸織草心機乱	Grasshoppers busy in the grass unsettle the heart;
雁陣結雲眼路遮	a line of geese bonding with clouds obstructs my view.
勝絶風流依造化	The beauty of this place is all because of Creation:
不斯人力以相加	any human effort to add something is pointless here.[18]

In the final couplet (l. 7) one encounters a word that does occasionally surface, albeit always in Sinitic texts of the Heian period, and that is often translated as "Nature": *zōka* 造化 (Creation), which refers to Heaven and Earth as the producer of all things. In other words, it is a physical force, and as such "Creation" could apply itself to the work of uncannily crafty human hands as well. Gardens provided that ideal space where "nature" could be recreated in such a way that the results of Creation were most visible.

18. *Honchō mudaishi* poem no. 462, *Honchō mudaishi zenchūshaku*, vol. 2, p. 427.

GARDEN VIEWS

That gardens in Heian Japan occupied a liminal position between the world of man-made objects and phenomena and materiality of the natural world is attested by *Iroha jiruishō*, which puts gardens in the category "earthly forms." Like pavilions, gardens are man-made, yet form part of a scenic view as a collective manifestation of natural phenomena. Motonaka Makoto has shown that Heian assessments of gardens focused on two core concepts: the grounds or the lay of the garden (*chikei*), and the view (*chōbō*).[19] With "view" Heian courtiers often referred to what was visible beyond the residence and the garden itself. In other words, gardens combine ideas of a represented natural world and of viewed landscapes. Japan's oldest extant treatise on garden design, the twelfth-century *Sakuteiki* (On creating gardens) opens with the exhortation that garden designs are best modeled after "landscapes in their innate disposition" (*shōtoku no senzui*).[20] It becomes apparent that landscape's inherent state lies less in its details than in the idea of an essence it embodies. Gardens must strip the natural landscape down to express it satisfactorily. As Thomas Keirstead observes, "The garden must mirror nature, but a natural landscape is emphatically not the desired result."[21] Gardens represent "nature" as summarized in a landscape so much more capably than nature itself manages, precisely because of their artifice.

Landscapes are constructs, cultural processes of human interaction with one's surroundings.[22] Like stellar constellations, landscapes exist in the eyes of the beholder and do not have meaning outside them. The English term "landscape" is intimately connected

---

19. Motonaka, *Nihon kodai no teien to keikan*, pp. 100–224, esp. p. 175.
20. *Sakuteiki*, ed. Hayashiya, p. 224.
21. Keirstead, "Garden and Estates: Medievality and Space," pp. 299–300.
22. Hirsch, "Landscape: Between Place and Space," pp. 2–9.

to painting, and likewise Heian discourse concerning scenes of the natural world and representations thereof is couched in the language of painting. Indeed, painting and garden design belonged to same, or at least very closely related, areas of expertise. *Sakuteiki* mentions a "Master (*ajari*) En'en" (?–1040), a garden designer who was also well known as a painter. En'en was dubbed "the painting master" (*e-ajari*) and is mentioned as the possessor of transmitted knowledge regarding the placement of stones.[23]

The term for landscape (*senzui*, var. *sansui*) used in *Sakuteiki* is literally "mountains and waters," and one sees that, true to this etymology, in Sinitic poetry and painting "landscapes" always are configured from bodies of stone or earth and of water. In fact, garden design, concretely, consisted of the art of "placing stones" (*ishi o tatsu*). The all-importance of stones and the ways to place them in a garden is also apparent from the existence in Heian Japan not just of garden architects but also of people specializing in the trade of "elegant specimens" of stones (*fūryū aru mono*), that is, "bizarre rocks and strange stones."[24] In addition, great attention was paid to the placing of stream beds. No garden was complete without channeled meandering streams (*yarimizu*) and a pond south of the main building. The overall sense one takes away from reading *Sakuteiki* is that in representing nature one outlines nature's essential features by marking space with stones and bodies of water. The plantings, then, are the "filling in" of the essential layout, creating an apparent hierarchy between streams and stones, which are fixed, and plants, which are seasonal. One may note that descriptions of gardens emphasize the immovable: they always contain flora, but the only fauna regularly mentioned are waterbirds.

---

23. *Sakuteiki*, p. 243.
24. *Gōdanshō*, pp. 32, 80–81, 500.

Anyone reading vernacular narrative fiction from the Heian court will at some point realize that certain categories of *realia* are described in great detail, whereas others are merely sketched. Minute varieties in clothing get much attention, for example, but spaces do not. Dwellings and gardens as a rule retain an abstract quality. As spaces, they seem to be adequately described as conforming to generic patterns. This helps to explain why Heian gardens look so much alike[25] and why contemporary scale models of Heian mansions tend to do so, too. This generic structure of gardens allowed for fluidity of a garden's function. Quite regularly after an owner's death, substantial mansions were donated to monastic organizations and became temples. Uji's Byōdō-in is only one such example. The metamorphosis from a private mansion's garden to a temple garden representing the Pure Land of the Amida Buddha did not necessarily require physical intervention; it was sufficient to reinterpret the garden's layout.[26]

THE GARDENS OF THE ROKUJŌ ESTATE

This brings us to a set of gardens designed by Genji together with his principal ladies. In Chapter 21 "Otome," at the height of his political power, two years after his appointment as chancellor (*dajō daijin*) at age thirty-three, he builds an extended villa and garden complex at Sixth Avenue. Here he will bring together six women dear to him. The text is not very clear about how exactly Genji comes into possession of this vast tract of land, but one-quarter of it had already

---

25. Hida, "Hiraizumi to Kyōto no teien no ruijisei," pp. 229–60.
26. On Pure Land gardens, see Motonaka, *Nihon kodai no teien to keikan*, 224–374; Ono, *Nihon teien no rekishi to bunka*, pp. 51–69. For examples other than Byōdō-in, see Ono, *Nihon teien no rekishi to bunka*, p. 52. Many of these temples grew out of chapel-like buildings already present on the estate.

been occupied by the former mansion of the Empress Akikonomu, and it is generally inferred that her mother, the Rokujō Haven, a former lover of Genji, left the property to Genji after her death. The building project of what becomes the Rokujō-in (Rokujō estate) quite literally lays the ground for the ten chapters that form the so-called Tamakazura sequence (from Chapter 22 "Tamakazura" to Chapter 31 "Makibashira") that is central to *The Tale of Genji*. This villa complex was divided into four sections, each of which was designated for an important woman in Genji's life. Hence, we may also say that the Rokujō-in aims to emulate the "rear quarters" (*kōkyū*) of the imperial palace complex; at the same time it functions as a physical summary of the tale so far.[27]

Genji had already experimented with the idea of bringing together different women in one ideal house. A few years earlier he refurbished his east pavilion at Nijō, which he inherited from his father, and partitioned it into separate lodgings with the intention of bringing both the lady called Falling Flowers (Hanachirusato) and his second formal wife, the lady from Akashi, to live together there (t283, 333). However, Rokujō-in is different. To begin with, its scale is enormous. Where a regular high-ranking noble's mansion would normally occupy one square city block (*chō* or *machi*) of approximately ten thousand square meters, Genji's new estate occupies "four *chō* of land at Rokujō and Kyōgoku" (t401), that is, a good ten acres.

More important, although earlier Heian fiction had created residences with gardens that cover comparably vast areas,[28] the Rokujō estate is designed according to a unique coordinating plan, one that

---

27. Field, *The Splendor of Longing*, p. 112; Shirane, *The Bridge of Dreams*, p. 129.
28. According to the fourteenth-century *Genji* commentary *Kakaishō* (Notes on rivers and seas), a model for Rokujō-in's overall garden design is found in *Utsuho monogatari* (Tale of the hollow tree, ca. 970–99). *Kakaishō*, 220.

hinges on its use of gardens. The four gardens, one for each section, express the identity of the women occupying that part of the mansion complex and may be thought of as their substitutes. At the same time, the gardens together form a full cycle: all are thematically organized by season. For practical reasons, but also symbolizing their correlation, the four sections are connected through roofed passageways. The text first introduces the bigger scheme of Genji's new estate:

> Genji's Rokujō estate was finished in the eighth month. Her Majesty had the southwest quarter, no doubt because that was where her residence had once stood. The southeast quarter was for himself [and Murasaki as well as Genji's young daughter by the lady from Akashi, Akashi no Himegimi]. He gave the northeast to the lady from his east pavilion [Hanachirusato, and eventually the young Tamakazura, too] and the northwest to the lady from Akashi. He had the existing hills and lake shifted about as necessary, changing the shapes of mountains and waters to suit each resident's wishes. (t402)[29]

Each garden's theme is expressed primarily through its plantings. Murasaki Shikibu's text is quite specific about these. The southeastern garden, for Genji and Murasaki, has as its theme spring; its plantings are five-needled pines (*goyō*), red plums (*kōbai*), cherry trees (*sakura*), wisteria (*fuji*), kerria roses (*yamabuki*), and rock azaleas (*iwatsutsuji*). The autumn garden in the southwest, for the Akikonomu Empress, has "trees certain to grow in rich autumn colors [*momiji no iro*]," autumn fields (*aki no no*), and flowers that "bloomed in all the profusion of the season." The summer garden in

---

29. For the technical terms of these four compass directions, see below. For the specifications of the plantings, see t402.

the northeast quarter, belonging to the lady called Falling Flowers and Tamakazura, is filled with plants that prove shade and cool—Chinese bamboo (*kuretake*), tall groves with depths of shade "as in a mountain village"—and furthermore has deutzia (*unohana*), orange (*hanatachibana*), pinks (*nadeshiko*),[30] roses (*sōbi*), peonies (*kutani*), and sweet flag (*sōbu*). Finally, the northwest wing's garden, for the lady from Akashi, has "a dense stand of pines [*matsu*] intended to show off the beauty of snow," "chrysanthemums [*kiku*] to gather the morning frosts of early winter," and oaks (*hahaso*), all appropriate for winter, as well as "a scattering of nameless trees transplanted from the fastnesses of the mountains." At another level, seasons also define the Rokujō estate narrative: the first eight chapters of the Tamakazura sequence progress along the cycle of a year, beginning in winter in Chapter 22 "Tamakazura" and ending in winter again in Chapter 29 "Miyuki."[31]

Although the four gardens collectively represent the full cycle of the four seasons, they are not arranged in cyclical order. That is, the seasons represented by the four gardens are not arranged clockwise or anticlockwise; if one wishes to follow the year's cycle, one must visit the four sections in a zigzag route. In fact, when Genji inspects the damage done by the typhoon that sweeps over the estate at the beginning of Chapter 28 "Nowaki," he does so in a clockwise route that underscores the hierarchy of the four quarters. Starting in his own spring section, he proceeds to the autumn section and from there to the winter quarter in the northwest, and on to the summer section in the northeast.

---

30. Since the eighth-century *Man'yōshū*, the *nadeshiko* was one of the "seven grasses of autumn," and as such one might be surprised to see it in a summer garden. The *Shinpen nihon koten bungaku zenshū* edition does not comment on this, but *waka* do exist that connect the *nadeshiko* to summer (e.g., *Shika wakashū* poem nos. 71–72, mainly because of its alternative name *tokonatsu* (everlasting summer).

31. Field, *The Splendor of Longing*, p. 113.

THREE VIEWS OF THE ROKUJŌ GARDENS

The larger designs of the Rokujō gardens follow the principle later outlined in *Sakuteiki*, that is, to think in terms of landscape and to understand that "landscape" is in essence the sum total of "the shapes of mountains and waters" (*mizu no omomuki, yama no okite*) through which Genji creates the layout of each garden. The generic quality of garden design allowed for reinterpretations of space, and indeed, the organization gardens of Genji's Rokujō estate can be understood through more than one morphological system.

The standard way to understand the gardens' noncyclical arrangement is to look at the organization of poetry anthologies. The overall design of the Rokujō-in is organized by season, as codified in *Kokin wakashū*, Japan's first imperial anthology of Japanese poetry (*waka*).[32] As noted, the first six of its twenty books are occupied with the four seasons: spring (Books 1–2; 134 poems), summer (3; 34), autumn (4–5; 145), winter (6; 29). Their respective spacing shows that an unequal appreciation of seasons overrides their cyclical progression: spring and autumn are more important than summer and winter. The more dramatic moments tend to take place in these two seasons, and it is this hierarchy that organizes the layout of the four sections of the Rokujō estate.

The two important gardens belong to the spring and autumn sections. They are the most colorful and will have the best extended views. Moreover, these two gardens are directly connected through their lake system. That the Akikonomu, or "autumn-loving," Empress secures such an important garden and the fact that its theme is

---

32. The main proponent of this rhetorical-poetic interpretation is Nomura, "Rokujō-in no kisetsuteki jikū." In English, see Field, *The Splendor of Longing*, pp. 111–25.

autumn is entirely logical. It is equally understandable that Murasaki, the one woman who is a constant and extremely close companion to Genji, but also the woman whom circumstances do not permit him to recognize as his official first wife, occupies the other prime season, spring.

The hierarchy of the two main seasons was constantly debated and is one strategy by which the subtle rivalry between Murasaki and the Akikonomu Empress is expressed. Once the Rokujō estate is ready, it is autumn, and the Empress sends Murasaki a box with autumn leaves and the words

"You whose garden waits by your wish to welcome spring, at least look upon these autumn leaves from my home, carried to you in the wind." (t404)

Murasaki, out of season, responds by filling a box with an artificial five-needled pine branch and writes back:

"They are trifling things, fall leaves scattered in the wind: I would have you see in the pine gripping the rock the truest color of spring." (t404)

This invitation is taken up in spring when in Chapter 24 "Kochō," ladies in waiting to the Akikonomu Empress visit Murasaki's spring garden and imagine themselves visiting a Daoist realm of immortals. In autumn again, Chapter 28 "Nowaki" opens with fading memories of spring and the glory of the autumn garden. "Autumn had always had more partisans than spring in the debate over which is to be preferred, and those who once favored that celebrated spring garden now turned, as people do, to look elsewhere" (t487).

Another, quite different set of interpretations is not based on poetical rhetoric, but on spatial organizations that are informed by divination systems from ancient China and by Buddhist traditions.

Sakuteiki regularly emphasizes the four directional animals, or "four deities," as yet one more organizing principle in garden design, because of their protective qualities: "By planting trees in the four cardinal directions of one's dwelling, one makes it a place completely protected by the four deities."[33] These four deities entered Japan in about the seventh century and are the Azure Dragon (*seiryō* var. *seiryū*; east, or left)[34] associated with spring and represented by a stream; the White Tiger (*byakko*; west, or right) or a broad avenue, representing autumn; the Vermilion Bird (*suzaku* var. *sujaku*; south, or front) or a pond, associated with summer; and the Black Turtle-Snake (*genmu* var. *genbu*; north, or back) or a hill, and representing winter. Lacking stream, avenue, pond, or hill, *Sakuteiki* specifies, one can replace these by planting respectively nine willows (*yanagi*), seven catalpa trees (*hisagi*), nine *katsura* trees, or three cypresses (*hinoki*). This "four directions" logic of geomancy informed the planning of the entire city of Heian-kyō, but operated on a smaller scale as well.

It will be noted that the organization of the Rokujō estate and its gardens does not adhere to the four principal compass directions, but is forty-five degrees off. Its four sections are oriented toward the southwest, southeast, northwest, and northeast, indicated in the original text by directions on the zodiac compass: "sheep-monkey," "dragon-snake," "dog-boar," and "ox-tiger," respectively. One practical reason for this deviation must be that the Rokujō estate had to adhere to the north–south, east–west grid of the Heian capital. Even in fiction, urban planning simply did not allow for an estate covering an area consisting of four square city blocks (*machi*) to upset the course of major roads and intersections. Within one block, one could

---

33. *Sakuteiki*, p. 243. For an introduction to the four directional deities in Japan, see Van Goethem, "Feng Shui Symbolism in Japan" pp. 35–48.

34. The orientation in traditional East Asia is always facing south.

organize an east–south–west–north orientation; on a scale such as Rokujō-in's, with four separate mansions, one could not. That said, *The Tale of Genji* does on occasion seem to force the four gardens of the Rokujō estate to snap to the rhetorical grid of the four deities and the seasonal associations of the four main compass points. The northwestern quarter of the lady from Akashi is called "western block," the lady called Falling Flowers lives in the "eastern direction," while Murasaki's southeastern garden is referred to as the "southern block."[35]

Even so, it is eminently clear that the governing principle of Rokujō-in's coordinating plan is a "four directions, four seasons" scheme. The first reference to such a garden organization is mythical: the story of Urashima Tarō's visit to the palace of the dragon king on the bottom of the sea, "where one can see a different season in each of the four directions."[36]

Another parallel is that with the early life of the Buddha, when as Prince Siddhartha he lived on his father's estate. His father built "mansions for the three seasons" (*sanjiden*): a warm one for winter, a cool one for summer, and a neither cold nor warm one for the two rainy seasons, which in India did not require separate treatment. There Siddhartha lived with his three wives, one in each mansion. In an early Chinese alternative life story, *Xiuxing benqi jing* (The sutra of the [Buddha's] practices and origins; early third century), with

---

35. Respectively, Chapter 21 "Otome," Chapter 22 "Tamakazura," and Chapter 28 "Nowaki." Tyler silently corrects this to "northwest quarter," "to the northeast," and "southeast quarter," respectively (t402, 422, 491, 493). To point out the obvious: these compass assignations do not match the seasons associated with these quarters. See also Mitani, *Monogatarishi no kenkyū*, pp. 407–09.

36. Ibid., pp. 414–15. The Urashima Tarō legend is an old one; versions of it, albeit without the "four directions, four seasons" gardens, appear in eighth-century *Tango fudoki* and *Man'yōshū*, and tenth-century *kanbun* versions exist as well. The idea that the dragon king's palace at the bottom of the ocean boasted gardens divided into seasonal quarters already existed in the Heian period, and is referred to in, for example, *Eiga monogatari*. William and Helen McCullough, trs., *A Tale of Flowering Fortunes*, p. 631.

an adaptation to China's climate, there is mention of four halls, one for each of the four seasons.[37] This parallel with the Buddha's living arrangements does on occasion surface in *The Tale of Genji*, for example when the fragrances of Murasaki's spring garden call forth the Buddha's realm.

> What delights there were to be seen, then, in the jewel-strewn garden before Genji's residence, and how poorly mere words convey the exquisite beauty of the gardens of his ladies! The one before the spring quarter, where the scent of plum blossoms mingled with the fragrance within the blinds, especially recalled the land of the living Buddha, although actually the mistress of the place lived there in peace and quite at her ease. (t431)

A third reading of the Rokujō garden ensemble, which takes one away somewhat from the notion of seasons per se, but does help to broaden the scope of what landscapes could signify in Heian court culture, is intimately tied to the idea of a genealogy of the Rokujō estate. Admittedly, the first explicit identification of Genji's estate with a historical but equally mythical estate in the same location, designed by another "Genji" (or Minamoto) minister, dates to the fourteenth century.[38] Medieval readers of *The Tale of Genji* associated Genji's estate with the "Riverside Mansion," or Kawara-in, for a number of reasons: both estates occupied roughly the same coordinates in the capital, both covered the equivalent of four square city blocks, both harbored fanciful landscapes, and both were built

---

37. *Konjaku monogatarishū*, vol. 1, p. 60; see also ibid., pp. 17–18, note 5 (where Siddhartha's three wives are mentioned). See also Mitani, *Monogatarishi no kenkyū*, pp. 416–17; Saeki, *Genji monogatari ni okeru 'kangaku*,' pp. 303–13.

38. *Kakaishō*, 220. Japanese studies that discuss the Rokujō estate in relation to Kawara-in and Minamoto no Tōru, as well as Uda, and the realm of the immortals abound. For a recent one, see Yuasa, "Hikaru Genji no Rokujō-in."

by sons of emperors turned commoner by taking the lineage name Minamoto. Kawara-in was the legendary estate of Minamoto no Tōru (822–95), a statesman and poet with a deep interest in the Daoist cult of immortals.[39] This heritage combined with a rhetoric dominant in both Sinitic literature and *waka* poetry to sketch ideal landscapes in terms of the immortals' realm. Tōru turned the gardens of the Rokujō estate into "an unknown land," the "middle islands" in their ponds calling forth the "mountain above the turtle," one of the three or five mythical mountains in the eastern sea where immortals dwell, of which Mount Penglai (Jp. Hōrai), or "turtle mountain," was the one in the middle (t442).[40]

Since the "certain estate" to which young Genji brings his lover Yūgao, with its "unkempt and deserted garden . . . , its ancient groves towering in massive gloom," was also identified by readers as Tōru's Riverside estate, the Rokujō grounds become a horticultural palimpsest (t64, 65). Ghosts not only of the Genji minister, then, but also of former lovers, including the dead Rokujō Haven, who bequeathed the estate to Genji in the first place, haunt the sculpted landscapes of Genji's gardens.

CONCLUSION

In *The Tale of Genji*, the natural world as mediated through and exemplified by gardens provides an understanding both of courtly cultural attitudes toward "nature" and of the emotions of the tale's protagonists as well as their respective relationships. A Heian garden

---

39. Frank, *Démons et jardins*, pp. 133–37.
40. The "Poetic Exposition on the Kawara Mansion" (*Kawara-in no fu*, ca. 971) by Minamoto no Shitagō (911–83) also explicitly ties Tōru's garden to Mount Penglai: "When it is clear, we look out from the immortals' terrace: / distant, Mounts Penglai and Yingzhou seem near." *Honchō monzui*, pp. 126–27.

presented nature broken down into the material and the tangible as well as landscapes reduced to their elementary constituents through stones and water. This nature was extremely codified and as such intimately connected with the human realm: the natural world explained as well as triggered emotional response. A garden's views and seasonal plantings combined to stress a hierarchy of seasons and of protagonists and to underscore dramatic moments. "Nature," then, is one fundamental means to unlock the world that *The Tale of Genji* represents.

WORKS CITED

Eiga monogatari. Ed. Yamanaka Yutaka, Akiyama Ken, Ikeda Naotaka, and Fukunaga Susumu. *Shinpen nihon koten bungaku zenshū*, vols. 31–33. Tokyo: Shōgakukan, 1997.

Field, Norma. *The Splendor of Longing in "The Tale of Genji."* Princeton, NJ: Princeton University Press, 1987.

Frank, Bernard. *Démons et jardins: Aspects de la civilisation du Japon ancien.* Paris: Collège de France, Institut des Hautes Études Japonaises, 2011.

Gōdanshō. Ed. Yamane Taisuke and Gotō Akio. *Shin nihon koten bungaku taikei*, vol. 32. Tokyo: Iwanami Shoten, 1997.

Hida Norio. "Hiraizumi to Kyōto no teien no ruijisei." In *Heiankyō to kizoku no sumai*, ed. Nishiyama Ryōhei and Fujita Masaya. Kyoto: Kyōto Daigaku Gakujutsu Shuppankai, 2012.

Hirata Yoshinobu and Misaki Hisashi. *Waka shokubutsu hyōgen jiten.* Tokyo: Tōkyōdō Shuppan, 1994.

Hirsch, Eric. "Landscape: Between Place and Space." In *The Anthropology of Landscape: Perspectives on Place and Space,* ed. Eric Hirsch and Michael O'Hanlon. Oxford: Clarendon Press, 1995.

Honchō monzui. Ed. Ōsone Shōsuke, Kinpara Tadashi, and Gotō Akio. *Shin nihon koten bungaku taikei,* vol. 27. Tokyo: Iwanami Shoten, 1992.

Honchō mudaishi zenchūshaku. 3 vols. Ed. Honma Yōichi. Tokyo: Shintensha, 1992–94.

Jackson, Reginald. "Scripting the Moribund: The Genji Scrolls' Aesthetics of Decomposition." In *Reading "The Tale of Genji,"* ed. Richard Stanley-Baker et al. Folkestone: Global Oriental, 2009.

Kagero Diary, The. Tr. Sonja Arntzen. Ann Arbor: University of Michigan Center for Japanese Studies, 1997.

Kagerō nikki. Ed. Kikuchi Yasuhiko, Kimura Masanori, and Imuta Tsunehisa. *Shinpen nihon koten bungaku zenshū,* vol. 13. Tokyo: Shōgakukan, 1995.

Kakaishō. Ed. Muromatsu Iwao. *Kokubun chūshaku zensho,* vol. 3, Tokyo: Kokugakuin Daigaku Shuppanbu, 1908.

Keirstead, Thomas. "Garden and Estates: Medievality and Space." *Positions* vol. 1, no. 2 (1993).

Kokin wakashū. Ed. Ozawa Masao and Matsuda Shigeho. *Shinpen nihon koten bungaku zenshū,* vol. 11. Tokyo: Shōgakukan, 1994.

Kokuhō Genji monogatari emaki. Nagoya: Gotō Bijutsukan, 2000.

Konjaku monogatarishū, vol. 1. Ed. Konno Tōru. *Shin nihon koten bungaku taikei,* vol. 33. Tokyo: Iwanami Shoten, 1999.

Kurata Minoru. "Shizen." In *Heian daijiten: Zukai de wakaru 'Genji monogatari' no sekai,* ed. Kurata Minoru. Tokyo: Asahi Shinbun Shuppan, 2015.

Makura no sōshi. Ed. Matsuo Satoshi and Nagai Kazuko. *Shinpen nihon bungaku zenshū,* vol. 18. Tokyo: Shōgakukan, 1997.

McCullough, William H. and Helen Craig McCullough, tr. *A Tale of Flowering Fortunes.* 2 vols. Stanford, CA: Stanford University Press, 1980.

Mitani Ei'ichi. *Monogatarishi no kenkyū.* Tokyo: Yūseidō, 1967.

Motonaka Makoto. *Nihon kodai no teien to keikan.* Tokyo: Yoshikawa Kōbunkan, 1994.

Nomura Sei'ichi. "Rokujōin no kisetsuteki jikū no motsu imi wa nani ka." *Kokubungaku* vol. 25, no. 6 (1980).

Okamoto-MacPhail, Aiko. "Interacting Signs in the *Genji* Scrolls." In *The Pictured Word,* ed. Martin Heusser et al. Amsterdam: Rodopi, 1998.

Ono Kenkichi. *Nihon teien no rekishi to bunka.* Tokyo: Yoshikawa Kōbunkan, 2015.

Owen, Stephen. *Readings in Chinese Literary Thought.* Cambridge, MA: Harvard University, Council on East Asian Studies, 1992.

Rodd, Laurel Rasplica and Mary Catherine Henkenius, tr. *Kokinshū: A Collection of Poems Ancient and Modern.* Princeton, NJ: Princeton University Press, 1984.

Saeki Masako. *Genji monogatari ni okeru 'kangaku': Murasaki Shikibu no gakumonteki kiban.* Tokyo: Shintensha, 2010.

Sakuteiki. Ed. Hayashiya Tatsusaburō. *Nihon shisō taikei,* vol. 23. Tokyo: Iwanami Shoten, 1973.

Sei Shōnagon. *The Pillow Book.* Tr. Meredith McKinney. London: Penguin Books, 2006.

Shimizu, Yoshiaki. "The Rite of Writing: Thoughts on the Oldest Genji Text." *Res* 16 (1988).

Shirane, Haruo. *The Bridge of Dreams: A Poetics of "The Tale of Genji."* Stanford, CA: Stanford University Press, 1987.

Shirane, Haruo. *Japan and the Culture of the Four Seasons: Nature, Literature, and the Arts.* New York: Columbia University Press, 2012.

Smits, Ivo. *The Pursuit of Loneliness: Chinese and Japanese Nature Poetry in Medieval Japan, ca. 1050–1150*. Stuttgart: Franz Steiner, 1995.

Takahashi Bunji. "Genji monogatari to shizen." *Kokubungaku: Kaishaku to kanshō* 65, 12 (2000), no. 835.

Van Goethem, Ellen. "Feng Shui Symbolism in Japan: The Four Divine Beasts." In *Theory and Reality of Feng Shui in Architecture and Landscape Art*, ed. Florian C. Reiter. Wiesbaden: Harrassowitz, 2013.

Yuasa Yukiyo. "Hikaru Genji no Rokujō-in: Minamoto no Tōru to Uda jōkō no Kawara-in kara." In *Genji monogatari no ishizue*, ed. Hinata Kazumasa. Tokyo: Seikansha, 2012.

Chapter 7

Rethinking Gender in *The Tale of Genji*

RAJYASHREE PANDEY

The questions we ask both of the contemporary world and of distant times and places are perforce animated by concerns and anxieties that belong to our own age. This is reflected in the centrality that we accord today to questions of gender, as well as in our use of it as an analytic category to help unravel the workings of power and the particular modes of domination and subordination that shape relationships between men and women. Gender is now seen as a constitutive and often unacknowledged feature of the ways in which not only literature, philosophy, and history, but even the more "objective" natural sciences have come to be discursively produced.

How we read *The Tale of Genji* is no exception. Today it can no longer be viewed simply as a charming tale of romance in which aristocratic men and women, governed by the "rule of taste," composed love poetry, played music, and engaged in amorous affairs. In recent academic writings, the focus has shifted to an exploration of how questions of gender are enmeshed in the refined games of courtship and conquest that are central themes in the work.[1]

An inquiry into gender is a distinctly modern undertaking, and it is above all academic feminism that has given it voice by using it as a central category of analysis. Exploring relationships between men and women in *The Tale of Genji* has necessarily entailed unveiling the inequality at the heart of gender relations in the text. Rather than adding to this growing body of literature, invaluable as it has been, my approach here, in keeping with the philosophical concerns of this book, is to offer instead a critique of contemporary approaches to the study of gender in the *Genji* by interrogating some of the foundational assumptions that have gone into the making of gender as a category and some of terms that are intimately intertwined with it, such as the body, sexuality, desire, agency, masculinity, and femininity.

I do so on the grounds that there has been little theorizing in academic writing on the *Genji* about how the category "gender" came to be produced in the first place, and how the debates that brought it into being as an analytical tool occurred within the specific context of the religious and philosophical traditions of the West. If we grant that gender is not only historically but also culturally variable, then as a conceptual category it may need to be stretched and rethought to be of service for explicating non-Western pasts.

My approach then is to begin by examining European debates on gender and considering some of the core assumptions that have gone into the making of this category. This serves as the necessary backdrop for demonstrating that it is only by rethinking these assumptions within the broader epistemic framework of what one might broadly call the East Asian[2] religious, philosophical, and medical

---

1. See Field, *The Splendor of Longing*; Bargen, *A Women's Weapon*; Sarra, *Fictions of Femininity*; and the articles in *Genji kenkyū*, ed. Mitamura et al., 10 vols .
2. By the "East Asian" tradition, I mean the complex nexus of Daoist, Buddhist, and Confucian ideas that circulated in China, Korea, and Japan in the premodern period.

traditions that we can decipher how gender functioned in medieval Japanese texts.[3] By doing so I hope to make visible the cultural variability of gender and to explore how it operates within the specific context of *The Tale of Genji*.

A BRIEF GENEALOGY OF SEX/GENDER

As a conceptual category, widely deployed in feminist writing, the term "gender," from the outset, served a political function. It was a response to the biological determinism that was at the heart of the claim that had been made since the eighteenth century that sexual difference was something inscribed on the body, a fact of nature that could not be changed, and hence the reason women were innately inferior to men. The category "gender" emerged precisely as a way of combating this logic, by arguing that social roles were not necessarily bound to sex and that sexual or biological difference did not determine intellectual and other differences. Gender became "a social category imposed on a sexed body."[4]

The view that sexual difference, grounded in the body, defined what it meant to be man or woman was a radical departure from conceptions of the body and the sexes that had dominated medieval and Renaissance thought in Europe. The body in these earlier periods was not seen as belonging to the sphere of nature, standing in opposition to and separate from the social or cultural realm. Gender boundaries

---

3. I use the term "medieval" to refer to works belonging to very different historical periods—from the Heian period texts such as *The Tale of Genji* to works in the Kamakura and Muromachi periods—on the grounds that, for all their differences, what gives these texts produced across different time frames a certain coherence is that none of the questions they raise, the issues they problematize, or the resolutions they offer can be properly understood outside of the Buddhist paradigm that frames the discursive possibilities available to them.

4. Scott, "'Gender': A Useful Category," p. 156.

were fluid, and the nature of the sexes was seen as interchangeable and permeable.[5] Until the seventeenth century, what prevailed was the "one-sex model," in which men and women were seen as having essentially the same sexual organs, and what distinguished men from women was merely that men's genitalia lay on the outside while those of women were inverted.[6]

The belief in the isomorphism of men's and women's anatomy did not, of course, mean that men and women were considered equal, for the assumption was always that the male constituted the normative model of which the female was simply an inferior version. However, what is significant is that neither the body nor its sexual organs were the privileged sites for the justification of particular social arrangements. To be one's gender, to occupy a particular place within the social order as a man or woman, was itself seen as part of the natural order. Sex did not function as a biological category any more than gender did as a social one.[7]

The developments within European history and science that produced a new understanding of women as constituted through their sex became the starting point for the feminist project of the sixties and seventies, which, while leaving unchallenged the idea that woman was constituted through her sexual attributes, sought nonetheless to question the assumption that her social roles inevitably followed from them. Women, it was assumed, were a self-evident grouping, whose members had been subjected to systematic neglect or vilification on the basis of their sex. Part of the new work undertaken by feminists was the attempt to "retrieve" women who had been silenced and written out of official historical, religious, and philosophical discourses.

---

5. See Bynum, "The Female Body and Religious Practice," pp. 185–87.
6. Laqueur, *Making Sex: Body and Gender*, pp. 19–20, 25–62, 63–113, 114–42, 150–54.
7. As Laqueur puts it, "Nature [here] is not therefore to culture what sex is to gender, as in modern discussions." See ibid., p. 29.

While the project of retrieval was invaluable, it was also fraught with problems. Underpinning much of this work was the assumption that "Woman" was a self-evident and pre-given transcendental category. Feminist debates since the eighties have increasingly engaged in questioning this understanding of "woman," or even of the more capacious, lowercase, pluralizing amendment "women," as a stable category.[8] The destabilization of "women" as a fixed category has had consequences for understanding what we mean by gender. Judith Butler has been a particularly influential voice, claiming that gender "ought not to be conceived as a noun or a substantial thing or a static cultural marker,"[9] but rather as "an activity, a becoming," whereby the iteration of words, acts, and gestures creates the illusion of fixed notions of "an interior and organizing gender core, an illusion discursively maintained for the purposes of the regulation of sexuality within the obligatory frame of reproductive heterosexuality."[10] For Butler gender is performative, and the binaries of sex/gender, man/woman, and hetero-/homosexuality are not facts or truths about the world that are made manifest through our actions. Rather it is the other way round: it is through the endless repetition of certain acts that we create the illusion of the stability of gender.

GENDER, SEX, AND BODY IN *THE TALE OF GENJI*

Many of the debates that I have outlined above are the necessary starting point for considering both the possibilities and limits of

---

8. See, for example, Riley, "*Am I That Name?,*" pp. 2–5, and Scott, "The Evidence of Experience," p. 202.

9. Butler, *Gender Trouble: Feminism and the Subversion of Identity*, p. 112.

10. Ibid., p, 337 .

applying the category "gender" to our analysis of *The Tale of Genji*. For all the differences between medieval Europe and Japan, both shared a conception of the cosmos as one in which the human and natural orders were integrally linked. This was a world in which men, women, animals, and supernatural beings inhabited a common cosmological order, often intermingling promiscuously with one another; nature was a living presence, yet to be reduced to a passive object, to be given meaning by the Man of Reason. As in medieval Europe, so in premodern China and Japan, the natural and the social were not conceptualized as two distinct categories. Male and female were understood to be at once natural and social, which meant that the distinction of sex and gender, which is premised on the division of the world into these two domains, had little purchase.

However, there were important differences between the two traditions that shaped understandings of the body, woman, and sex. Neither the "one-sex model" that dominated Western understandings of the body until the seventeenth century nor the sexual dimorphism that informed subsequent understandings of it is necessarily applicable to an interpretation of how "male" and "female" came to be constructed in premodern China and Japan. As Charlotte Furth argues, classical Chinese medical texts, which formed the basis of Japanese medical theories, conceived of the feminine (*yin*) and masculine (*yang*) principles as complementary aspects of the body, which were seen to interpenetrate both men and women. The ideal body was the androgynous one, which held together both elements, *yin* and *yang*, in perfect balance. In Chinese medicine "healthy males and females, when seen as a fertile couple, formed the matching *yin yang* opposites of homologous gender."[11]

The relationship between the body and mind was not the site of troubled debates in the East Asian traditions, in the way that it was in

11. Furth, *A Flourishing Yin*, p. 52.

Western thought. In both Daoist and Buddhist thought the two were envisaged as a mind-body complex,[12] in which the body was seen as a psychosomatic process, "something done, rather than something one has."[13] The six sense organs in the Buddhist framework include not only what we would categorize as physical attributes—the eye, the ear, the nose, the tongue, and the body—but also the mind/consciousness. The body in the East Asian tradition was not mere matter—the heart/mind was integral to its very constitution.

The word in the Japanese medieval lexicon that corresponds to the term "body," *mi* (身), unlike the word *shintai* (身体), which is used today to signify the physical body, made no distinction between the physical body and what we might call the psychic, social, or cultural body; indeed, *mi* extended beyond the body to signify a self, understood not as an individual subject or autonomous agent separate from society, but rather as one that was meaningful only as a social being. It is for this reason that one of the most common usages of the term *mi* was to signify a person's status or standing in the world. There are no words in the medieval lexicon for sex or gender: the term *mi* encapsulates both because the natural and the social domains are, in this schema, inseparable.

There is little evidence within the East Asian tradition to suggest that men or women formed an identifiable group that cohered around the specificity of their sexual attributes.[14] The terms *onna* (女) and *otoko* (男) in medieval Japanese cannot be conflated with the modern words for woman/women, *josei* (女性), and man/men (男性), which were not coined until the nineteenth century and which, as the character *sei*, or sex (性), demonstrates, were founded

12. For a more detailed consideration of how the mind and body work together, see Kasulis, "The Body—Japanese Style."
13. Ames, "The Meaning of the Body in Classical Chinese Philosophy," p. 168.
14. Barlow makes the same point in "Theorizing Women: Funü, Guojia, Jiating," p. 266.

on new biological understandings of men and women as constituted through their sexuality. When medieval texts speak of *onna no mi* (女の身), they mean more than the physical and sexed body that makes for womanhood; both her mental and emotional attributes as well as her relationship to others as a social being are involved in the constitution of what we might call the female body/self.

Mental and affective processes were understood as integral parts of the body's materiality, which meant that "thought" did not function as the other of "feeling" or emotion, and "form" was not the antithesis of "matter." In *The Tale of Genji*, for example, the word *kokoro* refers to both heart and mind; the verb *omou* encapsulates both feeling and thinking,[15] and the word for love, *koi*, makes no distinction between the physical and spiritual aspects of love.

It is therefore not surprising that sex and the body are not associated with sin or shame in *The Tale of Genji*. The text makes no attempt to mask the fact that men are interested in possessing women *sexually*. And yet, intriguingly, a striking feature of courtly texts written in Japanese such as *waka* poetry, women's diaries (*nikki*), and *monogatari*, or romances, of which the *Genji* is an exemplar, is that works in these genres make little mention of the sexual act or describe the physical characteristics of the bodies engaged in sexual pleasures. Unlike Victorian literature, this has little to do with a prudishness that required that ideal relations between respectable men and women be represented as chaste and companionate, and certainly never sexual.

The Tale of Genji favors an elliptical mode for alluding to the fact that a relationship has been sexually consummated. Ellipsis here constitutes a particular form of decorum, or reticence, which extends to food as much as it does to sex. We are far removed from the discourse of sexuality produced in modern societies that, in Michel Foucault's

---

15. Kasulis, "The Body—Japanese Style," p. 303.

words, "dedicated themselves to speaking of it [sex] ad infinitum, whilst exploiting it as *the* secret."[16]

Rather than isolating sex as a distinct domain of pleasure or shame, *The Tale of Genji* presents us instead with a world where the characters, narrators, and readers alike are all drawn into the pleasures of erotic and affective fulfillment. However, as we shall see in the next section, it is a measure of the degree to which the text is suffused with a Buddhist view of the world that in the end the seductions of worldly desires are illusory, leading inevitably to disillusionment and suffering, and even death and disaster.

GENDER, AGENCY, AND BUDDHISM IN *THE TALE OF GENJI*

All of Genji's major relationships in the text end badly. His principal wife, Aoi, possessed by the spirit of the high-ranking Rokujō Lady whom Genji treats with cavalier disregard, suffers and meets with an early death. The same is true for Yūgao, with whom he has a fleeting affair. Genji's ill-conceived marriage to the high-ranking Third Princess, who turns out to be a disappointment, results in his neglecting her. This in turn creates the conditions for Kashiwagi's transgressive sexual liaison with her. The attendant pregnancy and Genji's realization that the father of the child to come is Kashiwagi have disastrous consequences. Kashiwagi, shamed by Genji's unspoken censure, falls ill and dies. The Third Princess rushes to take the tonsure.

Genji, whose irresistible charms are often lauded in the text, is singularly unsuccessful in his romantic undertakings, even with

16. Foucault, *The Will to Knowledge*, p. 35.

Murasaki, the seemingly stable center of Genji's affective world, and in the end love brings unhappiness not only for the women he pursues but also for himself. He spends his last days after the death of Murasaki in isolation and despair, and he disappears from the text a broken man, unable to escape from the pain brought about by his worldly attachments.

After Genji's death, this pattern of amorous pursuits resulting in disaster is repeated with greater intensity in the Uji chapters. The eldest daughter of the Eighth Prince, Ōigimi, pursued by Kaoru, starves herself to death, refusing to give in to his advances. Her half-sister Ukifune, caught between the affections of Kaoru and Niou, attempts to drown herself, and eventually becomes a nun.

It is not surprising then, given the tragic fates of many of the women in the text, that scholars have focused on the suffering and helplessness of women to explore the nature of gender relations in the *Genji*. Often the fact that the work is written by a woman is taken as confirmation of the fact that underlying the highly aestheticized games of love, what the author seeks to expose is men's thoughtlessness and cruelty toward courtly women in a polygamous world. Despite the many privileges of education and wealth accorded to them, women cannot but suffer, caught as they are in oppressive patriarchal structures that shape gender relations in that society.

Framed by feminist concerns, the analysis of gender in the *Genji* sees in the text the presence of a consistent voice, that of a female author, who through the plot device of romance, exposes the unequal relations between men and women, which result in women's suffering and oppression. At the same time, the emancipatory project, built into feminism, demands that women be seen as agents, actively fighting oppression. Proof of women's resistance to male desire and the assertion of individual autonomy is found in the figures of Murasaki, who strives to distance herself from Genji by requesting repeatedly that she be allowed to take the tonsure; Ōigimi, who starves to death rather than give in to Kaoru's advances; the Rokujō Lady, whose angry spirit possesses and kills her rivals; and Ukifune, who is lauded as a woman who chooses her own destiny, achieving independence from men by taking the tonsure and giving expression to her new-found sense of self through her poetry.

Here I would like to propose a very different reading of women's suffering and their response to it, by problematizing the conceptual framework of agency, resistance, and oppression, which takes little account of the broader Buddhist episteme within which questions of suffering are thematized in the text. When we speak of "agency" to consider women's responses to oppression, what we consistently privilege is *human* agency, which presupposes the supremacy of Man, who replaces the gods as the maker of meaning in the world.[17] Gods, now stripped of their role as agents, are explained away as little other than projections of the human mind. Given that in the world of medieval Japanese texts gods, buddhas, men, women, animals, and even material objects alike worked as vibrant actors within a shared cosmological order, granting agency and consciousness only to human beings, is little more than an anachronistic ascription of our own worldview to an altogether different cosmology.

The unlikely union of Genji with the Akashi Lady when Genji is in exile in Suma is effected not through the personal agency of either of the protagonists but due to the intervention of a number of supernatural agents. In Chapter 13 "Akashi", the spirit of Genji's deceased father appears to him in a dream and urges him to follow the Sumiyoshi god to Suma. The father of the Akashi Lady also receives a divine message that instructs him to bring Genji from Suma to Akashi. It is the power of the Sumiyoshi god that the text credits for the miraculous bond between Genji and the Akashi Lady which results in the birth of a daughter who eventually becomes an empress, thereby securing

17. See, for example, Faure, *The Power of Denial*, pp. 331–32.

Genji's political fortunes and bringing true a prophecy made when he was born that he would rise to extraordinary heights.

Modern interpretations of the workings of gender and agency also cannot accommodate a view expressed in medieval Buddhist and literary texts alike that the dramas that unfold in men's and women's lives are less the consequences of their own actions performed in present lives than the mysterious manifestations of karma from previous existences. In the *Genji* many of the amorous entanglements in which women find themselves embroiled are viewed not through the prism of coercion or consent, but rather through the Buddhist notion of *sukuse*, fate or karma, a recurrent term in the text.

When the Fujitsubo Lady discovers that she is pregnant after the illicit and transgressive liaison forced on her by Genji, her stepson, she attributes this crisis to a "shocking destiny" (*asamashiki onsukuse*). Her attendant Ōmyōbu also views this situation as a reflection of the "inescapable bond" (*nogaregatakarikeru onsukuse*) between Fujitsubo and Genji (g1/233; cf. t97–98).[18] The Rokujō Lady, horrified by the malevolent work done by her spirit (*tama*), which leaves her body to attack her rivals, speaks in despair of actions that are beyond her control. She can only attribute them to the "wretchedness of her fate" (*sukuse no uki koto*). When Genji finds out that the child to be born to his wife, the Third Princess, is the fruit of Kashiwagi's adulterous relationship with her, he realizes that this misfortune is linked to his own adulterous relationship, many years earlier, with his father's wife Fujitsubo. He expresses his surprise at the way in which retribution for the betrayal of his father and the throne has occurred in this very lifetime rather than in the next, and he wonders whether his burden of sin will, as a consequence, be lessened in lives to come.

---

18. I draw these examples from Shirane's *The Bridge of Dreams*, p. 173. Tyler paraphrases these locutions as "the misery of her [sc. Fujitsubo's] lot" and "fate [that] had struck after all."

When Yūgiri, Genji's son, tries to possess Ochiba no miya sexually, she resists his advances, leading him to wonder whether it is the weakness of their karmic bond from past lives that accounts for her unequivocal rejection of him. Time and time again both men and women in the text read the circumstances that unfold in their lives as the workings of inexplicable causes and contingencies reverberating through past existences rather than primarily as consequences of their own actions as autonomous individuals who are entirely in control of their own destinies.

The modes of understanding that attribute agency to gods, spirits, and buddhas and grant power to actions performed in past lives for the events that occur in the present are at odds with conceptions of agency which presuppose that the individual, endowed with free will, is the author of her own actions. The imperative to attribute agency to female characters in the text produces celebratory accounts of women who recognize their agency and act to change their situation in the world. Passivity, in this reading of agency, while worthy of sympathy, is a failing given that each individual is responsible even for inaction. However, even passivity is not seen as an irrevocable condition, for it assumes the presence of a nascent consciousness, which, given the right circumstances, can be awakened such that an individual can finally come into her own and act in her own interest. The moral charge of celebrating agency often takes the form of treating it as conceptually interchangeable with the idea of resistance against relations of power and domination. This means that acts, particularly religious ones, that work in consonance *with* social conventions rather than *against* them cannot be granted real agency.[19] This has implications for how scholars interpret the act of taking the tonsure in *The Tale of Genji*.

---

19. I am drawing here on Mahmood's "Feminist Theory, Embodiment, and the Docile Agent," pp. 202–36.

TONSURE AND AGENCY

In medieval times, both men and women, regardless of their status in society or the circumstances that led to take religious vows, shared in the aspiration to become lay nuns or monks at some stage in life, in the hope of retiring from the world of social obligations and preparing for a favorable death. Scholars have singled out nunhood as one of the sites upon which women's response to Buddhism's "misogyny" came to be played out in the medieval period. Some have seen the act of tonsure as an act of resistance to unequal social arrangements: nunhood, in this reading, becomes the space of freedom.[20] Others, working within the same conceptual framework of agency, have claimed precisely the opposite, arguing that the practice of tonsure was proof of women's oppression and subservience in the face of patriarchal domination and Buddhist misogyny,[21] "a form of death in life."[22] Or in another manifestation of the idea of the individual as an autonomous being responsible for her actions, nuns are sometimes seen as complicit with Buddhist ideology, thereby contributing to the subjugation of other women.[23]

If we work within the framework of agency understood as either liberation or subjection, the particular reading that we favor becomes little more than an arbitrary choice. No one would deny that a woman taking the tonsure served a variety of ends, ranging from testing the affections of a lover whose attentions had flagged to withdrawing altogether from a relationship that had gone wrong.[24] Becoming

---

20. See Ruch, "The Other Side of Culture," p. 510.
21. See, for example, Ishida, "Bikuni kaidan: ama no tokui na seikaku," pp. 1–15; Hosokawa, "Sairinji sōji to ama," pp. 143–51. For a more nuanced reading of nunhood see Meeks, "Buddhist Renunciation and the Female Life Cycle."
22. Field, *The Splendor of Longing*, p. 189.
23. Faure, *The Power of Denial*, pp. 53, 78, 331–32. See also Kimbrough, *Preachers, Poets, Women and the Way*, p. 215.
24. See Laffin, *Rewriting Medieval Japanese Women*, p. 83.

a nun may well have been a consequence of unfortunate social circumstances, but to see these acts solely as manifestations of either empowerment or victimhood reduces medieval players to little more than versions of our own selves. If personhood in medieval Japan is located in the social, and if it is not imagined as an individual and secular identity, then agency in this context would have to be disentangled from nineteenth-century liberalism, which speaks an altogether different language of choice and self-determination.[25]

Women's tonsure was one socially available model for escaping from the trials of worldly life, as well as engaging in the performance of pious and virtuous deeds that worked not against but rather in conformity with the traditions and practices of medieval society. If we are insistent upon seeing this as a form of resistance, it would have to be, as Sanjay Seth notes in another context, "a very specific sense of 'resistance', one not closely tied to intentionality, and partly as a consequence of this, lacking heroic connotations."[26]

While it is true that it is as a tragic consequence of Genji's marriage with the high-ranking Third Princess that Murasaki expresses her desire to become a nun, her desire to do so is accorded a special place in the *Genji* because she is an exemplar of what is most valued in the Buddhist world, namely a pious disposition that encompasses the widely held aspiration to be born again in one of the Buddha's paradises. Murasaki is often likened to a bodhisattva, and her garden is associated in the text with the Pure Land of Amida Buddha. In the religious rituals performed in honor of Genji's fortieth year, the ceremonies organized by Murasaki are singled out as comparable to the "true Paradise." The seriousness of her intent to take religious vows

---

25. As Walter Johnson suggests, "[T]he term 'agency' smuggles a notion of the universality of a liberal notion of selfhood, with its emphasis on independence and choice." See his "On Agency," p. 115.

26. Seth, *Subject Lessons: The Western Education of Colonial India*, p. 33.

and her initiative in organizing the ceremonies for the recitation of the *Lotus Sutra* (*Hokke Hakkō*) demonstrate her commitment to the Buddhist Way, which offers the possibility of disengaging from worldly attachments and preparing for death. In the end she performs an exemplary death.

The aspiration to become a monk or a nun resonated as a profoundly charged affective trope in *The Tale of Genji* precisely because, within the context of a romance narrative, it served to dramatize the tension between the seductive power of affective attachments and the recognition that they had to be overcome in order to escape the suffering and pain that they inevitably caused. Murasaki's inability to take the tonsure lies in the fact that Genji will not allow it because, as he explains, he cannot imagine a life without her. The text tells us that Murasaki herself cannot bear to imagine the pain she will cause him if she leaves their conjugal life to become a nun. The emotional charge of the scene lies in the way in which the text stages the tension between the bonds of attachment and the profound pain involved in breaking them and in its use of the two central figures of romance in the text to enact it. To privilege gender alone makes us miss the larger philosophical concerns that are at work in the text and reduces it to a monochromatic representation of Murasaki as a woman who is denied her autonomy by her selfish and self-serving husband Genji.

It is notable that young men, unlike women in the *Genji*, are conspicuous in their failure to take the tonsure. In keeping with the conventions of *waka* and *monogatari*, men are the ones who pursue and initiate amorous affairs, and it is this role that locks them into an inescapable and endless cycle of attachment to worldly desires that come to be embodied in the women they pursue. Both the taking of the tonsure and the inability to do so carry multiple significations in the *Genji*, and neither is reducible to being seen solely through the prisms of gender and agency, understood in terms of a binary framework of domination and subordination. To do so eviscerates the text of the Buddhist worldview that frames the narrative, producing anachronistic readings, which turn the *Genji* into a secular text where piety becomes simply a displacement or metaphor that obscures (when read through the lens of "gender," "agency," and "resistance") the "truth" of the inequality and injustice of gender relations.

Many of the problems I have raised above are connected with the fact that the *Genji* is often read as a psychological novel, where men and women are treated not as textual figures but as representations of the real. This effect of verisimilitude is produced in no small measure through the changes to the original text effected by its English translations that require consistency of voice and tense, the breakup of long flowing passages into discreet sentences, and the homogenizing of multiple narratorial points of view in order to produce intelligibility. I raise this point because defamiliarizing the way we read the *Genji* is the first necessary step for understanding the complexity of the workings of gender in the text. If we take the original seriously, we may grant more readily that what is fascinating about the work is precisely the ways in which it works in multiple registers, at once a tale in which we are made profoundly aware of the fact that men's pursuit of women results in immeasurable suffering, particularly for the women who are the recipients of men's advances; as a profound Buddhist reflection on the deluded nature of all attachment; and as a work that seeks to elaborate upon and complicate the conventions and tropes of *waka* love poetry by wedding them with a rich and complex narrative prose. It is to this last aspect of the work that I turn next.

WAKA POETRY, GENERIC CONVENTIONS, AND GENDER IN *THE TALE OF GENJI*

The Tale of Genji has almost eight hundred poems (*waka*) interspersed within its long prose narrative. How gender is configured within the conventions of *waka* poetry, therefore, has a significant bearing on the ways in which amorous relationships play out within the text. *Waka* poetry's dominant themes are nature and love, both of which are expressed through a prescribed repertoire of images and vocabulary. The central figures of love poems are *otoko* (man) and *onna* (woman), who appear in the poems through terms such as *kimi* (you) and *hito* (male or female lover) or *ware* (I). These latter terms are used for both men and women alike. They indicate nothing about the gender, identity, or social status of either the poet or the one who is being addressed.[27]

When a poem is described as a woman's poem (*onna no uta*), what is at issue is not the sexual or personal identity of the composer of the poem, but rather the particular stylized role or persona to be adopted by the poet that is consonant with woman, not as a real, living being, but rather as a trope or an idea. Even when a poem is marked as anonymous or when there is no headnote that explains the circumstances under which it was composed, it is possible to infer which persona a poet has adopted.

This is because in the *waka* tradition, woman is always positioned as the one who waits and pines for her male lover, while man is the one who visits at night, and departs before dawn. He is the one who initiates the affair and composes the morning-after poem to which his lady is expected to respond. A poet, regardless of his or her biological sex (a category that has no real meaning in this context), can slip seamlessly into the persona of the waiting female or the male who visits.[28] It is through the performative stances adopted by poets

27. The capacious term *ware* in *waka* poetry does not correspond to the personal pronoun "I" in the English language, understood as an autonomous, freestanding, individual identity. *Ware* speaks to fluid, multiple selves that often blend into one another, inhabiting as they do the same experiential space. See Miyake, "The Tosa Diary," p. 63.

28. Michel Vieillard-Baron argues that it is the stance that the poet adopts in the composition, rather than his or her biological sex, that renders the work masculine or feminine. See his "Male? Female? Gender Confusion in Classical Poetry."

that *otoko* and *onna* come into being, albeit provisionally, within the discursive space of *waka* poetry.

Animals and plants are often metonymically associated with *otoko* and *onna*—morning glory (*asagao*), for example, is the face of a female lover in the morning; the child who is stroked (*nadeshiko*) is at once a flower as well as a girl who is much loved and raised into womanhood by a man, while *ominaeshi* (maiden flower) functions both as flower and "maiden." Through a thick web of connections the deer is figured as male, while the bush clover, for whom it/he pines, is associatively linked to the female.

The Tale of Genji's extraordinary achievement is to seamlessly blend the form and content of *waka* poetry with a sustained prose narrative and to make poetry the primary vehicle through which the thoughts and feelings of the central figures can be given expression. However, it is precisely the strong presence of poetry in the text and the observance of its codes and conventions that undo a reading of the *Genji* as if it were a nineteenth-century realist novel, where the fictional relations between men and women are more readily amenable to being read as reflections of the workings of gender in the real world.

Following the protocols of *waka* poetry, many of the central figures in *The Tale of Genji* are metonymically associated with flora and fauna drawn from nature. Nature here is not imagined as separate from the social world, which is why the four seasons constitute a rich source for the generation of both poetic and gendered associations. The feelings expressed in *waka* are diffuse and decentered, often echoing the rhythms and patterns observable in nature, and it is for this reason that both seasonal and love poems partake of a shared affective universe shaped by the inevitable passage of time.

For a character in a text to be imbued with a unique personality and psychological makeup, the minimum requirement is that she

have a name. And yet the characters in the *Genji* to whom we refer
with proper names, and to whom as a consequence we attribute a
fixed entity, are in fact identified in the text either by their official
ranks or titles, which frequently change with the passage of time, or
by their relationships with one another. Often they are known only
by the sobriquets they have acquired from a word in a poem they
have composed or in one addressed to them. This is the case for many
of the female characters in the text, such as Yūgao, Oborozukiyo,
Hanachirusato, Tamakazura, and Ukifune.

Waka poetry in the *Genji* destabilizes the notion that every
poetic composition, recitation, or allusion seeks to express individual thoughts and feelings, and that it is the lyrical expression of
a unique and singular self, whose emotions are found reflected in
nature. Following the established conventions and protocols of
poetry allows the figures in the text to give expression to experiences
that are not exclusive to them as autonomous individuals, but ones
that belong to readers, narrators, and protagonists alike, all of whom
inhabit a shared erotic and affective world.

GENDER AS PERFORMANCE IN *THE TALE OF GENJI*

Understanding how gender functions is clearly important in a text
such as the *Genji* that accords centrality to relationships between
men and women. In considering how gender is produced and how
it operates within the text, Judith Butler's work on performativity is
particularly pertinent, as it allows us to think outside of the binaries
of sex as a biological truth and gender as socially constructed and to
treat both as "truth effects" produced through the repeated iteration
of performative stances. For as I have argued earlier, the epistemic
framework within which texts such as the *Genji* were produced does

not conceive of gender as a social category that offers a corrective to the biological truth of sex.

In our own age, masculinity has often been constituted through an emphasis on muscles and physical strength, while femininity is made visible through breasts and the display of flesh. A striking feature of the *Genji* is that, of the vast majority of men and women who inhabit the text, there are very few whom we can conjure up in their fullness, as people composed of flesh and bone. Both the physical and psychic attributes that go into the making of the body often find expression in the robes within which the body is enveloped.[29] Genji is portrayed as an exemplar of beauty and radiance, but it is the casual refinement and elegance of his attire rather than his physical appearance that renders him a person of extraordinary beauty in the text.

Furthermore, there is little to differentiate men and women on the basis of their attire. This is why lovers often exchange and wear each other's robes without any implication that doing so is an act of cross-dressing. The beauty of the face and the physical aspects of the body are not accorded much significance and are often conveyed cursorily in highly stylized terms. The terms *okashi, utsukushi, namamekashi, rōtashi, medetashi, natsukashi,* and so on, which appear frequently in the *Genji*, convey a wide range of nuances, signifying different forms of allure: charming, beautiful, appealing, desirable, refined, youthful, and winsomely appealing. These terms, for the most part, are used for both men and women alike. One of the most potent markers of refined sensibility in the *Genji* is the ability of both men and women to express their feelings with tears. The image of the courtly aristocrat shedding tears, far from being a sign of effeminacy, maps onto an altogether different aesthetic, which renders the weeping man deeply attractive to both women and men.

---

29. See Pandey, *Perfumed Sleeves and Tangled Hair*, chaps. 2 and 3, for a more complete discussion of the connections between the body, robes, eroticism, and gender.

If gender difference does not register overtly through the body, clothes, and ideals of beauty, this does not mean that men and women in the text are indistinguishable one from the other or that their relationships are unmarked by the play of power. However, how gender comes to be coded depends on the context in which it is performed. Within the dense social world of the *Genji*, gender, status, age, and a highly aestheticized form of eroticism often crisscross, creating a multitude of possibilities. How gender and status intersect, for example, is open to at least two different readings.

In one, gender itself is fixed and stable but varies at its point of intersection with class. A serving woman, for example, has fewer privileges but perhaps also greater freedom because of her class. In this reading, her "womanness" is fixed, but the ways in which it plays out, in social terms, is determined by class. The categories are stable, and one could more or less represent the range of possibilities on a graph, where the vertical line is gender and the horizontal line class; where they intersect gives us a reading/representation of what it was like to be a serving woman, an aristocratic woman of the middling ranks, a woman belonging to the uppermost echelons of court nobility, and so on.

In the second reading, and one that informs my understanding of gender in the *Genji*, gender is performative and not fixed and given, and thus how it is performed—what constitutes being a woman—is itself shaped by class, which again, far from being stable, functions as a dynamic and fluid category. Gender in the *Genji* functions as a kind of script, and it is the specificity of the gendered performance, that is to say the particularity of the script that is enacted, that gives substance to the categories "male" and "female."

The anonymous twelfth-century fictional tale *Torikaebaya monogatari* (The tale of "If only I could change them back") exemplifies perfectly this idea of gender as something that is not a given but rather a matter of "becoming" through repeated performance.

The daughter of the Minister of the Right, Himegimi, is raised as a boy and takes her place at the court as a man, while her brother Wakagimi, brought up as a girl, enters court as a lady. It is through forms of rigorous self-fashioning, that is to say through the cultivation of particular emotional dispositions and forms of bodily comportment appropriate to their respective genders, that Himegimi and Wakagimi are able to transform themselves such that they can successfully take on their new gendered roles, regardless of their sexual attributes. "Words designating 'man' or 'woman' often appear with verbs that imply the mutability or superficiality of that very status."[30] In the end, *Torikaebaya monogatari* returns the two siblings to their proper gendered roles, but for much of the text it engages in playful inversions, whose effect is to expose the fictive nature of the fixity of gender as the basis of a stable identity.

It is the possibilities offered by different ways of "doing" gender that *The Tale of Genji* explores through the many romantic encounters at the heart of its narrative. Let us consider, for example, the significance of *déshabillé* in the text. In descriptions of Genji's clothing, we often find words such as *shidokenaku, uchimidaru, azaretaru, uchitoketaru,* and *yatsureru.*[31] All these terms convey a sense of casualness, careless ease, languor, and informality that render Genji a particularly erotic figure in the text. However, the potential of such an attire worn to arouse amorous interest is not consistently maintained and is always contingent on the complex intersections of gender and class. When Genji spies on Utsusemi and Nokiba no Ogi, the latter,

---

30. As Gregory Pflugfelder observes, "Words designating 'man' or 'woman' often appear with verbs that imply the mutability or superficiality of that very status—'becoming' (*naru, arisomu*), 'changing into' (*kawaru, kau*), 'making someone into' (*nasu, torinasu*), 'imitating' (*manebu*), 'behaving as' (*motenasu*), 'spending time as' (*tsugu*), 'getting used to being' (*narau, narasu, tsukainarasu, arinaru*), 'reverting to' (*narikaeru, kaeriaratamu*), and so on." See Pflugfelder, "Strange Fates: Sex, Gender, and Sexuality in Torikaebaya Monogatari," p. 355.
31. See Kawazoe, "Hikaru Genji no shintai" pp. 18–20.

he observes, is attired in thin white robes covered with a gown worn carelessly. Nokiba no Ogi's casual appearance, while not dissimilar to Genji's, is judged by Genji to be slovenly and somewhat coarse (*hōzoku nari*). This asymmetry could no doubt be readily explained by the fact that Nokiba no Ogi is a woman and that it is the foundational difference of gender that accounts for his reading of her bodily comportment.

However, Genji's assessment of Nokiba no Ogi is not reducible to the fact that she is a woman and that as a woman she is expected to be modest. Her failure to match her stepmother, Utsusemi, is a result of the fact that she makes no effort to emulate the comportment of highborn ladies and thereby merely confirms the insignificance of her own social stature. Here, status is of greater significance than gender. Gender alone is an inadequate guide for reading the asymmetries that are constitutive of all relationships in the text. For it is perfectly possible, in other contexts, for a noblewoman to evoke feelings of tenderness and desire even if she is dressed, like Genji, in informal garb. Kaoru's intense longing for the First Princess is awakened upon being treated, unexpectedly, to the pleasure of seeing someone of an exalted rank in thin summer robes. Kaoru, who is particularly sensitive to the privileges attendant on the accident of birth, recognizes beauty as something that inheres to the highest born. For Kaoru, the First Princess's light, transparent gown does not bespeak frivolity or carelessness—seeing someone of such exalted status in informal garb provides an erotic charge both because of the beauty of her form, revealed through her transparent clothes, and perhaps more significantly because Kaoru, a commoner, has been treated to the rare sight of a princess of the highest stature in casual attire.

However, status too is far from being a stable criterion for gauging the workings of the politics of desire. After all, not all princesses, however highborn, necessarily live up to men's amorous and erotic expectations. The Third Princess (Onna san no miya) proves to be a great disappointment to Genji despite her impeccable lineage. Kaoru's intense attraction to the First Princess is tied not only to her own noble lineage but also to his intense awareness of his own relatively inferior status. The shifting contexts within which amorous encounters take place are thus always imbricated in a variety of asymmetries and hierarchies, which sometimes work together and at other times pull in different directions, thereby attesting to the inadequacy of treating either gender or class in isolation, outside of the setting or stage (*bamen*) upon which they are brought into play.

GENDER AND LANGUAGE

My final example of the instability of gender is drawn from the assumed link between gender and language in classical and medieval Japanese texts. Japanese culture, by the tenth century, operated through two languages, Chinese and Japanese. Chinese was the official written language of the court, and all public, formal, political, and intellectual activities, which were conceived of as the exclusive domain of men, were expressed through this medium. Japanese became the language of women and came to be linked to the private, domestic, and affective spheres of courtly life. And yet these two languages did not function in literary texts as watertight or self-contained mediums.

One of the most striking examples of forms of linguistic/gender crossing is to be found in the diary *Tosa nikki* (The Tosa diary, ca. 935), written by the middle-ranking courtier and poet Ki no Tsurayuki. In the very opening lines of the text, Tsurayuki declares his intention to write the diary in the voice of a woman to see what she can do with a form that is said to be the exclusive domain of men. As Thomas Harper puts it, "[H]e will be both male and female, he will be both at once, and he will be so with words—which he can do because the boundaries of his two languages coincide so precisely with the boundaries of the two sexes."[32]

Because it is written in *hiragana*, the vernacular phonetic script, Tsurayuki's text is marked feminine. The use of *kanbun* expressions and the text's adherence to the protocols of diaries written in Chinese, noting with exactitude the month and year of each entry, render it masculine. This seamless journeying between two linguistic modes in which "both languages resound simultaneously"[33] is inextricably tied to the intermingling of both male and female voices, which are themselves produced through language. What Tsurayuki's text effects is a breakdown of both Chinese and Japanese, and male and female, such that they become porous, permeable, and indissolubly linked entities.[34]

While it is undeniably the case that women were expected to write in Japanese, in the woman's hand (*onnade*), and could not blatantly trespass on what was considered male terrain—*The Tale of Genji* is after all written in *hiragana*—we need to consider the significance of the fact that Murasaki Shikibu's writings are punctuated by an attempt both to display and to disavow her knowledge of Chinese. In her diary, *Murasaki Shikibu nikki*, she goes out of her way to record that her father regrets that she is not a man, given that she is very much better than her brother at learning Chinese, even though her knowledge has been acquired merely by eavesdropping on his lessons, and that as lady-in-waiting to the Empress, she secretly teaches her mistress how to read Chinese poems.[35]

Indeed, she works the theme of the assumed mismatch between gender and language into a fabled scene in *The Tale of Genji* where, on

32. Harper, "Bilingualism as Bisexualism," unpublished paper.
33. Ibid.
34. See Miyake, "The Tosa Diary."
35. Bowring, *Murasaki Shikibu: Her Diary and Poetic Memoirs*, p. 139.

a rainy night, a group of men appraise different types of women. One of the young noblemen speaks of a former ladylove, the daughter of a Chinese scholar who was once his teacher. She, he tells his listeners, was so accomplished in Chinese herself that she wrote beautifully in the language, and even helped him with his Chinese lessons. On one occasion, she informs him that she cannot meet him as she has caught a cold and that, having drunk a medicinal preparation made of garlic, she suffers from bad breath. Her explanation of why she is indisposed is delivered in a language that reeks of Chinese as strongly as her breath smells of garlic. Needless to say, the young man is turned off, and the scene ends with one of his friends commenting that in women knowledge of the Chinese classics is not an attractive quality (g1/85–88, t33–35).

It is not clear who is the object of ridicule here—the man who is intimidated by a woman who excels in Chinese or the woman who, oblivious to the divisions of language/gender, performs in Chinese. The construction of courtly women's gender rested upon the maintenance of a clear distinction between Chinese and Japanese. By bringing to life women such as herself who were in fact learned in Chinese, Murasaki Shikibu's work has the effect of demonstrating the performative nature of gender and exposing the fictive nature of the assumed isomorphism of gender and language.

CONCLUDING REMARKS

I have argued that for gender to be useful as an analytical category for understanding a text such as *The Tale of Genji*, it has to be dissociated from many of our contemporary assumptions about the body, sex, man, woman, justice, equality, individualism, agency, and so on. Gender difference is undoubtedly central to the generation of romance in the text, but difference is constituted not through man and woman understood as fixed and stable categories, defined by their bodies, but rather through the stylized performative modes that often follow the conventions of Japanese love poetry.

That gender and status intersect in the text is undoubtedly true, but how the two come to be aligned does not map onto a stable grid for what it means to inhabit a particular gender, and one's status within society is itself unstable and subject to change. Page girls, nurses, ladies-in-waiting, and so on all belong to the serving classes, but their status within courtly society varies greatly. Their performance of gender, likewise, is by no means uniform, producing a multiplicity of ways of being "woman."

Analyses of the working of gender in the *Genji* have focused primarily on the unequal relationships between men and women, to demonstrate how men's actions cause pain and suffering for the women with whom they establish amorous liaisons. This is turn has led to the imperative to find within the text instances of female agency, where women strive to establish their autonomy and offer resistance to unjust social arrangements.

However, as I have argued, if we attend to the broader religious and philosophic context within which the work is located, we see that the text, while being acutely sensitive to the pain and suffering caused by amorous entanglements, does not conceptualize relations between men and women through the language of social justice or human agency, but through an altogether different idiom that belongs to a Buddhist view of the world. Agency here is not the provenance solely of humans. Gods, buddhas, bodhisattvas, as much as the consequences of actions taken in previous existences, shape how romantic relations are forged and undone. Amorous attachments inevitably produce pain and misery, and it is the women in the *Genji* who suffer the most. However, unlike the men who fail spectacularly to do so, they are the ones who are able to renounce worldly life, which is the precondition for overcoming pain and suffering in the Buddhist worldview. It is a measure of the *Genji's* extraordinary power that it communicates in equal measure both the seductive nature of love and the illusory nature of its pleasures.

WORKS CITED

Ames, Roger. "The Meaning of the Body in Classical Chinese Philosophy." In Thomas P. Kasulis, Roger Ames, and Wimal Dissanayake, eds., *Self as Body in Asian Theory and Practice*. New York: SUNY Press, 1993.

Barlow, Tani. "Theorizing Women: Funü, Guoja, Jiating." In Angela Zito and Tani Barlow, eds., *Body, Subject and Power in China*. Chicago: University of Chicago Press, 1994.

Bowring, Richard. *Murasaki Shikibu: Her Diary and Poetic Memoirs*. Princeton, NJ: Princeton University Press, 1982.

Butler, Judith. *Gender Trouble: Feminism and the Subversion of Identity*. New York, 1990.

Butler, Judith. "Gender Trouble, Feminist Theory, and Psychoanalytic Discourse." In Linda Nicholson, ed., *Feminism/Postmodernism*. New York: Routledge, 1990.

Bynum, Carolyn. "The Female Body and Religious Practice in the Later Middle Ages." In Michel Feher, with Ramona Naddaff and Nadia Tazi, eds., *Fragments for a History of the Human Body*, part I. New York: Zone Press, 1989.

Faure, Bernard. *The Power of Denial: Buddhism, Purity, and Gender*. Princeton, NJ: Princeton University Press, 2003.

Field, Norma. *The Splendor of Longing in the "Tale of Genji."* Princeton, NJ: Princeton University Press, 1987.

Foucault, Michel. *The Will to Knowledge: The History of Sexuality*, vol. 1, tr. Robert Hurley. London: Penguin Books, 1998.

Furth, Charlotte. *A Flourishing Yin: Gender in China's Medical History, 960–1665*. Berkeley: University of California Press, 1999.

Genji kenkyū, 10 vols. Mitamura Masako et al., eds. Tokyo: Kanrin shobō, 1996–2005.

Hosokawa Ryōichi. "Sairinji sōji to ama." In Ōsumi Kazuo and Nishiguchi Junko, eds., *Shirīzu josei to Bukkyō, Sukui to oshie*, vol. 4. Tokyo: Heibonsha, 1989.

Ishida Mizumaro. "Bikuni kaidan: Ama no tokui na seikaku." *Musashino joshi daigaku kiyō* 18 (1978).

Johnson, Walter. "On Agency." *Journal of Social History* 37, 1 (2003).

Kasulis, Thomas P. "The Body—Japanese Style." In Thomas P. Kasulis, Roger Ames, and Wimal Dissanayake, eds., *Self as Body in Asian Theory and Practice*. Albany: State University of New York Press, 1993.

Kawazoe Fusae. "Hikaru Genji no shintai to yosōi o megutte." *Murasaki* 34, 12 (1997).

Kimbrough, Keller. *Preachers, Poets, Women and the Way: Izumi Shikibu and the Buddhist Literature of Medieval Japan.* Ann Arbor: University of Michigan, Center for Japanese Studies, 2008.

Laffin, Christian. *Rewriting Medieval Japanese Women: Politics, Personality, and Literary Production in the Life of Nun Abutsu.* Honolulu: University of Hawai'i Press, 2013.

Laqueur, Thomas. *Making Sex: Body and Gender from the Greeks to Freud.* Cambridge, MA: Harvard University Press, 1990.

Mahmood, Saba. "Feminist Theory, Embodiment, and the Docile Agent: Some Reflections on the Egyptian Islamic Revival." *Cultural Anthropology* 16, 2 (May 2001).

Meeks, Lori. "Buddhist Renunciation and the Female Life Cycle: Understanding Nunhood in Heian and Kamakura Japan." *Harvard Journal of Asiatic Studies* 70, 1 (June 2010).

Miyake, Lynne. "The Tosa Diary." In Paul Schalow and Janet Walker, eds., *The Woman's Hand: Gender and Theory in Japanese Women's Writing.* Stanford, CA: Stanford University Press, 1996.

Pandey, Rajyashree. *Perfumed Sleeves and Tangled Hair: Body, Woman, and Desire in Medieval Japanese Narratives.* Honolulu: University of Hawai'i Press, 2016.

Pflugfelder, Gregory. "Strange Fates: Sex, Gender, and Sexuality in Torikaebaya Monogatari." *Monumenta Nipponica* 47, 3 (Autumn 1992).

Riley, Denise. *"Am I that Name?": Feminism and the Category of "Women" in History.* Minneapolis: University of Minnesota Press, 2003 (originally published 1988).

Ruch, Barbara. "The Other Side of Culture." In Kozo Yamamura, ed., *The Cambridge History of Japan: Medieval Japan,* vol. 3. Cambridge: Cambridge University Press, 1990.

Sarra, Edith. *Fictions of Femininity: Literary Inventions of Gender in Japanese Court Women's Memoirs.* Stanford, CA: Stanford University Press, 1999.

Scott, Joan Wallach. "The Evidence of Experience." In Gabrielle Spiegel, ed., *Practicing History: New Directions in Historical Writing after the Linguistic Turn.* New York: Routledge, 2005.

Scott, Joan Wallach. "'Gender': A Useful Category of Historical Analysis." In Joan Wallach Scott, ed., *Feminism and History: Oxford Readings in Feminism.* Oxford: Oxford University Press, 1996.

Seth, Sanjay. *Subject Lessons: The Western Education of Colonial India.* Durham, NC: Duke University Press, 2007.

Shirane, Haruo. *The Bridge of Dreams: A Poetics of "The Tale of Genji."* Stanford, CA: Stanford University Press.

Vieillard-Baron, Michel. "Male? Female? Gender Confusion in Classical Poetry (*Waka*)." *Cipango—French Journal of Japanese Studies* 2, English selection (2013).

Chapter 8

Murasaki's "Mind Ground"

A Buddhist Theory of the Novel

MELISSA MCCORMICK

Over the course of its roughly millennium-long reception, *The Tale of Genji* was viewed by many readers as a text that was profoundly Buddhist in nature, one that was best understood through the interpretive tools of Tendai Buddhist thought in particular.[1] This means that *The Tale of Genji* was deemed a philosophical text to which one could turn to think through not only issues of morality and ethics, but fundamental metaphysical questions about the nature of truth, our perception of the phenomenal world, and the phenomenal world's relationship to language. Some of the most explicit evidence that readers approached and understood the tale through a Buddhistic

---

1. In explaining the idea of "original enlightenment" or an inherent buddha nature in Japanese thought, Jacqueline Stone defines Chinese T'ien-t'ai (Tendai in Japanese) as one of "the great totalistic systems of Chinese Buddhist thought . . . which envision the world as a cosmos in which all things, being empty of independent existence, interpenetrate and encompass one another. These systems are both ontological, in explaining all concrete phenomena (*shih* 事) as nondual with truth or principle (*li* 理), and soteriological, in showing liberation to consist of insight into this unity." See Stone, *Original Enlightenment and the Transformation of Medieval Japanese Buddhism*, esp. pp. 6–7.

framework comes by way of *Genji* commentaries, a cumulative tradition of exegesis that continued for more than five hundred years.[2] This might surprise those accustomed to seeing *The Tale of Genji* examined primarily in secular aesthetic terms and categorized as a courtly romance centered around the amorous exploits of an imperial prince. A Buddhist view of the tale may also seem to be at odds with some of the work's qualities considered most appealing—its compelling plot and affective poetry, its wealth of detail concerning Heian life and court customs, and its vividly drawn characters of all moral persuasions, with their accessible humanity and seemingly lucid psychological interiority. Most of all, instances in the tale of ironic distance, humor, and even anti-Buddhist sentiment suggest an author who scrupulously avoided overt didacticism of any kind, as though the tale were written from a familiar secular humanist perspective. In this way, *The Tale of Genji* satisfies the demands of readers of modern novels, and surely for this reason its Buddhist elements may seem placed there only to "add a dash of melancholy" to the work.[3]

2. The earliest extant *Genji* commentary, *Genji Explicated* (*Genji shaku*, 1160) by Sesonji Koreyuki (d. 1175), is in fact contemporaneous with the earliest extant text of *The Tale of Genji* (the illustrated scrolls in the Tokugawa and Gotoh Art Museums). There are more than one hundred separate examples of premodern *Genji* commentaries, most which have yet to be studied in detail. One of the earliest to mention Murasaki Shikibu's Tendai Buddhist lineage and how an understanding of Buddhism was key to interpreting the tale was the *Genchū saihishō* (The most secret gleanings from the Suigenshō commentary, ca. 1313 (rev. 1364)). The text purports (as its title indicates) to excerpt the most hidden teachings from the partially lost *Genji* commentary of Minamoto no Chikayuki, the *Suigenshō* (mid-thirteenth century). For the text in Japanese of the *Genchū saihishō* see Ikeda, ed., *Genji monogatari taisei*, vol. 7. See also Tasaka, *Genji monogatari kyōjushi ronkō*. The highly influential *Kakaishō* (River and sea commentary, ca. 1387) by Yotsutsuji Yoshinari (1326–1402) continued in this vein, as did many of the commentaries produced in the fifteenth and sixteenth centuries, some of which will be referenced below. Lewis D. Cook presents a provocative overview of *Genji* commentaries in "Genre Trouble"; and for an excellent study of the entire history of *Genji* commentary combined with in-depth analysis of several premodern examples, see Kern, "Changing Perspectives on a Classic." Seminal studies in Japanese include Ii, *Genji monogatari chūshakushi no kenkyū: Muromachi Zenki*.

3. The quote is from Buruma, "The Sensualist," a review of Dennis Washburn's 2015 English translation of *The Tale of Genji*.

In fact, a backlash against a Buddhist interpretation of the tale started to gain momentum in the early modern period with the distinctive voices of commentators such as Kumazawa Banzan (1619–91). Armed with the philosophical tools of Neo-Confucianism and its inherent pragmatism and clear-cut morality, Banzan made a forceful case against the long tradition of Buddhist-oriented *Genji* commentaries in his own treatise on the tale.[4] As James McMullen has shown, Banzan was concerned above all with the implications of Buddhist notions of karma, transmigration, and any hint of predeterminism that might contradict the self-motivated morality at the core of his Confucian ethics. No writer was more influential in denying the validity of a Buddhist view of *Genji*, however, than Motoori Norinaga (1730–1801), whose treatise, *"The Tale of Genji": A Little Jeweled Comb* (*Genji monogatari Tama no ogushi*, 1799), incited a tenaciously secular approach to *Genji* criticism for generations to come. Norinaga rightly bristled at the idea that such a sublimely complex work of literature could be reduced to having a single Buddhist aim, a view that he believed the medieval commentaries promoted. He took note of the marked difference between the tale and Buddhist or Confucian moral texts that were intended to "encourage virtue and castigate vice" and criticized theories of the work that did not account for the fullness of its presentation of the human condition and emotion.[5] Norinaga arrived at his own theory of *mono no aware* (a sensitivity to the nature of things), which in essence gave him a framework for elaborating upon the tale's internal logic, in the process allowing him to create one of Japan's first sustained works of literary criticism. His interpretation took hold, and Norinaga's characterization of medieval

4. The treatise is called the *Discursive Commentary on the "Genji"* (*Genji gaiden*, late seventeenth century) and is Banzan's attempt to view the tale as consistent with Confucian philosophy; see the indispensable volume by McMullen, *Idealism, Protest, and the "Tale of Genji."*

5. See Thomas Harper's translation and introduction to Norinaga's treatise in Harper and Shirane, eds., *Reading "The Tale of Genji,"* pp. 411–506.

commentaries as steeped in superstition and arcane allegoresis was taken largely at face value from that point forward. On the other hand, annotators of *The Tale of Genji*, including the editors of modern editions of the tale, have always kept the medieval commentaries close at hand. Aside from their Buddhist framing, they constitute the most authoritative sources for understanding the difficult original text and Heian period culture and history and provide interlinear glosses on etymology, word definitions, debates on the meaning of passages, and lengthy citations of the sources of Murasaki's allusions from classical Japanese poetry and Chinese classics to official histories.

Given the level of erudition found in the medieval commentaries and the clear awareness of the text's complexity that they demonstrate, this essay questions whether the Buddhist foundations of the tale that they espoused should not be examined more closely. It suggests, moreover, that these texts in some ways prefigure modern theories of the novel that champion its capacity to elicit from the reader a unique form of empathic understanding.[6] In this regard, it is worth examining one of the main claims of these commentaries: that the Buddhist discourse on attaining insight into the nonduality of phenomena could be used as a means to illuminate the nature of the tale and to explain its value. The premodern *Genji* commentaries do not elaborate in great detail how the principles they espouse may be applied to the narrative, which may have been reserved for the oral teachings of which the written commentaries are often simply remnants. The analysis that follows therefore will pay close attention to the passages that do treat the topic in the commentaries, but it will also examine a number of largely unstudied pictorial artifacts produced in tandem with those texts for the crucial evidence they provide about

---

6. The description by Martha Nussbaum, for example, of how novels can function as "vehicles for Aristotelian morality" through their ability to engage the emotions and elicit an empathic response from the reader will be relevant; Nussbaum, *Love's Knowledge*, pp. 95–96.

how certain readers understood *Genji* as a philosophical text into the early modern period. This volume is, however, concerned with the *Genji* text itself, not its long history of reception and exegesis, which might take us far afield from the Heian period literary and philosophical interests of its author. To be sure there are sections in the *Genji* commentaries that approach the kind of allegorizing and numerological allegoresis so carefully studied by Susan Klein in the context of medieval commentaries on the *Tales of Ise*, which accord with medieval "revelatory" modes of reading and interpretation that are anachronistic to Murasaki Shikibu's era.[7] Moreover, it is important to keep in mind that the commentators under discussion had religious and political ties to Tendai institutions whose strength post-dates *The Tale of Genji*. But on balance the essence of the Tendai worldview, or "Tendai paradigm,"[8] advocated by the medieval texts and artifacts to be examined here, would have been familiar to the *Genji* author. Within her tale, which, to be sure, exemplifies the nonsectarian and ecumenical approach to religion characteristic of Heian courtiers, there are prominent references to Tendai texts. As Haruo Shirane and others have pointed out, meditative Tendai Buddhism and its promotion of salvation through one's own efforts, derived from the belief that the buddha nature is inherent in the individual, was one influential form of Buddhism in *The Tale of Genji*.[9] Examining the ideas of subsequent readers who attempted to understand the novel

7. Klein, *Allegories of Desire*. Later attempts to make the number of *Genji* chapters homologous to the twenty-eight chapters in eight fascicles of the *Lotus Sutra* by grouping certain chapters together, or to expand the chapters from fifty-four to sixty to make them match the sixty foundational texts in Tendai, are examples that suggest this kind of allegorizing approach.

8. Maeda, "Paradaimu to shite no bukkyō," pp. 254–72.

9. Shirane, *The Bridge of Dreams*, pp. 183–84. Also see Misumi, *Genji Monogatari to Tendai Jōdokyō*, 1. The Tendai monk Genshin (942–1017) and his *Essentials of Salvation* (*Ōjōyōshū*, 985) highly influenced Murasaki's thinking. As Robert F. Rhodes has argued, Genshin attempted to make Pure Land Buddhist teaching compatible with Tendai systems of meditation and accessible including the *nenbutsu* invocation, which is best understood as "Buddha contemplation"; see his *Genshin's Ōjōyōshū*, pp. 1–11.

holistically through the lens of Tendai philosophy may thus bring us closer to the intellectual heart of the tale than previously imagined, adding another dimension to our understanding of the relationship between Buddhist philosophy and literature.

BUDDHISM AND THE DEFENSE OF FICTION

More fundamental than Murasaki Shikibu's own affinities to Buddhist ideas, however, is the fact that she did not conceive of her tale from the perspective of a secular, postnaturalist writer. She inevitably sought to connect her characters, their actions, and their lives to the patterns of the universe as they were understood in Heian Japan, whether by Confucian, Buddhist, *kami*-centered, or other beliefs.[10] These were integral components of Murasaki Shikibu's endeavor; indeed it would be impossible to imagine a writer of her time period creating a narrative of this scale and ambition in which characters were merely representations of the particular or the self in a modern novelistic sense. Although *Genji* meets many of the criteria associated with the modern novel—irony, subversion, multivocality—it is fundamentally concerned with what Lukács terms "essences" that structure the tale.[11] Literature, and poetry in particular, were understood as more than the personal expression of an individual—rather, in its highest form, as a process by which latent patterns of the universe become

10. The secondary literature on these topics in Japanese is vast, but one recent work of note that demonstrates how the tale is structurally interwoven with beliefs and protocols of *kami* worship is Han, *Genji monogatari ni okeru kami shinkō*. This study and others show the benefit of considering how Murasaki juxtaposed different philosophical systems in the formal construction of the work.

11. See Lukács, *The Theory of the Novel*. Borrowing Lukács's schema of the history of the novel, Genji would be more analogous to the hero of an ancient Greek epic than the alienated protagonist of the modern novel because his character is premised on the notion that meaning inheres in the relationship between the individual and the universe.

manifest, filtered through human consciousness.[12] The author of *The Tale of Genji* could not have attempted to elevate the *monogatari* as a genre, which she certainly was doing, by presenting the struggles and triumphs of her characters as unconnected to a larger, unseen order of things. Without the sense of a latent force motivating her characters and events, her *monogatari* would never rise above the pejorative stereotype of tales that circulated in the Heian period. The locus classicus for the belittlement of tales is the preface to a work of true Buddhist didacticism contemporary with *Genji*, *The Three Jewels* (*Sanbōe*, ca. 984). It warns against the frivolous depiction of relations between men and women in *monogatari* and admonishes the reader to "not let your heart get caught up even briefly in these tangled roots of evil, these forests of words."[13] But as a preface to a compilation of Buddhist didactic tales with one goal in mind, it also takes issue with the lack of purpose of *monogatari* and the way they are written, describing them as nothing more than "meaningless phrases like so much flotsam in the sea, with no two words together that have any more solid basis than does swamp grass growing by a river bank."[14] In many ways, *The Tale of Genji* can be seen as one long rebuttal to this notion of the meaningless episodic nature of tales in the way it sustains its plot, which has its own internal consistency, across so many chapters. In other words, there are unifying principles at the heart of Murasaki's tale that many commentators over the centuries chose to articulate in Buddhist terms.

---

12. See Owen, *Traditional Chinese Poetry and Poetics*, for example, on the nature of the Chinese couplet as pattern and his discussion of analogy and the notion of a correlative cosmos. Also helpful is Tomiko Yoda's analysis of the function of *waka* in the tale and her critique of interpretations that would understand it as pure lyric expression or through the lens of post-Romantic poetry; see her "Fractured Dialogues."

13. Kamens, *The Three Jewels*, p. 93. In Japanese, Mabuchi et al., eds., *Sanbōe; Chūkōsen*, p. 6.

14. Kamens, *The Three Jewels*, p. 93.

Later commentators felt justified in proclaiming the Buddhist intent of *The Tale of Genji* because of specific references to Tendai. A scene in Chapter 10 "Sakaki" for example shows Genji studying the foundational texts of Tendai, among them *The Great Calming and Contemplation* (Ch. *Mohe zhiguan*, J. *Makashikan*) by Zhiyi (538–97), the meditation text in which the practice and doctrine of Tendai were most fully explained.[15] There are also the metanarrative references to Buddhist ideas in the famous "theory of tales" (*monogatari ron*), or "defense of tales," embedded in Chapter 25 "Hotaru."[16] There Genji enters into a debate about the value of fiction with the character Tamakazura, the secret daughter of Genji's rival Tō no Chūjō. Genji has been harboring Tamakazura in his Rokujō mansion under the false pretense that she is his long-lost daughter, thus establishing an ersatz parent and child relationship taken as truth by those around them. The middle-aged Genji finds the young woman Tamakazura alluring, reminiscent as she is of her mother, his deceased lover Yūgao, and Genji's sexual overtures toward her are relentless. The scenario creates an interesting tension in which Genji's desire can be viewed as incestuous if interpreted according to the pair's false projected reality, as opposed to their private truth, of which the reader is aware. The author thus establishes an ingenious and highly charged context for a discussion about the merits of fictional tales, as a conversation between two characters whose situation forces the reader into a heightened awareness of truth, falsity, and representation. This mise-en-abyme thus functions as a correlative to the dialogue, which develops into a statement on the link between the perceived reality

---

15. There are of course literary reasons for depicting Genji perusing this recondite opus, such as demonstrating the depth of the protagonist's philosophical capabilities, but to later commentators with Tendai affiliations the scene was interpreted as doctrinally significant.

16. The "defense of fiction passage" seems to have been influenced by the rhetorical structure of the *Lotus Sutra*. See Abe Akio, "Murasaki Shikibu no bukkyō shisō," cited by Shirane, *Bridge of Dreams*, p. 245 n. 4.

of fiction and the nature of truth in the Mahayana Buddhist understanding of phenomenal experience.

The passage begins when Genji enters a room in which he sees
Tamakazura immersed in reading illustrated stories and he begins
criticizing her for allowing her heart to be moved by pointless tales,
in which "the truth would be very rare" (g3/210–11; *makoto wa ito
sukunakaramu*). His observation echoes the language of previous
criticisms of tales, as in the *Sanbōe* preface, as potentially deleterious
to women, who tend to be easily swayed by their romantic content.
But the passage is constructed to lead to a defense of *monogatari*,
and it does so gradually by next having Genji begin to concede the
positive aspects of the affective power of fiction: "even among this
mass of falsehoods we find some stories that are properly written and
exhibit enough sensitivity to make us imagine what really happened"
(w519). Yet he still labels fictional tales "falsehoods" (*soragoto*), until
Tamakazura rebukes him, calling attention to Genji's own spinning
of lies. After this, Genji's rhetoric shifts once more and he begins to
praise *monogatari*, claiming that tales are in fact better than official
histories: "Tales have provided a record of events in the world since
the age of the gods, whereas histories of Japan like the *Nihongi* give
only partial accounts of the facts. The type of tales you are reading
provide detailed descriptions that make more sense and follow the
way of history" (w520). Finally, Genji describes how tales are written and the importance of including both good and bad examples in
fiction. This allows for an analogy to be drawn between tales and the
teachings found in Buddhist sutras:

> "For that reason, the narrow-minded conclusion that all tales
> are falsehoods misses the heart of the matter. Even the Dharma,
> which was explicated for us through Sakyamuni's splendidly
> pure heart, contains 'expedient means' (*hōben* 方便), those
> parables that he told to illustrate the truth of the Law. They may

seem contradictory to parts in the sutras and will raise doubts in the mind of an unenlightened person. However, if you carefully consider the matter, you realize that all have a single aim. The distinction between enlightenment and delusion is really no different from the distinction between the good and the bad in tales such as these. In the end, the correct view of the matter is that nothing is empty." (w520, modified)

Because of the self-reflexive nature of this paragraph, it was long perceived as the author of *Genji* using Genji the character to mount a Buddhist argument for the relevance of fiction. The claim goes so far as to analogize the use of negative examples, or evildoing characters, with the expedient means found in the teachings of the Buddha. Only the unenlightened would take the expedient means of the sutra, or of the tale, at face value, unable to perceive the single aim of the Dharma, whatever expedient form it may take. The passage paved the way for an understanding of the tale as infused with an awareness of Buddhist nondualism. The final phrase is the most evocative in this regard, for here Murasaki Shikibu invokes the notion that enlightenment, or "Bodhi-wisdom" (*bodai*), is indistinguishable from delusion, or "passionate attachments" (*bonnō*). The seeming paradox comes from the belief that all phenomena are interpenetrating and interdependent. According to this doctrine then, even what one may perceive to be evil acts found in the tale are expedient means to Buddhist liberation, and like everything else, they cannot exist apart from Bodhi-wisdom; both are constitutive of each other.

This may seem to be nothing more than a convenient rationale for depicting as many illicit scenes of romance as possible, or at least enough for Murasaki to keep her readers interested with "the strange and wondrous details of bad behavior," as Genji also mentions in the defense of fiction. In the lines immediately following the passage cited above, when Tamakazura rejects his advances, Genji presses her further, accusing of her of being unfilial in a way that contradicts the Buddhist Law. This seems to prefigure works of later medieval litera-ture that put to sardonic use the trope "the passionate attachments are indistinguishable from Bodhi-wisdom" (*bonnō soku bodai*). The "defense of tales" passage is thus complex and contradictory and entertaining, and as Richard Okada argued, it is therefore important that we not "universalize either the 'critique' or the 'defense' and turn them into self-standing 'arguments' or controlling metaphors of the tale. They form arguments, but the intertextual forces keep them pulled in specific directions related to class, gender, and genealogi-cal concerns."[17] Many of the medieval *Genji* commentary authors, although their multifaceted texts covering all aspects of the tale and its intertexts were far from reductive, continued to promote the Buddhist philosophical framework precisely as a controlling meta-phor. Rather than reducing the tale to a pedantic work of overt reli-gious didacticism, as Norinaga and others believed it did, however, the approach had the potential to allow for a holistic appreciation of the tale in all of its multivocality, subversiveness, and self-aware inter-textuality, the very techniques and qualities that allow it to transcend the didactic and the straightforward.

ENTERING THE FOUR GATES TOWARD PRAJÑĀ-WISDOM

In the mid-seventeenth century, for example, when the scholar and poet Matsunaga Teitoku (1571–1653) recounted what he had learned about *The Tale of Genji* from his teacher Kujō Tanemichi (1507–94), he began by explaining the tale's relationship to Tendai

---

17. Okada, *Figures of Resistance*, p. 231.

Buddhist thought.[18] In the course of his verbal teachings, Tanemichi had explicated *Genji* according to the idea that it contains "profound insights beyond discourse," a notion that he summed up as the "theory of cessation and insight" (止観の説 *shikan no setsu*), taken from Zhiyi's treatise and its exegetical legacy.[19] He explained that, "as a story written according to the Buddhist Dharma, it differs from usual tales, with profound insights in its every poem and every word." According to Tanemichi, *The Tale of Genji* is suffused with insights based on nondualistic thinking, a theory that was significantly premised on the idea that Murasaki Shikibu had mastered Tendai meditative practice.

Nothing crystallizes this Tendai theory of the author and her tale better than a group of portrait icons of Murasaki Shikibu that began to appear by the late sixteenth century and continued into the eighteenth century (Figure 8.1). The genre represents a type of image that was hung as a Buddhist icon in the so-called Genji Room at Ishiyamadera temple, where legend had it that Murasaki Shikibu had conceived of the idea for *The Tale of Genji*.[20] Such paintings depict Murasaki Shikibu with brush in hand, usually with ink and paper on her writing desk, and include three square cartouches at the top of the composition.[21] These cartouches,

---

18. Teitoku recounts Tanemichi's words in *Taionki* (Record of a debt of gratitude, ca. 1644–48), p. 35; . This passage is singled out for discussion in Maeda, "Paràdaimu to shite no bukkyō," p. 254.

19. The phrasing, a "theory of *shikan*," seems to be unique to Tanemichi, and perhaps something only communicated verbally in the lectures, exclusive teachings, and transmission of knowledge between teacher and disciple that were an essential part of the culture of *Genji* commentaries. Nevertheless, Tanemichi is drawing upon a long tradition of explicating *Genji* using the ideas in the *Makashikan*). For these ideas in Tanemichi's own commentary (1575), see also Nomura, ed., *Mōshinshō*. .

20. Katagiri, "Tendai shimon no san wo motsu Murasaki Shikibu zu," pp. 155–60. Also see McCormick, "Ishiyamadera and the Buddhist Veneration of Murasaki Shikibu."

21. This type of Murasaki icon is still hung with a small altar before it in the Genji Room adjacent to the main hall at Ishiyamadera. For more historical detail on the function of Murasaki

Figure 8.1 Tosa Mitsuoki (1617–91). *Portrait Icon of Murasaki Shikibu.* Edo period, seventeenth century. Hanging scroll, ink and color on silk, 90.5 × 52.7 cm. Ishiyamadera Collection, Shiga.

called *shikishi*, bear striking calligraphic inscriptions beginning on the far right with the so-called four gates ("four stages of contemplation," *shimon* 四門) of Tendai, followed by two *waka* poems from Murasaki Shikibu's personal poetry collection in the central cartouche and one in the cartouche on the far left. The four gates correspond to four stages of contemplating phenomena, and their inclusion here in a position that amounts to a preface for the painting announces the work's allegiance to the *shikan* theory of *Genji*.[22] As Katagiri Yayoi pointed out in her study of these images, numerous medieval *Genji* commentaries present Murasaki Shikibu as a figure within the Dharma lineage of Tendai, as someone who had mastered the "three discernments in one mind" (*isshin sangan* 一心三観).[23] The "three discernments" (*sankan* 三観) are methods of contemplation from within phenomenal experience.[24] Thus, these texts assert that the *Genji* author had contemplated phenomena from the perspective of "emptiness" (nothingness, or the void, *kū* 空), "conventional existence" (a temporary acceptance of provisional reality, *kari* 假), and ultimately "the middle" (*chū* 中). To arrive at the middle is to understand simultaneously phenomena as both empty and provisionally existing and thus interdependent

Shikibu icons, see McCormick, "Purple Displaces Crimson"; and "'Murasaki Shikibu Ishiyamadera mōde-zu.'"

22. Although many *Genji* commentators were affiliated with Tendai institutions, the four gates were not exclusive to Tendai, and the *shikan* theory of *Genji* could be understood as a general expression of nonduality, making the paintings appropriate for installation at Ishiyamadera, a Shingon Buddhist temple.

23. Katagiri, "Tendai shimon no san o motsu Murasaki Shikibu zu," pp. 156–58. In addition to the *Genchū saihishō* (ca. 1313), the *Kakaishō* (ca. 1387), the *Rōkashō* (1504), and *Mōshinshō* (1575) mentioned above, other medieval *Genji* commentaries that mention Murasaki's Tendai credentials include *Genji monogatari teiyō* (1432) by Imagawa Norimasa, which provides commentary on all 795 *waka* in the tale as well as summaries of the chapters.

24. As described by Neil Donner and Daniel B. Stevenson in their "Introduction" to the recent complete translation of the *Makashikan*. See Zhiyi, *Clear Serenity, Quiet Insight*, tr. Swanson, p. 8.

and nondual. Thus having calmed her mind to a state of cessation (*shi*止), fixated on Prajñā-wisdom and free from delusional thinking, Murasaki achieved transcendent insight (*kan* 観) into an ultimate nondualism between subject and object, self and other, and all phenomena.

The calligraphy inscription of the four gates on the painting cites a further parsing of the three truths and the three discernments, presenting the methods of contemplation as a tetralemma (Figure 8.2):

    (a) existence (有門)
    (b) nothingness (emptiness 空門)
    (c) both existence and nothingness (亦有亦空門)
    (d) neither existence nor nothingness (非有非空門)

In this scheme, the extremes of existence and nothingness, (a) and (b), are similar to the three discernments and the three truths, but

Figure 8.2 Detail of Figure 8.1.

the middle, the ultimate synthesis, is broken down more precisely, as (c) and (d), to convey the state when "existence and emptiness are 'simultaneously illumined and simultaneously eradicated'. When all vestiges of dualism (that is, root nescience) vanish, the transcendent and unalloyed middle—the third and absolute truth—is revealed."[25] Virtually all of the medieval *Genji* commentaries mention the four gates, with the most detailed explication of the philosophy found in the opening section of *Genji monogatari teiyō* (1432).[26] The painting of Murasaki Shikibu at work writing her masterpiece paired with a textual expression of what is achieved through "cessation and insight" thus posits for *The Tale of Genji* a philosophical origin story that goes well beyond the general trope of divine inspiration.

If *The Tale of Genji* was to be posited by later commentators as an embodiment of the principle of nondualism, that means its words had to be understood as functioning symbolically, as a manifestation of the ultimate truth. The first person to theorize this notion in relation to Japanese literature was the twelfth-century figure Fujiwara no Shunzei (1114–1204), who explicitly linked Zhiyi's "cessation and insight" to poetic composition. In his poetic treatise *Korai fūteishō* (Poetic styles from antiquity the present, 1197), Shunzei cites the opening passage of the *Makashikan* and goes on to draw an analogy between the ineffable state of *shikan* and the "deep mind" (*fukaki kokoro*) of poetry. As Esperanza Ramirez-Christensen has argued, Shunzei implies that the "poetic experience is essentially similar to the religious state of meditation and that the ontological existence of the poem is best conceived

---

25. Donner and Stevenson, "Introduction," p. 11.
26. Inaga, ed., *Imagawa Norimasa, Genji monogatari teiyō*, pp. 10–12. As a cumulative tradition of exegesis, the commentaries necessarily cite previous commentaries, including statements about the four gates, which might make the repetition seem rote.

in terms of Tendai's three-dimensional view of reality."[27] Although space limitations do not allow for elaboration here, commentators like Tanemichi, quoted above, were very much the inheritors of Shunzei's rhetoric.[28]

The tetralemma on the painting of Murasaki Shikibu is best seen as providing a means of understanding Murasaki Shikibu's writing, like Shunzei's use of *Makashikan* in articulating a method for composing and evaluating Japanese poetry. It does this by asking the viewer metaphorically to pass through the four gates on the right cartouche and then, with the mind prepared, to read the subsequent two *waka* poems by the author to the left. Both *waka* come from the collection of Murasaki Shikibu's verse where they are presented with headnotes and between other verses that contextualize them to a certain extent as grief poems, the first said to have been written sometime after the death of her husband:

Kokoro dani	Is there a fate
Ikanaru mi ni ka	That could at very least
Kanau ramu	Bring satisfaction?
Omoishiredomo	The truth I realize
Omoishirarezu	But cannot yet accept.[29]

27. The translations of Shunzei's treatise are from Ramirez-Christensen, *Emptiness and Temporality*, p. 88. See Bushelle, "The Joy of the Dharma," p. 222, for the correspondence between Shunzei's *kokoro, kotoba*, and *sugata* and the threefold truth.

28. Tanemichi and others traced their *Genji* scholarly lineage back to Shunzei through his son, the famous poet, calligrapher, and scholar Fujiwara no Teika (1162–1241). It is important to stress, however, that Shunzei's poetics were not exclusively Buddhist, as discussed in Riley Soles, "The Ecstasy of the Text," while investigating more fully the ritual context for Shunzei's Buddhist understanding of *Genji*, as undertaken by Bushelle in "The Joy of the Dharma."

29. Translated by Bowring, *Murasaki Shikubu, Her Diary and Poetic Memoirs*, p. 234. The poem (no. 56 in the collection) has no preface and follows directly from no. 55, which was said to have been written after the mourning period for her husband had ended.

The second poem follows a headnote that explains how Murasaki composed upon reading through the old letters of a recently deceased female friend, also a serving lady at court:

Tare ka yo ni	Who will read it?
Nagaraete mimu	Who will live forever
Kakitomeshi	In this world
Ato wa kiesenu	A letter left behind
Katami naredomo	In her undying memory.[30]

Within the narrativized frame of the anthologized collection, which presents the poems in chronological order, the two verses can be interpreted as personal reactions to specific circumstances. But as poems that reflect upon the nature and limited temporality of human existence, one can see how they would be selected and repurposed for use on Murasaki Shikibu portrait icons, the ultimate goal of which was to link *The Tale of Genji* to Tendai Buddhist beliefs. The poems are decontextualized from the facts of Shikibu's life as presented in the poetry collection, but the preface cartouche of the four gates gives them a new context, asking that they be read as metaphors for the Tendai approach to understanding reality.

When viewed through the frame of the four gates, which asks that one attempt to see an ultimate reality beyond the phenomenal world, each word in the first poem may be perceived as Buddhist in meaning. Rather than questioning her worldly "fate" and whether it will bring "satisfaction," the poet in the first poem may therefore be asking more abstractly if there is no "body"

---

30. Ibid., p. 255.

(*mi*) that can be brought into alignment (*kanau*) with "mind" (*kokoro*). The second half of the first poem shows that the verse focuses entirely on a perceiving subject who paradoxically states that, though she may "contemplate and reach understanding" (*omoishiredomo*), she "cannot contemplate and reach understanding" (*omoishirarezu*). The repetition of the compound verb "to contemplate and know" (*omoishiru*) in positive and negative form recalls the affirmative–negative dialectic between existence and nonexistence (or nothingness) in the four gates. Read this way, the first poem could be taken to describe contemplative practice and the process of moving through the different levels of discernment. Or more abstractly, the poem's implied thinking subject cancels itself out through the parallelism of the phrasing, poetically rehearsing the negation of the conventional self that must precede a discernment of the middle.

The second poem on the painting relates to *mujōkan*, the awareness of the impermanence of existence, through the voice of a poet who notes the irony of the written word enduring beyond the evanescent life of the writer. Although this poem has been interpreted as expressing the author's anxiety over making a mark in the world and leaving a name for herself as a writer, the application of the Tendai filter to the verse can produce a very different interpretation. The poem also calls attention to the lack of inherent meaning of the written word and its dependency on the perceiving subject to imbue it with value. The poem asks if "anyone will live on in this world to read" (literally "see," *mimu*) these letters, these "traces that do not disappear" (*ato wa kiesenu*), thus imagining a future in which the letters have become empty signifiers, meaningless until they are interpreted by a reader. The idea that the written word is contingent accords with notions about the provisional nature of language, as found in the preface to the *Makashikan*:

> Through great compassion [the Buddha] has pity on all who have not heard [the Dharma, and therefore expounds the Dharma with provisional indicators such as words]. It is as if by raising a [round] fan you replicate [the image of] the moon that is hidden behind a range of mountains, or by [artificially] shaking a tree you can teach about [the nature of] air when the wind has stopped.[31]

The passage goes on to warn about becoming trapped and too reliant upon texts, and calls for reading with insight, to see beyond the literal. By using the image of the round fan that stands in for the hidden moon, it shows the central place of metaphor as a mechanism for perceiving the ultimate reality of which the written word can be a manifestation.

This second poem by Murasaki, by envisioning a future world from which the poet and the poem's readers have also departed, emphasizes the mutability of existence, which was an integral part of Buddhist philosophy and which some commentators considered to be the central point of *The Tale of Genji*. It is this awareness of impermanence (*mujōkan*) that allows an individual to emulate the compassion of the Buddha, the radical empathy that comes from understanding the indivisibility of self and other. And it was the ability of *The Tale of Genji* to spark a profound understanding of impermanence in its readers through a narrative that traces an entire arc of a human life that made it essential to those who posited the author's enlightened mind. Kujō Tanemichi, whose belief in a "*shikan* theory" of reading *Genji* was described above, wrote elsewhere that "to understand the principle (*kotowari* 理) [that all that flourishes must fade] in the most profound

31. Zhiyi, *Clear Serenity*, tr. Swanson, vol. 1, p. 126.

way, nothing compares to reading *The Tale of Genji*."[32] For Tanemichi and others, Buddhism and literature were thus mutually reinforcing; fiction could be an effective and worthy vehicle for conveying Buddhist truth, but to understand the deeper meanings of the text one needed to grasp the philosophical apparatus of *shikan*. The portrait icon of Murasaki thus provides a model for understanding how to use *shikan* to understand her fiction as well, modeling a mode of reading and interpretation beneath the surface level of the text.

MOONLIGHT AND METAPHYSICS: SUMA AND AKASHI

The question remains as to how Buddhist philosophy could be used to interpret specific narrative moments in *The Tale of Genji* itself. Some hints in the commentaries appear in sections devoted to explaining the mysterious absent chapter, "Kumogakure," blank for all but its title. The chapter comes after Genji's final appearance in the tale in Chapter 41 "Maboroshi" and is thought to have stood in for a depiction of Genji's death, which many believed would have been beyond expression in words.[33] Medieval commentators used this chapter as an opportunity to expound upon the Tendai paradigm, and in the process, a nascent theory of fiction based on the "three truths" began to emerge. The author of the *Genji monogtari teiyō* for example explains how reading the fictional tale (*tsukuri monogatari*) relates to the three truths: to consider the deaths of characters is to contemplate phenomena through "emptiness"; understanding the character of the Kiritsubo Emperor as a symbol for, or analogous to, the historical figure of the

---

32. See Kujō, *Genji monogatari kyōenki*, p. 670.
33. In a translator's note (w881–82) Washburn succinctly outlines the debates about the original existence of this chapter.

Daigo Emperor (r. 897–930) is said to be akin to contemplating "provisional" reality; and finally, the wordless "Kumogakure" chapter is a perfect expression of the ultimate truth of "the middle," an expression of the void that encompasses both emptiness and contingent reality. The scheme of the three truths could thus facilitate an understanding of the tale as a whole, and its details, while enriching the experience of literary symbolism—essentially holding two things in one's mind at once. The experience of reading literature could therefore be linked to the so-called provisional gate, one that Tendai teachings enjoined disciples to undertake as one step on the path to enlightenment.

While elaboration of a Buddhist theory of the tale in the commentaries is minimal, another type of Murasaki portrait icon showing the author at the temple of Ishiyamadera composing her tale is useful in this regard because of its citation of a passage from Chapter 12 "Suma" (Figure 8.3). The painting depicts the popular genesis story for *The Tale of Genji* in which Murasaki's initial writing of her tale occurs not within the environs of the imperial court, but at the Buddhist temple just outside the capital:

> Charged by her highness the Imperial Consort with the task of writing *The Tale of Genji*, Lady Murasaki travelled to the temple of Ishiyamadera to pray for inspiration. On the fifteenth night of the eighth month she looked out over Lake Biwa, calmed her mind and gazed upon the moon's glowing orb reflected on the surface of the water, and suddenly the idea was born. She picked up her brush, but with no paper at hand, she reached for the scrolls of the *Great Perfection of Transcendent Wisdom Sutra* (S. *Prajñāpāramitā*, J. *Daihannyakyō*) resting on the Buddhist altar, and turning them over wrote the Suma and Akashi chapters.[34]

34. These are key elements of the legend found in medieval texts and painting inscriptions; see McCormick, "Purple Displaces Crimson."

Figure 8.3 Tosa Mitsuoki (1617–91). *Murasaki Shikibu at Ishiyamadera*. Edo period, seventeenth century. Hanging scroll, ink and color on silk, 86.0 × 46.5 cm. Ishiyamadera Collection, Shiga.

Such passages claim for *Genji* an originary moment rooted in meditative practice and further wrap the tale's authorship in spiritual imagery, by among other things depicting it as having been inscribed upon the back of a Buddhist sutra. Other versions of the legend suggested that Murasaki Shikibu was herself an incarnation of the bodhisattva Kannon sent into the world to set her readers on the righteous path of Buddhist devotion. In much the same way that Murasaki and Kannon are two and yet one, the temple of Ishiyamadera was said to be indistinguishable from the bodhisattva realm of Potalaka. The artist has composed a painting that on the surface appears to depict a straightforward image of a court lady writing at her desk, but for the initiated it functions as a visual metaphor for an enlightened being, at the moment of achieving stillness and insight by clearing her mind and meditating on the reflection of the moon.

The legendary date of the tale's creation is also important, as the increasing illumination in the course of the lunar cycle is a simile in the *Makashikan* for gradual enlightenment, which achieves perfection on the night when the moon is at its fullest, the fifteenth of the eighth month. It is on that night, which Zhiyi likened to have an expression of complete and perfect Buddhahood, that Murasaki Shikibu meditates on the moon and is enlightened. According to a *shikan* theory of the novel, that achievement of Buddhist insight merges with the writing of the tale, which is said to begin with a scene from "Suma." That scene describes Genji seeing the brilliant moon shining over the sea at Suma, where he has been living in self-imposed exile, and he recalls that it is the fifteenth of the eighth month. The painting explicitly connects the full moon that Murasaki gazed upon at Ishiyamadera to the moon gazed upon by her protagonist through the inscription that floats above the temple to the left of the moon in the upper register of the painting. It cites several lines and verse from the "Suma" chapter:

The full moon rose vivid and bright, bringing back memories to Genji. "That's right . . . tonight is the fifteenth." Staring up at the face of the moon, he lovingly imagined the music that would be playing on a night like this at the palace, with all the ladies gazing out at the night sky. When he murmured a line from Bai Juyi— "Feelings for acquaintances of old, now two thousand leagues distant"[35]—his attendants could not restrain their tears. With indescribable yearning he recalled the poem Fujitsubo sent him complaining about how the "ninefold mists" kept her from the palace. As memories of this and other moments came to him, he wept aloud. He heard a voice saying, "The hour is late." However, he could not bring himself to retire. (w277)

Miru hodo zo	Only while I watch
Shibashi nagusamu	For that moment, comes solace,
Meguriawan	But round to meeting
Tsuki no Miyako wa	With the Moon Capital—how far
Haruka naredo mo	Is that circle's joining still.[36]

Genji longs for the music at the palace and imagines those in the capital gazing up at the same moon. He recites a line by Bai Juyi (772–846) also composed on the fifteenth night of the eighth month in which the poet longs for his friend far away and remembers those he has left behind. The moon at Suma functions as a pivot mentally transporting Genji and the reader back to the capital and emphasizing his isolation on the coast. It is at once a melancholic and a beautiful device that allows the reader to briefly embody the perspective of Genji, of Fujitsubo and others in the capital, and of Murasaki the author—all sharing this vision of the moon.

35. *Baishi wenji* (*Hakushi monjū*) *juan* 14, no. 724, cited with commentary in g2/516.
36. Here quoted in the translation of Cranston, *A Waka Anthology*, p. 764.

The invocation of the "Suma" chapter in the *Genji* origin myth thus creates the perfect meditation on the Buddhist notion of nonduality. The moon is of course everywhere at once, and thus functions as a master metaphor for the way the buddha nature infuses every particle in the universe. The motif of the moon in the narrative creates a focal point for the switching of subject positions and enables a narrativized example of intersubjectivity between fictional characters and between the author and her protagonist contemplating the same moon on the same night. The *shikan* theory of the novel seems to say that the flash of insight that poetry has the capacity to engender may also arise from such moments in fiction like *The Tale of Genji*. The theory hinges upon a sensitivity to language and seeing within the figural moon (or in other characters such as the word for sky/void) the potential for metaphysical meaning. It allows for a reading of the tale in which a moon is never merely a moon, but might always be a metaphor for enlightenment, and in which nothing should ever be taken too literally.

When such intersubjectivity is linked with empathy, literary allusion can be tinged with Buddhist morality. The citation of a poem by Bai Juyi in the "Suma" passage, for example, composed on the same night of the year and thus beneath the same full moon, seems to collapse time and space in a way that accords with the nondualistic ideal. It frames Genji's own sorrow as a sentiment that had been felt in the past by the ancient poet and that would be felt again in the future, suggesting the continuous mind and delusional notion of short-term temporal divisions. Intertextuality thus becomes an expression of Buddhist belief and its attendant morality. What therefore might be taken as a lyrical expression of personal loneliness and longing in fact recalls Shunzei's comments on how poetic grace or beauty (*yūgen*) should reflect an achieved state of "insight into the profoundly moving character of things (*aware no fukaki koto*)," rooted in "human feeling" (*hito no nasake*). Esperanza Ramirez-Christensen

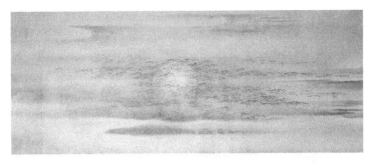

Figure 8.4 Tosa Mitsusada (1738–1806). *Scenes from the Suma Chapter of The Tale of Genji.* Edo period, eighteenth century. Handscroll, ink and light colors on paper, 38.1 × 949.9 cm. Harvard Art Museums, Cambridge, MA.

has explained Shunzei's understanding of "human feeling" as not "feeling as individual subjective emotion, but rather invoked in the context of an interpersonal, or dialogical, reciprocal relation—of a compassion extended by the one eliciting a profound response in the other," which he linked to an awareness of and sorrow for the human condition (*mujōkan*).[37] That the image of the moon on the water in the "Suma" passage becomes an emblem for the eradication of dualist thinking and the fixation point for the luminous quiescence of cessation and contemplation of *shikan* was undoubtedly grasped by certain readers. When the artist Tosa Mitsusada illustrated the scene of Genji contemplating the moon in exile (Figure 8.4), for example, he chose to depict nothing but a softly glowing orb merging with the blue waves and the white clouds, a ghostly image that comes in and out of focus, at once a moon above the clouds and a shimmering reflection on the water, casting the light of a metaphysical moon on the shores of Suma.

While the words of Shunzei noted above referred specifically to poetry, a fictional work like *Genji* could have evoked the existential

37. Ramirez-Christensen, *Emptiness and Temporality*, p. 82.

intersubjectivity of Zhiyi's philosophy through its mode of narration. *The Tale of Genji* has long been characterized as a psychological novel, earning its title because of the preponderance of characters who are "always thinking about what other characters are thinking."[38] A few paragraphs before the passage from "Suma" quoted on the paintings, for example, Genji's actions toward his men stem from an attempt to show that he understands their thoughts. Genji speaks a verse out loud to himself that reflects upon the sadness of those dependent on him and lamenting his absence in the capital:

Koiwabite	Weary with yearning,
Naku ne ni magau	Weeping, now the cries that come
Uranami wa	Mingle with the waves . . .
Omou kata yori	Waves that break before the wind
Kaze ya fukuran	That blows for the longed-for land?[39]

Hearing his poem, his attendants were startled awake. Seeing how splendid Genji looked, they were overcome by emotion, and as they arose unsteadily they were quietly wiping their noses to disguise their tears.

Genji wondered, *How must my attendants feel? For my sake alone they have come wandering with me to this sorry existence, having left behind their comfortable, familiar homes and parted with parents and siblings from whom even the briefest absence would be hard to bear.*[40]

---

38. See, for example, Raymond Mortimer's 1925 review of Waley's translation of *Genji*, "A New Planet"; and recent work on *Genji* and theory of mind. See Vincent, "Sex on the Mind: Queer Theory Meets Cognitive Theory." .
39. Here quoted in the translation of Cranston, *A Waka Anthology*, pp. 762–63.
40. The italics are from the Washburn translation, where they are used to indicate a character's interior monologue.

Such musings made him miserable, but then he realized that it must make his attendants feel forlorn to see him so down-hearted like this. And so, during the days that followed, he diverted them with playful banter, and in moments of idle leisure he would make scrolls with poems. He also drew remarkable-looking sketches and paintings. . . . Before coming to Suma he had heard about the views of the sea and mountains here . . . he depicted those rocky shores—their incomparable beauty truly surpassed anything he had imagined—in charcoal sketches of unrivalled skill. (w275)

Certainly, the poems in the *Genji* can reflect the tropes of post-language thinking prized in Tendai Buddhist aesthetics, but they are also situated within an established narrative world that enables a reader to see the morality of nonduality in practice. Genji's experience of exile as a nadir in his personal and political trajectory functions in many ways in the novel, but from a spiritual point of view, it creates an isolated meditative environment for the character in which he can be shown to exhibit a new awareness for the pain and suffering of others. And the author makes sure to show that he does not wallow in his grief but, as in the passage above, understands that he must ease the suffering of his loyal men. He subsequently distracts them with banter and marvelous paintings and drawings that capture the awesome physical landscape around them. Genji thus acts dutifully, engaging in moral behavior (easing the pain of his men) derived from a projection of thought that is itself a simulation of nondualistic thinking. Genji's morality is not derived from a higher power, but from an autonomous self that uses the power of the mind to determine proper action. In this particular example Genji's morality accords with the Middle Way of emptiness. Moreover, Genji comforts his men by aesthetic means: recognizing the sublimity of the landscape around him, he captures its beauty in images to uplift them. In so doing he becomes an artist whose creations are motivated by human feeling, showing the moral dimension of beauty. The paintings, because of their inherent affective power, will help Genji to emerge victorious in the overall trajectory of the novel; these are the very paintings created in Suma and Akashi that in the famous "picture contest" of Chapter 17 "Eawase" help his team win Emperor Reizei's favor, and later they symbolically affirm the ascendancy of Genji's daughter as empress. This daughter, whose mother is the woman Genji meets in Akashi, will in time make Genji the grandfather of an emperor, and it is her rise and that of her family that stands as the most important subplot of the tale. The author thus links her protagonist's moral actions to a plot structured with the force of Buddhist causality.

This essay has attempted to explore how figures in history who engendered the notion of a Buddhist philosophical foundation for *The Tale of Genji* might have actually applied a "theory of *shikan*" to reading the tale. Two different types of Murasaki Shikibu portrait icons produced in the milieu of Tendai *Genji* commentaries were used as models for reading and interpretation. With explicit references to Buddhist philosophy in their inscriptions in one type, and a key passage from the "Suma" chapter of the narrative in the other, the paintings provide an impetus for thinking about how essential ideas about nonduality, and by extension the morality of empathy, were applied to the *Genji*. The commentaries and paintings, although dating from the medieval to the early modern period, represent a strain of thought and a Buddhist relationship to language that was familiar to the *Genji* author herself. The commentaries were never solely Buddhist in focus, and even the patrons of the Murasaki Shikibu portrait icons were not single-minded in their approach to the tale. When Genji empathizes with his men in Suma and gazes out at the moon over the water, he does not achieve Buddhist insight, but goes on to struggle with his own self-professed sexual proclivities and lapses in

judgement and morality. *The Tale of Genji* contains no perfectly virtuous Buddhist exemplars, and even the question of whether Genji
successfully manages to renounce the world in the Buddhist manner
after he apparently determines to do so remains ambiguous at the
end of the chapter in which he makes his last appearance. In fact, the
author of *Genji* often makes a point of matching seemingly serious
Buddhist references with subsequent passages that appear to under-
cut any possibility of a didactic message. The *shikan* or Buddhist theory of the tale, however, accommodates these contradictions, even
embraces them. And while the theory was constructed upon the idea
of the perfect Buddha mind ground of Murasaki Shikibu, in actuality
it hinges upon the response of the reader, who is given the power to
envision her text as more than words.

ACKNOWLEDGMENTS

I wish to thank Ryūichi Abe, Ethan Bushelle, Edward Kamens, James
McMullen, and Riley Soles for their invaluable comments on drafts
of this manuscript.

WORKS CITED

Abe, Akio. "Murasaki Shikibu no bukkyō shisō." In *Genji monogatari kenkyū josetsu*,
    vol. 1. Tokyo: Tokyo Daigaku Shuppankai, 1959.
Buruma, Ian. "The Sensualist." *New Yorker* 91, no. 20 (2015): 64.
Bushelle, Ethan. "The Joy of the Dharma: Esoteric Buddhism and the Early Medieval
    Transformation of Japanese Literature." Dissertation, Harvard University, 2015.
Cook, Lewis D. "Genre Trouble: Medieval Commentaries and Canonization of *The
    Tale of Genji*." In *Reading "The Tale of Genji": Sources from the First Millennium*,
    edited by Thomas J. Harper and Haruo Shirane. New York: Columbia University
    Press, 2015.
Cranston, Edwin A. *A Waka Anthology*, vol. 2: *Grasses of Remembrance*, Part
    B. Stanford, CA: Stanford University Press, 2006.

Donner, Neil, and Daniel B. Stevenson. "Introduction." In Zhiyi, *Clear Serenity, Quiet Insight: T'ien-t'ai Chih-i Mo-ho chih-kuan*, vol. 1. Translated with commentary by Paul L. Swanson. Honolulu: University of Hawai'i Press, 2018.

Han Jonmi [Han Chong-mi]. *Genji monogatari ni okeru kami shinkō.* Tokyo: Musashino Shoin, 2015.

Ii Haruki. *Genji monogatari chūshakushi no kenkyū: Muromachi Zenki.* Tokyo: Ōfūsha, 1980.

Ikeda Kikan, ed. *Genji monogatari taisei.* 8 vols. Tokyo: Chūō Kōronsha, 1956.

Imagawa Norimasa. *Genji monogatari teiyō.* Edited by Inaga Keiji. Vol. 2 of *Genji monogatari kochū shūsei.* Tokyo: Ōfūsha, 1978.

Kamens, Edward. *The Three Jewels: A Study and Translation of Minamoto Tamenori's "Sanbōe."* Ann Arbor, MI: University of Michigan, Center for Japanese Studies, 1988.

Katagiri Yayoi. "Tendai shimon no san o motsu Murasaki Shikibu zu: den Kano Takanobu hitsu-bon o chūshin ni." In *Ishiyamadera to Murasaki Shikibu: Genji monogatari no sekai*, edited by Reizei Katsuhiko, Iwama Kaori, and Katagiri Yayoi. Ōtsu-shi: Daihonzan Ishiyamadera, 1991.

Kern, J. Christopher. "Changing Perspectives on a Classic: Pre-Modern Commentaries on the First Chapter of the *Tale of Genji.*" PhD diss., Ohio State University, 2014.

Klein, Susan Blakeley. *Allegories of Desire: Esoteric Literary Commentaries of Medieval Japan.* Cambridge, MA: Harvard University Asia Center, 2003.

Kujō Tanemichi. *Genji monogatari kyōenki*, no. 319. *Monogataribu* of *Gunsho ruijū*, vol. 17. Tokyo: Zoku Gunsho Ruijū Kanseikai, 1993.

Kujō Tanemichi. *Mōshinshō.* Edited by Nomura Seiichi. *Genji monogatari kochū shūsei*, vols. 4–6. Tokyo: Ōfūsha, 1980–81.

Lukács, Georg. *The Theory of the Novel: A Historico-Philosophical Essay on the Forms of Great Epic Literature.* Translated by Anna Bostock. Cambridge, MA: MIT Press, 1971.

Maeda Masayuki. "Paradaimu to shite no bukkyō: Genji monogatari to tendai kyōgaku." In *Sawarabi, Genji monogatari no kanshō to kiso chishiki*, vol. 39, edited by Suzuki Kazuo, Kansaku Kōichi, et al. Tokyo: Shibundō, 1998–2005.

Matsunaga Teitoku. *Taionki.* Edited by Kodaka Toshio. Nihon koten bungaku taikei, vol. 95. Tokyo: Iwanami Shoten, 1964.

McCormick, Melissa. "'Murasaki Shikibu Ishiyamadera mōde-zu' ni okeru shomondai: Wa to kan no sakai ni aru Murasaki Shikibu zō." *Kokka* 1434 (April 2015).

McCormick, Melissa. "Purple Displaces Crimson: The *Wakan* Dialectic as Polemic." In *Around Chigusa: Tea and the Arts of Sixteenth-Century Japan*, ed. Dora Ching, Louise Cort, and Andrew Watsky. Princeton, NJ: Princeton University Press, 2017.

McCormick, Melissa. "Ishiyamadera and the Buddhist Veneration of Murasaki Shikibu." In John C. Carpenter and Melissa McCormick, eds. *The Tale of Genji: A Japanese Classic Illuminated.* Metropolitan Museum of Art, 2019.

McMullen, James. *Idealism, Protest, and the Tale of Genji: The Confucianism of Kumazawa Banzan (1619–91)*. Oxford: Clarendon Press, 1999.

Minamoto Tamenori. *Sanbōe; Chūkōsen*. Edited by Mabuchi Kazuo, Koizumi Hiroshi, and Konno Tōru. *Shin nihon koten bungaku taikei*, vol. 31. Tokyo: Iwanami Shoten, 1997.

Misumi Yōichi. *Genji monogatari to tendai jōdokyō*. Tokyo: Wakakusa Shobō, 1996.

Mortimer, Raymond. "A New Planet." *The Nation and the Athenaeum* 37, no. 12 (1925).

Motoori, Norinaga. *"The Tale of Genji": A Little Jeweled Comb*. Translated by Thomas Harper. In *Reading "The Tale of Genji": Sources from the First Millennium*, edited by Thomas Harper and Haruo Shirane. New York: Columbia University Press, 2015.

Murasaki Shikibu. *Genji monogatari*. Edited by Abe Akio, et al. Shinpen nihon koten bungaku zenshū, vols. 20–25. Tōkyō: Shōgakkan, 1994–98.

Murasaka Shikibu. *Murasaki Shikibu, Her Diary and Poetic Memoirs: A Translation and Study*. Translated by Richard Bowring. Princeton, NJ: Princeton University Press, 1982.

Nussbaum, Martha. *Love's Knowledge: Essays on Philosophy and Literature*. Oxford: Oxford University Press, 1990.

Okada, H. Richard. *Figures of Resistance: Language, Poetry, and Narrating in "The Tale of Genji" and Other Mid-Heian Texts*. Durham, NC: Duke University Press, 1991.

Owen, Stephen. *Traditional Chinese Poetry and Poetics: Omen of the World*. Madison: University of Wisconsin Press, 1985.

Ramirez-Christensen, Esperanza. *Emptiness and Temporality: Buddhism and Medieval Japanese Poetics*. Stanford, CA: Stanford University Press, 2008.

Rhodes, Robert F. *Genshin's Ōjōyōshū and the Construction of Pure Land Discourse in Heian Japan*. Honolulu: University of Hawai'i Press, 2017.

Shirane, Haruo. *The Bridge of Dreams: A Poetics of the "Tale of Genji."* New York: Columbia University Press, 1987.

Soles, Riley. "The Ecstasy of the Text." Dissertation, Yale University, 2018.

Stone, Jacqueline Ilyse. *Original Enlightenment and the Transformation of Medieval Japanese Buddhism*. Honolulu: University of Hawai'i Press, 1999.

Tasaka Kenji. *Genji monogatari kyōjushi ronkō*. Tokyo: Kazama Shobō, 2009.

Yoda, Tomiko. "Fractured Dialogues: Mono No Aware and Poetic Communication in *The Tale of Genji*." *Harvard Journal of Asiatic Studies* 59, no. 2 (1999).

Vincent, J. Keith. "Sex on the Mind: Queer Theory Meets Cognitive Theory." In *The Oxford Handbook of Cognitive Literary Studies*, edited by Lisa Zunshine. New York: Oxford University Press, 2015.

Zhiyi. *Clear Serenity, Quiet Insight: T'ien-t'ai Chih-i's Mo-ho chih-kuan*. 3 vols. Translated with commentary by Paul L. Swanson. Honolulu: University of Hawai'i Press, 2018.

FURTHER READING

Bargen, Doris G. *A Woman's Secret Weapon: Spirit Possession in "The Tale of Genji."* Honolulu: University of Hawai'i Press, 1997.

Bowring, Richard, tr. *The Diary of Lady Murasaki.* Translated and introduced by Richard Bowring. London: Penguin Books, 1996.

Field, Norma. *The Splendor of Longing in the "Tale of Genji."* Princeton, NJ: Princeton University Press, 1987.

Harper, Thomas, and Haruo Shirane. *Reading "The Tale of Genji": Sources from the First Millennium.* New York: Columbia University Press, 2015.

Kamens, Edward, ed. *Approaches to Teaching Murasaki Shikibu's "The Tale of Genji."* New York: Modern Language Association of America, 1993.

LaMarre, Thomas. *Uncovering Japan: An Archaeology of Sensation and Inscription.* Durham, NC: Duke University Press, 2000.

McCormick, Melissa. *"The Tale of Genji": A Visual Companion.* Princeton, NJ: Princeton University Press, 2018.

McMullen, James. *Idealism, Protest, and "The Tale of Genji": The Confucianism of Kumazawa Banzan (1619–91).* Oxford: Oxford University Press, 1999.

Morris, Ivan. *The World of the Shining Prince.* Harmondsworth: Penguin, 1964

Pandey, Rajyashree. *Perfumed Sleeves and Tangled Hair: Body, Woman, and Desire in Medieval Japanese Narratives.* Honolulu: University of Hawai'i Press, 2016.

Pekarik, Andrew. *Ukifune: Love in "The Tale of Genji."* New York: Columbia University Press, 1982.

Seidensticker, Edward G., tr. *The Tale of Genji.* 2 vols. London: Secker & Warburg, 1976.

Shirane, Haruo. *The Bridge of Dreams: A Poetics of "The Tale of Genji."* Stanford, CA: Stanford University Press, 1987.

Tyler, Royall. *A Reading of "The Tale of Genji."* Charleston, SC: Arthur Nettleton, 2014 and (slightly reformatted) Blue-Tongue Books, 2016.

Waley, Arthur, tr. *The Tale of Genji* (one volume edition). London: George Allen & Unwin, 1935.

INDEX*

aesthetic order. *See* aesthetics
aesthetics
    aesthetic juxtaposition, 18, 84
    aesthetic model, 113–14, 120–21
    aesthetic order, 20–21, 22, 31, 102, 103,
        106, 112–13, 116–17, 122–23
    aesthetic society, 111
    aesthetic sublimation, 91–93
    and calligraphy/character, 24, 175–77,
        183, 190–91, 193–94, 197
    categories of, 78–79n.7
    order of, 113–14
    Tendai Buddhist, 285–86
agency, 31, 84–86, 87–88, 89, 90n.13, 120–21,
    124, 132–33, 228, 235, 240, 253–55
ajari, 212–13
Akashi, Japan, 5, 45, 49–50, 73, 75, 76–77,
    196, 285–86
"Akashi" (Chapter 13), 44, 48–49, 196, 237–38
Akashi Empress (character), 72, 76–77,
    90–91, 157–58, 201
Akashi Lady (character), 42n.7, 47, 72,
    73–75, 76–79, 126–27, 147, 215,
    216–17, 237–38
Akashi Monk (character), 149–50
Akashi Mother (character), 157–58
Akashi no Himegimi (character), 181, 195
Akashi no Kimi (character), 195, 196
Akashi Novice (character), 40, 45, 196
Akashi Princess (character), 157–58

aki konomu, 156–57
Akikonomu (character), 40, 53–54, 77–78,
    122–23, 129–30, 131, 156–57, 193–94
Akikonomu Empress (character),
    216–17, 218–19
aki no no, 216–17
Ames, Roger, 103, 104–5
Amida (Buddhist deity), 10–11, 214
Analects, 94–95, 103, 106
An Lushan rebellion, 93
Aoi (character), 44, 55, 82–83, 87, 152–53,
    154–55, 156, 235
"Aoi" (Chapter 9), 87, 167–68
Ariwara no Yukihira, 33–34, 75
artifacts, 17–18, 137, 138–39, 143,
    177–78, 260–62
Asagao (character), 54–55, 57–58, 59,
    156, 193–94
"Asagao" (Chapter 20), 39, 54–55
Aston, W. G., 14–15, 19–20
Autumn Foliage excursion, 74–75
azaretaru, 249–50
Azure Dragon (deity), 219–20

Bai Juyi, 33–34, 162–63, 281, 282–83. *See also*
    Bo Juyi
Bargen, Doris, 93n.18, 128n.34
Basho (Nishida Kitarō), 96–98
basso ostinato, 102
Bates, Stanley, 176, 197–98

*This index is the work of a freelance indexer, not this volume's editor.

Fujiwara no Teika, 24, 172, 173, 273
Fujiwara regents, 79–80
Fujiwara Yukinari, 192–93
fumi, 87–88, 94–95
fumimagahu, 171
fūryū aru mono, 213
fusū, 204–5

ganmon, 81
gardens, 26, 27–28, 34–35, 202–4, 210, 212,
    214, 218, 223–24, 241–42
Garfield, Jay L., 95
garlic lady (character), 87–88
genbu, 219–20
Genchū Saihishō (Fujiwara no Akihira),
    257–58n.2, 268–71n.23
gender, 2, 8, 10–11, 29–31, 69–70, 84–87,
    227–55, 266–67
"Gender in Japanese Art" (Chino), 84–86
General Theory of Relativity, 111
genius loci, 91–93
Genji (character), 15–16, 17, 19–22, 23,
    25–27, 28–29, 30, 31, 32–35, 36–66,
    68–69, 72–78, 79–80, 81, 82–83,
    87–88, 91–93, 101–2, 104–5, 106–7,
    108–13, 114, 116–30, 131, 132–33,
    143–44, 145–48, 149–50, 152–57,
    158, 160–61, 162–63, 164, 165, 166,
    167–68, 181, 183, 184, 185, 186, 187,
    188–89, 190–91, 193–96, 201, 207,
    214–19, 222–23, 235–36, 237–38,
    241–42, 247, 249–51, 264–65,
    266–67, 268–71, 277–78, 281,
    282–84, 285–87
Genji Explicated (Sesonji Koreyuki),
    257–58n.2
Genji minister (character), 223
Genji Monogatari. See *Tale of Genji, The*
Genji monogatari no kōsō to kanshibun
    (Kazuyoshi), 90n.13
Genji monogatari teiyō (Imagawa Norimasa),
    268–71n.23, 271–72
Genji monogatari to haku Kyoi no Bungaku
    (Kazuyoshi), 90n.13
genmu, 219–20
genre, 3–4, 257–58n.2, 262–63
"Genre Trouble" (Cook), 257–58n.2
Genshin, 260–62n.9

geomancy, 26–27, 28–29, 111
God of Sumiyoshi (deity), 46, 47
gojūshu, 172
Gongsun Long, 94–95
Gosen wakashū, 163–64
goyō, 216–17
Greco-Roman philosophy, 94–95
guilt. See shame and guilt
gyōsho, 178

Haapala, 175–76n.1
Hachi no miya (character). See Eighth Prince
hagi, 202–3
"Hahakigi" (Chapter 2), 18, 30–31, 54, 87–
    88, 106–7, 191
hahaso, 216–17
Hall, David, 103, 104–5
Han, 262–63n.10
Hanachirusato (character), 77–78, 156, 215,
    216–17, 220–21, 245–46
"Hanachirusato" (Chapter 11), 162–63
"Hana no en" (Chapter 8), 44–45,
    82–83, 87
hanatachibana, 216–17
hand. See calligraphy
Han Dynasty, 75
hare, 84–86, 87–88, 89
Harper, Thomas, 251–52
Haruo Shirane, 205–6, 260–62
Hase, Japan, 209
Hasedera, 143–44, 143–44n.8
"Hashihime" (Chapter 45), 49, 64–65
"Hatsune" (Chapter 23), 195
Haven. See Rokujō estate
Heaven, 26–27
Heian
    courts, 8–10, 20, 26, 29, 70, 90, 106,
        114, 203–4, 205–6, 212, 214,
        222–23, 260–62
    gardens, 202–3, 204, 212, 214, 223–24
    literature, 62, 63, 86–87, 89, 205–6, 209,
        211, 215–16, 260–62
    monogatari, 160
    period, 5–8, 9–10, 16, 17, 18–19, 31,
        69–70, 75, 79–80, 83–84, 89, 90, 95–98,
        108–9, 152, 175–76n.2, 176–77, 178,
        203–4, 205–6, 212, 213, 221n.36, 257–
        58, 259–60, 262–63, 262–63n.12